D1563453

*African American Women
and Christian Activism*

African American Women and Christian Activism

NEW YORK'S BLACK YWCA, 1905–1945

JUDITH WEISENFELD

HARVARD UNIVERSITY PRESS

Cambridge, Massachusetts
London, England   1997

To the memory of James M. Washington,
with gratitude for his faith in me and my work

Library of Congress Cataloging-in-Publication Data
Weisenfeld, Judith.
    African American women and Christian activism : New York's Black
    YWCA, 1905–1945 / Judith Weisenfeld.
        p.   cm.
    Includes bibliographical references (p.   ) and index.
    ISBN 0-674-00778-6
    1. YWCA of the City of New York—History—20th century.
    2. Church work with Afro-Americans—New York (State)—New York.
    3. Young women—New York (State)—New York—Religious life.
    I. Title.
    BV1393.B58W45 1997
    267'.597471'0996073—dc21   97-21901

Acknowledgments

I HAVE BENEFITED from the support and assistance of many people in the course of researching and writing this book. Archivists and librarians at the New York City Young Women's Christian Association, the National Board of the Young Women's Christian Association, the Princeton University Library, the Columbia University Library, and the Schomburg Center for Research in Black Culture of the New York Public Library proved invaluable in the research phases. The Ford Foundation, the Fund for Theological Education, Barnard College, and the Ann Whitney Olin Foundation all supported my work over the past few years.

Friends and colleagues at Princeton, especially Albert J. Raboteau, John F. Wilson, Eugene Lowe, Albert G. Miller, and Timothy Fulop, read and commented on the dissertation that contributed to this larger project. Linda Green, Zita Nunes, Maggie Sale, Karen Van Dyck, Priscilla Wald, and Angela Zito could not have been better colleagues or friends in providing strong, caring readings in the wonderfully encouraging atmosphere of our writing group. Without question, their thoughtful criticism has marked this book for the better. The friendship and intellectual exchange I have shared with Terry Todd have anchored me for many years. I also want to thank Diane Burhenne, Celia Deutsch, Martha Hodes, Richard Newman, Michele Rubin, and Debo-

97053

rah Valenze, as well as Margaretta Fulton at Harvard University Press, for their advice and support. And Timea Szell's humor and enthusiasm, her unfailing care, and her high scholarly standards have enriched me and my work in countless ways.

Contents

Introduction

$\mathscr{I}$N HER AUTOBIOGRAPHY, Pauli Murray recounts one of the most significant decisions of her early life in choosing to move from Durham, North Carolina, to New York City in 1928 to attend college. Seeking to avoid the humiliations of additional years of segregated education in the South, Murray enrolled at Hunter College, living with relatives in the predominantly white neighborhood of Richmond Hill, Queens. In the spring of her first year in college, she welcomed the opportunity to move into the Emma Ransom House residence of the African American Young Women's Christian Association (YWCA) on West 137th Street in Harlem.[1] Her cousin, the director of the residence, offered her part-time work at the switchboard and elevator. Murray recalled, "That summer at the YWCA was a heady experience for an eighteen-year-old—no schoolwork to burden me, no accounting to anyone for my goings and comings, no restraints on time as long as I was in by midnight, and a whole city to explore in my free hours."[2] In addition to the pleasure of her newfound freedom and the enjoyment of contact with other young African American women studying and working in the city, Murray also remembered the importance of interacting with the women who staffed this YWCA. These women, she wrote, provided "role models in the pursuit of excellence." Indeed, Murray had many female role models in her life, from her schoolteacher aunt who adopted her to Hunter College faculty, to the staff of the YWCA, all of whom contributed to her development as a civil rights activist, a lawyer, and eventually one of the first women to be ordained an Episcopal priest in the United States. She pays moving tribute to the deep influence of all these women in her life. The YWCA provided a particularly inspiring atmosphere at that time in her life: "None of these women would have called themselves feminists in the 1930s, but they were strong, independent personalities who, because of their concerted efforts to rise above the limitations of race and sex and to help younger women do the same, shared a sisterhood that foreshadowed the revival of the feminist movement in the 1960s."[3]

Although her achievements made her extraordinary, Murray at the same time was typical of the kind of young woman to whom this YWCA reached out. Orphaned at a young age, she nevertheless grew up embraced by a loving family whose members emphasized the potential for her to be anything she chose in spite of the restrictive and humiliating realities of the Jim Crow South. Once when Murray complained to her aunt about their poverty relative to more affluent black residents of Durham, her aunt retorted angrily, "Your family stands with the best. It's not what you have but what you *are* that counts."[4] Murray's family impressed upon her the importance of standing with "the race" and of understanding American history and the place of African Americans within that history. With the strong grounding provided by her family, Murray set out to achieve beyond the boundaries set by the racism of segregation in the South.

Murray's arrival in New York City in the late 1920s marked for her and for many other African American migrants a new kind of freedom not possible in the South. She recalled, "That first trip to New York [to visit colleges] had been the most exciting experience of my young life. . . . Most of all I was impressed because we could sit anywhere we chose in the subway trains, buses, and streetcars, and there was no special section for colored people in the movies. I knew then that someday I would live in New York."[5] The excitement of the North, of New York, and of college rapidly became tempered by the harshness of the Great Depression, however. As a poor student in difficult times, Murray found the atmosphere of the YWCA particularly nurturing and supportive and an integral part of the excitement of New York City.

As the personal interactions and contacts at the YWCA proved significant for her, so too did the spiritual grounding of the institution and the individuals she met there. Murray wrote, "There was also a spiritual dimension in these associations which contributed to my growth. I recall a single encounter that made a lifelong impression."[6] She described meeting a YWCA worker while doing a shift on the elevator one evening. The woman, whom she had never seen before, handed her a small comb with a Japanese design painted on it. The woman explained that because she had lost her temper in a discussion with someone in the lobby, she wanted Murray to have one of her precious possessions. Murray saw in this encounter a model of the kind of spiritual discipline that she should cultivate in her own development as a leader. Her experiences at the YWCA exemplify the type of interactions with and support of young women that motivated black women in New York to establish a YWCA in 1905.

~~~ THIS BOOK tells the story of African American women in the New York City YWCA over the course of a forty-year period. These women came together from a variety of backgrounds and personal experiences, but all committed themselves as "willing workers" (as one young women's club within this YWCA called itself) to a number of projects. These emphasized nurturing young black women and improving the daily living conditions and life opportunities of black women and men in New York. The leaders of the organization themselves emerged from communities and educational institutions that consciously fashioned them as workers in and for their communities, and they took up the responsibility with vigor.[7]

Although for most people the image of the YWCA today has little to do with religion, the organization nevertheless originated from the Christian commitments of its founders. An acknowledgment and understanding of the religious concerns of the women of New York's African American YWCA are important to my examination. Faith was vital to the women involved in the institution, and in keeping with the YWCA's stated mission of "bringing about the kingdom of God among young women," they held a place for Protestantism in their work. In addition, the book explores new ways to understand the connections between religious belief and black women's collective action. To a large extent, scholars have ignored the degree to which late-nineteenth- and early-twentieth-century African American women's activist projects, most notably the national club movement, remained deeply grounded in evangelical Christian concerns. African American women in the YWCA, both at the national and local levels, similarly approached social reform questions from their perspective as Christians committed to the possibility of divinely aided social progress. Thus, a firmly drawn division between "secular" and "religious" does not prove productive for understanding these women's work. Examining the YWCA, a bridge between the secular and the religious, provides a new perspective on the religious lives of black women and one that does not place religious expression in a narrow context.

Also informing this work is the issue of how we study women's religious experiences in contexts in which institutions foster male leadership and support male voices in the public arena. The venue of the YWCA allows us to explore black women's religious experiences at the perimeter of "the black church"—the group of institutions generally placed at the center of discussions of African American religious life. In studies that pose "the black church" and its male leadership as the exclusive arena for understanding black religiosity, those of us interested in women's lives are too often forced to remain satisfied with examining the background or the supporting roles played by black women. In taking up New York City's African American YWCA, I join other scholars of black women's history who make the perspective of the women the starting point. Thus, the institution emerges as a significant (although not the only) site from which many African American women expressed their religiosity in ways that complemented their church lives.

This is also a local study that places African American women at the center of the story of early-twentieth-century black New York and establishes them as significant actors in the life of the city in ways that most works on black New York—generally focusing on the artists and writers of the Harlem Renaissance period—do not. The story begins, significantly, years before the development of Harlem as a community of African Americans, thus locating the foundations of their work elsewhere, in the life of black New York in other neighborhoods. As a result of this broadening of the traditional scope of black New York history, I explore the contributions of African American women to black New Yorkers' developing sense of community in this period. In addition, I am concerned with the various roles that black women played in Harlem's growth and its emergence as a center of black life and culture in this period.

In placing African American YWCA women at the center of this particular telling of New York's story, I am also choosing to privilege black Protestant life in the city over the new religious movements that developed in black urban communities in the 1920s and 1930s. The rejection of traditional forms of Christianity as inappropriate for African Americans is a significant commonality among new movements such as the Commandment Keepers (who identify as black Jews), the Nation of Islam, Father Divine's Peace Mission Movement, Daddy Grace's United House of Prayer for All People, and Marcus Garvey's Universal Negro Improvement Association among others. Various scholars have done excellent work setting these movements in the context of a religious search by many African Americans for new ways to construct their identities. While these movements represent an important component of African American religious history, in this period most African Americans' primary religious affiliation remained Christian. And black Protestant life provides the backdrop for the story of New York's African American YWCA.

In addition to telling a story of a particular group of African American women in New York City, this work also emphasizes the impact of the city's African American women on discussions of national and international issues within black communities. Connections with other local black women's organizations, with national black women's groups, with mixed-sex African American organizations, and with interracial civil rights and religious groups all became important avenues for black YWCA women in New York to express and act on their concerns beyond the local arena. Exploring these connections reveals the institution and its leaders as part of a complex web of networks and organizations, through which African American women entered public discourse on a range of American issues. Through this approach we can begin to see the degree to which local organizations were the foundation for the emergence of national organizations, such as the National Association of Colored Women, in the late nineteenth and early twentieth centuries.[8]

Along with other recent works on African American women's organizing, I emphasize the importance of recognizing connections between black and white women's organizations.[9] By this I do not mean that black women merely mirrored, in some "black" way, the kind of work in which white women engaged. Instead, the history of the New York City YWCA reveals a dynamic involvement between black and white women, marked by significant areas of commonality, as well as much conflict. Importantly, understanding that the African American women who founded a YWCA organization in New York City sought out a connection *after* having already constituted their own group significantly alters an assumption, common in previous scholarship on American women's activism, that the great majority of black women's organizations had their roots in the process of "splitting off" from white women's groups. Here we have an independent African American women's group that chose to ally itself, over a period of many decades, with white women, largely on the grounds of common bonds of religious commitment. Nevertheless, such alliances were not free of discord. For African American women in the New York City YWCA, however, such discord often motivated them in important ways and reinvigorated their commitment. These women constructed their identities as Christian activists in an arena in common with white women in the YWCA, and also used various conflicts between the two groups to help create a sense of solidarity among themselves as African American women engaged in Christian activism.

The question of the relationship between class and community identity for African American's is also important in this study. It is difficult to discuss issues of class among African Americans in the late nineteenth and early twentieth centuries because they are often bound up with present-day political issues within African American communities and among scholars of African American history. Often scholars with commitments to preserving an image of a "pure" African American folk idiom or culture present relatively privileged African American women in clubs and church groups—privileged by virtue of income, education, skin color, church affiliation, or a variety of other class indicators—as enforcing "inauthentic" standards of behavior and impressing aspirations derived from middle-class white America upon less privileged black communities. Rather than viewing African American women in the New York City YWCA as mimicking white women, this study examines them within an existing black middle class that constituted a vibrant sector of African American life throughout the late nineteenth and early twentieth centuries. In situating these women's experiences in the context of their historical moment, I hope to counter views that, retroactively, evaluate such women according to strict standards of class, ideological, and lifestyle indicators as the markers of "authentic" and "inauthentic" blackness throughout all of African American history.[10]

Wealthy, middle- and working-class, rural and urban African Americans *all* represent significant positions in varied, complex, and overlapping communities. Certainly the relatively privileged leaders of the organization sometimes experienced conflict with the working poor who constituted the majority of the membership. Sometimes they even constructed their identities and the African American YWCA's institutional identity over against particular visions of the poor. Nevertheless, sustained examination of the institution's history over time reveals a great degree of complexity in the cross-class interaction that occurred. The women of this YWCA saw the values and standards that they embodied as organic to their experiences as African American Christian women and, where they shared values with white YWCA women, did not view themselves as imposing foreign elements onto their communities.

THE STRUCTURE of the book follows the chronological development of the institution, and the periodization reflects my interest in examining this particular YWCA in the context of the broader YWCA's era of conscious segregation. Thus, the narrative ends in the late 1940s when the national YWCA began to move away from its commitment to segregation. While African American women in the organization objected to, found offensive, and doggedly fought the segregated nature of the work, ironically, the period of segregation provided an opening for development and growth that fully integrated work might not have allowed.

In telling the story of New York City's African American YWCA, I have been guided by the number and kinds of sources that have survived. The majority of institutional records, such as the minutes of board meetings, correspondence, and even annual reports for the African American branch of the New York City YWCA, no longer exist. For the most part, my work relies on the experiences, histories, and perspectives of the changing group of women who comprised the leadership of the institution. Neither the names nor the voices of most of the members who participated in activities at this YWCA survive in the records of the New York City YWCA, and we find few indications elsewhere. The absence of the perspective of the larger membership of the institution necessarily shapes the way the narrative develops. However, the narrative that does emerge from the viewpoint of the leadership nevertheless constitutes a significant angle on an important story. I remain committed to presenting this story as merely one way of telling the story of African American YWCA women in New York City. Rather than viewing the particular sources available to me as a limitation, I have joined others in taking up the challenge of revealing African American women's strategies, challenges, and contributions to American life.

~ 1

"Bend the Tree While It Is Young": Institutional Alliances/ Institutional Appropriations

*F*ROM THE FALL OF 1907 through the spring of 1908, Addie Waites Hunton and Elizabeth Ross placed themselves in the difficult position of defending to African American women activists the segregated policies of the white-dominated Young Women's Christian Association (YWCA). Hunton and Ross, the first African Americans employed at the national level of the YWCA, used their positions to respond to a new policy established by the recently formed National Board of the YWCA that required new YWCAs in cities to affiliate as branches of existing YWCAs. In effect, this generally meant that African American YWCA organizations had to subordinate themselves and become branches of white city associations in order to receive recognition at the national level. The new policy, put into effect in the spring of 1907, emerged as a reluctant group of white YWCA leaders sought to come to terms with the appeal of the YWCA movement among African American women and their agency and forcefulness in founding local YWCA organizations for black communities.

The National Board sought two related outcomes. First, the new policy placed the concerns of white segregationists above all others in this national organization. The requirement that African American YWCAs seek recognition through local white associations allowed both southern and northern white YWCAs to deny access to black women at will. Second, the board's policy made concrete the belief that African

American women's work could best be supervised through a relationship of "stewardship." In this way, the board reasoned, it could monitor and restrict the level of African American women's agency within the organization and maintain "standards" by admitting only those associations "worthy" of the title YWCA. This proved to be a critical juncture in the life of the YWCA in the United States. African American women had demonstrated their interest in the organization by their work and involvement in it, and at this point, the national YWCA declared its unwillingness to view black women as equals, even in the context of Christian activism.

The National Board employed Addie Waites Hunton and Elizabeth Ross[1] to investigate and evaluate the involvement of African American women in the YWCA, to help create a sense among black female activists of what "worthiness" meant in the YWCA context, and to maintain that standard, thereby accommodating black women to a subordinate role. In the winter of 1907, Hunton visited African American YWCA groups in black colleges and in various cities, reporting to the National Board that only four of the city associations—those in New York, Brooklyn, Baltimore, and Washington—proved "worthy" of being called YWCAs. Hunton did not, however, make clear the specific criteria for worthiness in her writings, but each of these associations had established a physical plant for the work, offered devotional programs, and had a management board of active volunteers. Ross continued the investigative work in 1908. Her report to the National Board following her survey reveals her own conflicts about her role as an employee of the National Board and as an intermediary between the National Board and African American women in the YWCA.

Ross's 1908 report reveals the locus of the struggle between the African American women's organizations that called themselves YWCAs and the national structure of the YWCA. In some of these organizations, she wrote, much of the work fell outside the bounds of YWCA interests as defined by the National Board. The board felt that kindergartens, Epworth Leagues, Sunday schools, and "rescue work" with "fallen" women all fell outside the scope of the YWCA, as did the attention that many black groups gave to the elderly and to children.[2] For the National Board, true YWCA work focused exclusively on fostering religious awakening in young, self-supporting Protestant women as a supplement to their church attendance. Locating within a YWCA religious activities that might be seen as a substitute for church involvement thwarted achieving the goal, as did educating children and providing services for the indigent poor. The National Board charged Hunton and Ross with upholding this standard.

But Ross's reports to the National Board also articulate many of the frustrations with the 1907 policy of African American women both in the YWCA and outside it. How were they to believe that the YWCA truly desired to meet their needs when it made their associations and needs subordinate to those of white women? What should they think of situations like the one that existed in Little Rock, Arkansas, where white YWCA women, with the tacit approval of the National Board, prevented local African American women from even forming an association? Ross remained deeply concerned about how to justify the policies and at the same time keep African American women supportive of the YWCA and solidify their faith in the organization. As a sociologist, Ross understood the complexities surrounding institutional survival. Both she and Hunton, whose career up to this point had been focused on administering educational institutions, notified African American women that they felt the YWCA's process of certifying new associations for affiliation with the National Board would ensure institutional stability and prevent new groups from failing.[3] Such stability, they asserted, would enhance the public image of African American female activists.

The most difficult aspect of Hunton and Ross's role as mediators, however, remained the YWCA's failure to include African American women fully in its work, fashioning, instead, a rigidly segregated structure. For black women interested in the movement, this structure clearly indicated inadequate concern for extending the YWCA's influence in African American communities, as well as reluctance to recognize black women's work. Ross reported in 1908 that women she spoke with expressed

> a general feeling of doubt about the philanthropic and Christian basis of Association work generally . . . When I have been often asked to tell why the National Board has not shown more interest in city work for colored people and has refused one association [in a southern city] which has sought membership in the National movement, I must confess that although I did the best I could, my

defense has not been sufficiently formidable to convince inquirers of the truth of our sincere interest in them and their work.[4]

Thus, Ross herself remained frustrated by her own need to justify the National Board's policy as an issue of real institutional standards and uniformity rather than overt racism.

The YWCA had been a significant arena for cooperative work between African American and white women since the late nineteenth century. In the organization, African American and white women could meet on the common ground of desire to secure a place for evangelical Christian belief and practice in the lives of young women, as well as concern for improving the material conditions in which these women lived. Despite a history of racist policies and painful incidents of racism, African American women continued to build organizations on the model of the YWCA, and they continued to seek affiliation with the National Board. Weighing the YWCA's record, it is difficult to understand the enduring presence of African American women from the late nineteenth century on. What could the YWCA offer these women that would make bearable the indignity of working through a segregated branch system? Why did they choose to remain with the YWCA in light of other possibilities for organizing, in particular, African American women's own approaches to social service in the late nineteenth and early twentieth centuries? How did African Americans in the YWCA negotiate their own vision of their individual and collective place over against the desires of the white leadership?

The white leadership of the YWCA sought to build an institution that would last beyond the generation of the founders, and one that could speak with a unified voice to social, cultural, and political issues on the American scene. In order to accomplish this, white YWCA leaders sought to present the workings of this institutional structure as "natural" and as removed from human construction as possible. In this way, the institution would "take on a life of its own" and no longer depend on individual personalities for its survival. The YWCA's status as an institution of evangelical Christianity facilitated this process because, as Peter Berger's work has demonstrated, religion functions as the most productive mechanism of legitimation by inserting divine intention into institutions of human construction.[5] Thus, because of the YWCA's fundamentally religious goal—to spread evangelical Christianity among young women—the leadership could see and convey its structure as conforming to a divine vision for Christian women in late-nineteenth-century America. Although there was, in fact, a certain degree of flexibility built into the operations of the YWCA—the negotiation between local contexts and national structures emerges as one example—the concerns of white leaders for institutional stability and legitimation often resulted in efforts to extend a veil over black women in an attempt to conceal the human agency of white American women in creating and maintaining the organization.

African American women's continuing commitment to the YWCA reflects a confidence in their own ability to engage and transform the movement and its institutional structures in significant ways. As one African American activist wrote, the goal of black women's work should be to "bend the tree while it is young," and she called on women to direct particular attention in their work to young people.[6] This metaphor aptly applies to the goals black women articulated for institutions of evangelical Christianity such as the YWCA. African American women saw possibilities for themselves within the YWCA precisely because of their ability to see the constructed nature of its institutional structure. They understood the potential for influencing the direction and future of the YWCA, as well as appropriating aspects of its structure that suited their goals within their own communities. In effect, they set out to bend this particular tree—the developing YWCA—to provide shade and security for as broadly cast a group as possible. The struggle of black women to ally themselves with the possibilities they saw inherent in the YWCA structure and the attempt of white leaders to appropriate black participants and contain their potential to claim its discourse for their own purposes characterize much of the history of black and white women in the YWCA.

In addition to the issue of institutional stability and the legitimation of the YWCA's structure and purpose, white women in the YWCA struggled with the question of cultural interaction between themselves and African American women. In the late nineteenth and early twentieth centuries, white leaders of the YWCA tended to view this interaction as the meeting of two wholly discrete racial/cultural groups, and to obscure many of the historical, social, and cultural points of identity between them. In his work on the uses of constructed images of racial difference in colonialist literature, Abdul R. JanMohamed argues that the most innovative European colonialist literature is that in which the author can both bracket his or her own particular cultural grounding and recognize the historical, social, economic, and political factors that create differences between European subjects and cultural Others. Historical grounding and the ability to see potential sites of meeting lead, for JanMohamed, to the possibility of a genuine meeting of self and other.[7] While white women in the YWCA often sought to appreciate the material circumstances in which African American women found themselves, they failed to meet black women in the YWCA on mutual ground. African American women in the YWCA tended to exhibit greater awareness of the arenas in which the syncretism of which Jan-Mohamed speaks *already* existed by virtue of shared historical and discursive experience between African American and white American women. At the same time, they affirmed their cultural and historical uniqueness, in part, through organizing in arenas separate from white women and, in fact, often separate from black men as well. Thus, African American women's attraction and commitment to the YWCA since the late nineteenth century represented a skillful balancing of their own history of organizing within black communities and interpretations of the possibilities inherent in the YWCA's evangelical Christian foundation and its institutional structure.

African American Women and the Politics of Racial Uplift

African American women's collective action for the benefit of their communities represents a tradition with roots deep in the experience of slavery in America. Enslaved African American women developed networks to support each other in childbirth, child rearing, and the provision of health care, in addition to assisting black men to meet their own needs. Their free counterparts during the same period organized female benevolent societies, reading groups, antislavery societies, and religious associations to provide similar services to free blacks. Antebellum free northern black working women gathered in groups like the Colored Ladies Benevolent Society of Detroit, the Colored Female Produce Society, the Afric-American Female Intelligence Society, and the Daughters of Africa.[8] Excluded from the support provided to white Americans by the government and white benevolent institutions, black women participated in an African American struggle to build an alternative institutional structure.

To a significant degree, African American women's organizing in the late nineteenth century remained deeply connected to the work of black churches. In the African Methodist Episcopal (AME), African Methodist Episcopal Zion (AMEZ), Colored Methodist Episcopal (CME), and black Baptist, Presbyterian, and Episcopal churches, African American men and women created a space from which they could resist the attacks of white America on the political, economic, and spiritual well-being of their communities. While inequality and inhumanity remained pervasive in the larger American society, African Americans could live out their own social teaching on "the fatherhood of God and the brotherhood of man"[9] within the bounds of black churches.

From the beginnings of the independent black church movement in the late eighteenth century, these institutions provided a venue for free blacks in particular to engage in political struggle, and by the end of the nineteenth century, black churches in black communities had embraced multiple roles. With the entrenchment of Jim Crow at the end of the nineteenth century and the attendant exclusion of African Americans from electoral politics, black churches functioned as an authenticating mechanism for political leadership. Alexander Crummell, Francis Grimké, Henry McNeal Turner, Walter H. Brooks, Daniel Alexander Payne, and Alexander Walters—among the most powerful voices in late-nineteenth-century black America—emerged from the ranks of the clergy of these churches. Black churches became centers of community economic development, providers of education, and venues for social interchange, thus becoming a "public sphere" mediating between African American communities and white American society.[10]

However, the tendency to speak of "the" black church serves to erase a host of complexities inherent in the grouping of these churches in the late nineteenth century. Although we may speak of commonalities of approach to political engagement, agreement on certain theological issues, and the common desire to build religious community that takes seriously both culture and race, no such entity as "the" black church truly exists. In fact, African American religious history (indeed, like American religious history) appears marked by fragmentation as much as by unity. Theological disputes, disagreement on the question of political involvement, and differing notions of the role of race in creating religious community (particularly for those African Americans in predominantly white denominations) loom as among the most significant reasons for this fragmentation.

Second, the tendency to view "the" black church as the only arena through which African Americans could organize or deliver services to their communities ignores the diverse other means black Americans created for just these purposes. Secret societies, literary clubs, banks, insurance companies, burial societies, newspapers, scholarly organizations, card clubs—all proved central to the functioning and survival of African American communities in the late nineteenth century. Such organizations sometimes had connections with black churches and sometimes functioned independently.

In the same way, African American women used Christian concerns and experiences in black churches to ground their work in social service organizations. As early as 1793, black women from Philadelphia's Free African Society, the cornerstone of the black independent church movement, founded the Female Benevolent Society of St. Thomas, a mutual aid society. This model of denominationally based women's organizations became central to the development of African American women's movements in the late nineteenth and early twentieth centuries. Black women proved vital to the operation of the churches as a public sphere for social action. Women's societies in the churches contributed to the financial resources of their institutions and fostered a sense of community for women that served to support the development of leadership skills. These skills, especially the ability to marshal financial resources, became central to the growth of black church missions in Africa, the Caribbean, and the American South.[11]

At the same time, black churches—although the primary arenas through which opposition to racial domination took place and the principal authenticators of black male political leadership—proved to be sites of conflicted experiences and meanings for black women. Late-nineteenth-century debates in black churches over the question of women's participation in the ordained roles of minister, elder, and deacon arose, in part, in response to the persistence of preaching women earlier in the century.[12] By the end of the century, the impact on black men of shifting constructions of gendered notions of race became equally important in leading to attempts to subordinate black women within the churches. In the post-Reconstruction era, white America asserted, through an emphasis on the notion of the innate criminality and hypersexuality of black men, the belief that black men were unsuitable for suffrage. In the South, in particular, the solution fixed upon for containing black communities was a radical policing of contact between African Americans and whites through both legislative means and the threat and practice of lynching. These practices, aimed primarily at subordinating African American men to white men, thereby "feminizing" them, necessarily affected the lives of African American women. Black women were expected to assume a place in a racialized hierarchy that placed them not only below white men but also below white women and black men. In addition to the negative impact that white America's gendered construction of race had on black women, the struggle of African American men to construct their own vision of "manhood" within their own communities also often worked to constrain black women.

The general debate over the "proper" relation of African American women to African American men struggling for "manhood rights," as men often called citizenship rights in this period, clearly had an impact within the public sphere of black churches. In black Baptist churches, women faced opposition on the part of some male clergy to a range of their activities, including the formation of Bible bands and the development of women's organizations at the state level. As Virginia Broughton, a feminist theologian and central figure in founding a Baptist women's convention in Tennessee, writes in her memoirs,

> Ministers and laymen, who looked with disdain upon a criticism that came from a woman, and all those who were jealous of the growing popularity of the woman's work, as if there was some cause of alarm for the safety of their own positions of power and honor, all rose up in their churches, with all the influence and power of speech they could summon to oppose the woman's work and break it up if possible.[13]

As with other forceful, public black women like Sojourner Truth and Ida B. Wells, Broughton's opponents sought to discredit her by questioning whether she was, indeed, a woman by labeling her "mannish." Daniel Alexander Payne, one of the most important AME bishops in the nineteenth century and a central figure in shaping the denomination's gendered policies, remained adamantly opposed to according women leadership roles. Payne opposed both women's preaching and ordination and, instead, advocated that women cultivate the role of "domestic educator" and function as the anchor of the family.[14] The Rev. J. H. A. Johnson of Hagerstown, Maryland, supported Payne's position in an article in the *A.M.E. Church Review*, asserting that

> It is hereby admitted that [woman] is ordained as an auxiliary to man's moral worth . . . She, whether as a wife or a daughter, was made for the home circle and for man's protection . . . Here she performs her duties and finds enough to do without going into questionable fields of labor. Here, whether married or single, she can always find employment that will redound to the glory of God.[15]

For Johnson and others of like mind, part of the church's role should be to emphasize that women's identities existed only in relation to men. Wife and daughter could benefit the family, church, race, and nation only by assuming roles that supported men's work.

Anna Julia Cooper, one of the most prominent black intellectual figures of the nineteenth century, spoke before an 1892 meeting of black clergy in the Protestant Episcopal Church and cried out for these men to recognize the importance of women in the ongoing advancement of African Americans: "Now the fundamental agency under God in the regeneration, the re-training of the race, as well as the ground work and starting point of its progress upward, must be the *black woman* . . . No other hand can move the lever. She must be loosed from her bands and set to work."[16] Despite the opposition of powerful men, African American women participated in various aspects of life in the black churches and engaged both women and men in discussion about the role of Christian women in the process of "racial uplift," the most common term during this period for African American collective action toward political, economic, and moral progress.

In the late nineteenth and early twentieth centuries, questions of the meaning of African American experience, of the nature of community and identity, and of the future destiny of African Americans occupied center stage in African American discourse. Black Christians sought God's purpose in allowing the experience of slavery and God's vision for the future. The Rev. James Theodore Holly, the Protestant Episcopal bishop of Haiti, for example, asserted that God had a plan to carry out the salvation of humanity through dispensations in which the various races of humanity, corresponding to the sons of Noah, would play particular roles. The work of people of African descent would effect the final phase of the plan.[17] For many African American theologians in this period, the destiny of African Americans remained inextricably linked to the Christianization of Africa, and these theological statements fueled the growing missionary work of black and white churches.

Others situated African American destiny firmly in the American context. Mrs. M. E. Lee put forward this position in her poem, "Afmerica," published in 1885 in an AME church periodical.

> Afmerica! her home is here!
> She wants or knows no other home,
> No other lands, nor far nor near,
> Can charm or tempt her thence to roam.
> Her destiny is marked out here.
> Her ancestors, like all the rest,
> Came from the eastern hemisphere,
> But *she* is native of the *West*.
> She'll lend a hand to Africa
> And in her elevation aid.
> But here in brave America
> Her home, her only home is made.
> No one has power to send her hence;
> This home was planned by Providence.[18]

Lee's use of "Afmerica" represents attempts by some black Americans to assert their Americanness in the context of ongoing discussions among whites and blacks of colonization schemes—that is, the expulsion or "repatriation" of people of African descent to parts of Africa. In this sixteen-stanza poem, Lee traces the integral part that African Americans played in the building of America and foretells a future in which the nation embraces its diversity. "O turbulent America!" Lee declared. "So mixed and inter-mixed, until throughout this great Columbia all nationalities at will become thine own, thy legal heirs." Lee placed women at the center of this future in a variety of spheres from the home to education, medicine, the arts, religion, and politics.

Whether African Americans saw God as working out African American destiny primarily in the context of Africa or America or both, all agreed that God's plan would entail human agency. In the period from the end of Reconstruction to World War I, dubbed "the nadir" by historian Rayford Logan,[19] African Americans debated the politics of racial uplift to determine what form of human agency God's plan would require. The politics of racial uplift in the late nineteenth century encompassed a broad spectrum of opinions but tended to emphasize racial solidarity and action from within the community on behalf of all African Americans. Thus, most racial uplift activists saw a strong organizational base as a critical component of any approach to racial uplift. Articulators of philosophies of racial uplift, across a range of approaches, called for African Americans to marshal their means and create institutions of civil society that could mediate between African Americans and white Americans and hasten the progress of the race. A number of fundamental points of agreement emerged among racial uplift activists in looking ahead to the new century, including clear, easy identification of the wrongs committed against African Americans. They also agreed that, despite the shameful treatment blacks had suffered, African American achievement not only could be demonstrated but must be demonstrated as part of an organizationally based strategy for uplift.[20]

As one means of highlighting the positive aspects of the state of black America, the turn of the century saw the proliferation of race history books by both black and white Americans. Works like William Wells Brown's *The Rising Sun: Or the Antecedents and Advancement of the Colored Race* (1874), George Washington Williams's *History of the Negro Race in America from 1619–1880* (1883), and Joseph E. Haynes's *The Negro in Sacred History* (1887) laid the groundwork for many that would follow. With the new century, the titles became ever more hopeful, with Booker T. Washington's *A New Negro For a New Century: An Accurate and Up-to-Date Record of the Upward Struggles of the Negro Race* (1900), J. J. Pipkin's *The Story of a Rising Race: The Negro in Revelation, in History, and in Citizenship* (1902), Mary Helms's *The Upward Path, The Evolution of a Race* (1909), and multiple volumes of J. W. Gibson and W. H. Crogman's *The Progress of a Race, or the Remarkable Advancement of the Colored American.*

In this period, the black press built on earlier achievements and emerged as a central component of institution building among African Americans to aid the cause of racial uplift. Countless articles in the black press highlighting African American history and progress accompanied the race history books, and a wider audience found the periodicals accessible. Newspapers like the *New York Age*, the Baltimore *Afro-American*, the Chicago *Defender*, and the *Washington Bee*, and magazines like the *Colored American Magazine*, the *Christian Recorder*, *The Crisis*, and the *A.M.E. Church Review* all had national circulations and multiple readers for each printed copy. The black press, then, became an important means of conveying aspects of the philosophy of racial uplift and for women to present their own perspectives in the discussion. Most important, newspapers and magazines aided the process of creating a sense of peoplehood around common experiences and concerns as articulated in the press. For black women, this function of the press proved to be crucial to the formation of a national club to address their needs. The Boston-based *The Woman's Era* magazine, founded in 1893, consciously addressed a national audience, with reports from regional correspondents in New York, Kansas City, Denver, Washington, Chicago, and New Orleans. Through the magazine's identification of issues relating to black women's lives and through its audience base, *The Woman's Era* mobilized women to form a national organization at the end of the nineteenth century.

Black women who participated in the national club movement devoted serious attention to the politics of racial uplift. Local clubs and state federations affiliated under the umbrella of the National Association of Colored Women (NACW) in 1896 in order to promote women's voices in African American movements for political, social, and economic progress. Not distinct from the traditions of black women's organizing in the churches, the club movement grounded itself in churchwomen's assertion that their work would prove central to the future of African Americans. Fannie Barrier Williams, a founding member of the NACW, termed the increasing prominence of women in uplift work "The Awakening of Women."

> Our women, thus organized, have it in their power to supplement the blessed influence of the churches, the moulding forces of the schools . . . , to such an extent as to link their efforts with the best results of woman's work in these latter days of the nineteenth century . . . The standard of life in the aggregate amongst us is not high, it is our blessed privilege to elevate it . . . Thus shall we have

a conscious share in whatever is true, beautiful and good in the destiny of this republic.[21]

Williams articulated a common theme in the club movement, that African American destiny remains a fundamentally American destiny and that the American future depends deeply on the progress that African Americans can wrench from the hands of a reluctant white society. Club women insisted that progress would be effected, in large measure, by the actions of the "respectable" on their own behalf and on behalf of those African Americans in more difficult circumstances. The NACW's motto, "Lifting As We Climb," reflected this approach.

The founding of the NACW also occurred in the context of particularly harsh assessments of African American women by white journalists, historians, and "scientists." As Evelyn Brooks Higginbotham and others have demonstrated, from slavery on, white America defined black women in ways that continually placed them outside of the constructed category of "woman" in America. White society considered a woman's proper sphere to be her home, but black women worked— most often for white women in their homes.[22] Moreover, a growing cadre of "experts" located the source of "the Negro problem" in African American women. This literature constructed African American women as icons of unbridled sexuality, as betrayers of men, and as irredeemably impure. One white southern woman reported on her "experiences of the race problem" in the early twentieth century.

Degeneracy is apt to show most in the weaker individuals of any race; so negro women evidence more nearly the popular idea of total depravity than the men do . . . [T]hey are the greatest menace possible to the moral life of any community where they live. And they are evidently the chief instruments of the degradation of the men of their own race. When a man's mother, wife, and daughters are all immoral women, there is no room in his fallen nature for the aspirations of honor and virtue . . . I cannot imagine such a creation as a virtuous black woman.[23]

In responding to such attacks, African American women in both church and club revealed their own difficult relationship to these questions and the degree to which they internalized and feared the vision of themselves as uncontrolled sexual beings. The strategies devised by black female activists sought to address racialized constructions of gender generated from sources external to black communities but, at the same time, often did not seek to mitigate the effects of the internalized fear.

In their club work, African American women placed home life at the center of their concerns, acknowledging that they saw needed adjustments in black family life as their critics maintained. In their writings and speeches, club women and church workers emphasized careful attention to the home and to the raising of children as crucial to women's contributions to racial uplift. In a symposium on "Woman's Part in the Uplift of the Negro Race," published in the *Colored American Magazine* in 1907, this theme predominated. One club woman wrote, "Our part in the uplift of the race is to do as much as any other race of women, and much more in some respects. We are a peculiar people in that we have the great distinction of being colored people. We in our homes should begin by teaching our children that the honor of the race is with them and that they must hold it ever sacred." And another: "Our women have and are preparing themselves to help lift their race to a higher plane. Only in forty-three years we have been taught the importance of having a substantial foundation on which to erect the building of our lives, so important, I believe, of the many places our women are filling today. We should begin in the home. Home influence is either a blessing or a curse, for good or evil."[24] While club women focused attention on encouraging the building of Christian homes, by no means did this serve as a call for women to remain supportive and invisible in the home to the exclusion of other activities. In their club work and church work, African American women emphasized that community service was equally important to women's contribution to uplift work and that, through their presence, they could "bend the tree" of the racial uplift movement to be responsive to the particular needs of women.

Although the end of the nineteenth century saw the creation of large national movements like the NACW and the Woman's Convention of the National Baptist Convention among African American women, their coming together with many goals in common did not always obscure the various underlying tensions. These national organizations also represented sites of conflict and arenas in which African American women hashed out issues of both individual and community identities. Class, color, education, religion, region, sexual politics, and age all formed lines by which club and churchwomen on both the local and national level demarcated their territory. Given the common goal of racial uplift and the "politics of respectability,"[25] the question of who could best represent the finest of "black womanhood" and help move all African Americans toward the goal remained for club women. Was a college degree a necessary part of her credentials? Should she be a member of one of the black church denominations? Should she be young or older? Married or not? Southern? Northern? Would that woman come from among the black elite?

Black club women fiercely played out all of these issues within the NACW in its first years, but the question of skin color proved to be the most difficult. Although white America constructed a two-tiered racial system in which "one drop" of "black blood" made one black, African American communities often made variations in skin color much more meaningful. For African Americans, light skin color often brought substantial advantages, including more ready access to education and employment, as well as leadership in black communities. While color alone did not lead to privilege, for club women seeking to build a national movement, the issue of how to deal with the color hierarchy proved difficult.

NACW members elected Mary Church Terrell, the Oberlin-educated, light-skinned wife of Robert Terrell (an influential lawyer, educator, and judge), as the NACW's first president. By the 1906 biennial convention in Detroit, the question of the relationship between color and leadership had come to the fore. Josephine B. Bruce, the wife of former Senator Blanche K. Bruce and a member of Washington, D.C.'s black elite, emerged as a strong candidate for the presidency of the NACW. Many convention delegates saw the possibility of Bruce's leadership of the organization as deeply problematic. For an organization dedicated to the uplift of African Americans, some argued, how could a woman, light enough to be taken for white, be an appropriate leader? One delegate asserted, "We prefer a woman who is altogether a Negro, because, while the lighter women have been the greatest leaders and are among the most brilliant in the Association, their cleverness and ability is [sic] attributed to their white blood. We want to demonstrate that the African is as talented."[26] Bruce withdrew from the election and the darker-skinned Lucy Thurman prevailed.[27] The women who spoke against Bruce's candidacy felt that to reinforce white Americans' notion that their own genetic influence made some African Americans successful and respectable would only hinder the cause. Paradoxically, their argument both opposed white racism and reveals a great deal of fear that, in fact, it was the presence of "white blood" that elevated some African Americans. Nevertheless, the club women chose to underscore the achievements of the more "purely" African among them as part of their commitment to racial uplift.

As with color, class became an issue of contention for activist club and churchwomen. For African Americans during the late nineteenth and early twentieth centuries under the burden of a society in which categories of class remained highly racialized, the indicators of class entailed much more than income or family wealth. No amount of money could have kept Ida B. Wells from being ejected from the "ladies" car of the Chesapeake, Ohio, and Southwestern Railroad in 1873 or Rev. Elijah Love and his party from the East Tennessee, Virginia, and Georgia Railroad in 1889, nor could it have saved countless other victims from such harassment.[28] For most white Americans, all African Americans belonged in the same class, one determined primarily on the basis of race. Within African American communities, however, status distinctions rested on other clear factors, including color, education, income, family history, virtue, and church affiliation. The fact that many of the leaders of the national club movement came from the black elite constituted, for some critics, evidence of the bankrupt nature of club life.

Nannie Helen Burroughs, an educator and influential figure in the black Baptist women's movement, articulated a familiar critique of club women.

> Negro women have had a mania for club life. But did you ever stop to think that the clubs and federations among us are doing actually nothing for the benefit of the masses? Women who constitute them are of "the kid glove order" who think themselves too good to work among the lowly and who do little to tone up our club life. They leave the platform and applause after a flowing paper talk on some burning race question and retire to their parlors where whist and euchre and merry music are indulged in until early morning. They live unconcerned and at ease while four million of their black sisters are out yonder in the cold, in the bonds of iniquity and the galls of bitterness. The fact is that the secular clubs existing under

the good name of charity are only agencies to bring together certain classes at the exclusion of the poor, ignorant women who need
to be led by the "educated class."[29]

The women who led the national club movement objected to the
assertion that they did nothing to benefit the masses of black women.
Many of them argued that, in fact, the status distinctions that they made
ultimately benefited the cause of racial uplift. For many club women,
demonstrations of status distinctions to white America began the process of reformulating the racialized construction of class in America and
thereby led to a meritocracy in which an individual is recognized for her
achievements, regardless of racial status. Certainly, these women saw
themselves as more advanced in terms of education, virtue, and respectability than the masses of black women, but they also promoted an
ideology that insisted on linking their own advancement to that of poor
black women. The discourse around this issue reflects the attempt to
make class and status distinctions among black Americans and, at the
same time, affirm a bond among all African American women. But the
program for racial uplift often did involve establishing a normative
category for "black womanhood," one that prescribed and proscribed
codes of dress, behavior, speech, and manner of worship. These issues
of contention in the national club movement—class, status, color,
respectability—reveal the concerns of the women involved, as well as
the difficulties of attempting to create a univalent image of black
women leaders for both white and black society.

The issue of cooperative work between African American and white
American women, often on the agenda of the club movement, also
proved to be a significant question in the history of African American
women's work in churches. Both conflict and cooperation loom as
themes in this "unlikely sisterhood," as Evelyn Brooks Higginbotham
has termed it.[30] The treatment of Josephine St. Pierre Ruffin, one of the
nation's most important black club women, at the 1900 convention of
the white General Federation of Women's Clubs was indicative of one
of the most significant areas of conflict for black club women. Ruffin,
attending the conference as a representative of her Boston Woman's
Era Club, was refused admission because she was a representative of
an African American club. Told that the white representatives would
seat her as a delegate only if she represented a "white club," Ruffin

refused and someone attempted forcibly to retrieve the written credentials given to her. This incident, representative of ongoing conflict between black women's and white women's clubs over the question of
recognition of black women's work, turned, in Fannie Barrier Williams's estimation, on white women's fear of "social equality."[31]

However, in other times, places, and arenas, African American and
white American women worked together toward common goals. In an
era of hardening Jim Crow, southern black and northern white Baptist
women cooperated to fund and operate evangelical missions in the
southern United States in which they linked religious education with
literacy, race history lessons, and the cultivation of women's leadership.[32] While conflict also sometimes emerged in these moments of
cooperation, joint efforts between black and white women in religious contexts during the late nineteenth and early twentieth centuries
proved significant. The YWCA served as one of the central organizational structures in which women from varied backgrounds met
through a bond of dedication to Christian service.

YWCA Social Reform Work

The Young Women's Christian Association in the United States had
been functioning for almost a half century by the time African American women in New York City founded a YWCA in 1905. The work of
the organization in this country had its origins in New York City during
a series of Protestant revivals in 1857 and 1858. These religious revivals, occurring in other northern cities in the same period, arose in the
context of the financial panic of 1857, after the failure of the Ohio Life
Insurance Company, and the economic depression that followed. A new
spirit of cooperation across the lines of the predominantly white Protestant denominations characterized this series of revivals, and at some
point, a group of white women participating in the Fulton Street revival
in New York separated to form a daily prayer circle in order to address
women's spiritual needs in an arena constructed by women. In 1858 this
group organized formally as the Ladies' Christian Union, which would,
in 1870, give rise to the Young Ladies' Christian Association of New
York.[33]

Both of these evangelical organizations fostered in white women the
experience of conversion in which they would come to "know Jesus

Christ as Savior and Lord."[34] The women who directed the growth of this association, primarily members of New York City's wealthy white elite, felt certain that they themselves had experienced this conversion, and so, in coming together, they sought to determine how they could most effectively evangelize others. For this New York City association as well as for other Christian women's associations being formed in other cities, the target group became young white working women who did not attend any church. By holding prayer meetings in factories, these evangelical activists hoped to entice working women first to participate in the YWCA and, ultimately, also to become active members of evangelical Protestant churches.

Bible study sat at the center of the YWCA's activity in the organization's earliest years. Bible classes at the YWCA did not function as sessions in which open discussions of biblical passages or themes took place, but rather as meetings during which working women heard an address and joined in prayer and devotion preceding and following the talk. The classes in New York became quite large, numbering over two hundred participants by 1876. YWCA workers in New York and in other city associations carefully emphasized to their membership that participation in Bible class and prayer services in no way substituted for church attendance. The association's work focused on developing a personal relationship with members in order to guide them into churches or, in some cases, back to churches. The New York City YWCA's 1881 annual report outlined the approach that teachers of Bible study should take: "By frequent personal intercourse with each scholar the teacher becomes acquainted with her history, with the influences that surround her at home and at work, learns her peculiar temptations, visits her when in sickness or in sorrow, sends a kind note of enquiry if she be absent from the class, and is thus qualified to impart the sympathy, the wise counsel and the soul help of which each stands most in need."[35]

The Bible would also function as an avenue to literacy for working women. Clearly, YWCA Bible study did not encourage poor women to engage in biblical exegesis, independent thinking, or an individualist approach to Christian scripture. This firmly guided approach to Bible study in the early YWCA confounds the traditional evangelical emphasis on the individual's direct experience of the divine word and reveals the ways in which the wealthy white women of the YWCA saw class as a factor that mediated religious experience. The 1878 report of the New York City YWCA remarked that "It has been noticed of late that women of culture and refinement form a much larger proportion of the [Bible] class than heretofore; and we rejoice accordingly, for while all are precious in our sight, as in the Master's, we cannot but feel that the brighter and more numerous the talents devoted to His service, the greater the work accomplished for Him."[36] While "refined" women constituted a brighter Christian light for the YWCA, poor women were not beyond being brought to a level where they too could serve as Sunday school teachers and missionaries, and the YWCA set this as one of its goals for Victorian America.[37]

The YWCA's program of lunchtime prayer meetings for white working women in factories began to be supplemented in the 1870s by more lively activities in the association building designed to attract women and thereby guide them into the Bible class.[38] Light calisthenics classes, cooking clubs, industrial training classes, traveler's aid assistance for new arrivals in the city, and a residence counted among these new undertakings. Lecture programs, commonly offered at the YWCA, covered a broad range of topics. The 1879 lecture series at the New York City YWCA included talks on "Growing Old Gracefully," "Spinster Authors of England," "The Good Elements of Communism," "Inside Japan," and "Bees." Many of these programs could also be found in other women's Christian associations springing up around the country. While the specific methods may have varied, these groups remained aware of each other's work and clearly saw themselves as working toward the same goal of extending Christian influence to urban white women.[39]

The policing of white women's bodies in a variety of ways, as well as controlling the relationship of these bodies to public space, proved central to the YWCA's approach to dealing with issues affecting the lives of urban women. YWCA literature emphasized the physical toll that work took on white women, as well as the spiritual and psychological implications of labor. One report asserted,

> The sources of recreation for women are fewer, while their nature requires greater relaxation. The ten, twelve, even fourteen hours of daily toil exhausts their feeble frames and depresses their spirits, creating an absolute need of cheerful social influences to refresh

them for another day's toil. Of necessity they cannot safely mingle in general society with the same freedom as young men.[40]

YWCA programs, as a result of these concerns, stressed that body, spirit, and mind were connected in the body, the temple of God. Bodies should be cared for and properly developed as part of the individual's duty to God. These concerns grounded the organization's focus on "physical culture," or exercise. But the YWCA also emphasized that women's bodies could not have the same relationship to public space as did men's. While the space of the factory had been opened to these women as laborers, the YWCA identified a central part of its mission as keeping women from the dance hall, the saloon, and the street. The YWCA thought of its building as an alternative public space, constructed by women and functioning as an extension of the Christian home.

Like the Young Men's Christian Association (YMCA), founded in the United States in 1851, the YWCA's early approach to forming or reforming young women emphasized "character building." As David I. Macleod has demonstrated, the YMCA sought to address fears among white, middle-class Americans that precisely those things that made them middle class—sedentary occupations, extended education, and an extended youth—were "feminizing" them and draining them of some essential principle, thereby lessening the chances that their boys could become effective leaders. Organizations like the YMCA and the Boy Scouts sought to develop specific methods to ensure proper adolescent development especially for boys.[41]

Some of these organizations, influenced by the work of G. Stanley Hall, placed his recapitulation theory of human development at the center of their programs. Hall, in his mammoth two-volume work, *Adolescence: Its Psychology and Its Relations to Physiology, Anthropology, Sociology, Sex, Crime, Religion and Education*, asserted that individual human development parallels that of the progress of civilization through its various stages. During boyhood, for example, boys engage in "gang" behavior, a behavior Hall saw as an indication of the "tribal" stage of development. With this particular understanding of young people, the YMCA and the Boy Scouts made available organized activities to allow adolescents to act out their "savage" urges under adult supervision and provide assistance for the transition from stage to stage.[42]

Girls required a different program. In "primitive" civilization, Hall asserted, the roles of men and women were similar; the divergence of these roles reflects the advanced stage of white American civilization. Hall understood women's desire to return to equality with men as "natural," but, ultimately, as serving to diminish the energy available for the United States to move to the next stage of civilization. Hall, then, saw gender as constructed against "nature" in order to build "civilizations." Therefore, the education of girls should be restricted in order to socialize them into roles that would prove most beneficial to society as a whole. This he termed "broadening by retarding." Educators should carefully retard women's intellectual development in order to bring forward their "intuitive natures." An ideal curriculum for girls would include nature studies, household studies, and, most important, religion, a woman's natural domain. Hall argued vociferously against coeducation and higher education for women, based on the "scholarly consensus" that excessive mental activity results in infertility in women or the creation of "bachelor women," that is to say, unmarried women or, worst of all, lesbians.[43]

Hall saw certain races as adolescent and in need of similar guidance to civilization. "Most savages," Hall wrote, "in most respects are children, or, because of sexual maturity, more properly, adolescents of adult size. Their faults and virtues are those of childhood and youth. To commercialize and oppress them with work is child labor on a large scale. Without them our earthly home would be left indeed desolate."[44] Hall's view of African Americans as an "adolescent race" incorporated aspects of fear of black sexuality as well as the construction of people of African descent as "natural" and "childlike."

The YMCA developed "character-building" programs grounded in Hall's view of human development and gender roles. The YMCA's methods of character building varied from city to city but clearly centered on fostering character in young men in an environment separate from women. Although women had been present in the YMCA through women's auxiliaries dating back to the 1850s, the auxiliaries focused on assisting the men in their work rather than on providing services for women. Men tolerated the presence of women and used their enthusiasm for YMCA work, as an extension of supportive domestic roles, to raise funds and to assist in organization and administration, but never allowed women to become fully part of YMCA work. The

YMCA emphasized its belief that boys must be contained and trained for leadership and that "manliness" had to be cultivated in them. While the organization framed this in terms of guiding boys' development into adulthood, YMCA leaders also saw this "manliness" over against "femininity." And women could not create "manly" men.[45]

The YWCA modeled itself, in part, on the YMCA work that preceded it. Women in the YWCA often described their organization as a "character-making instrument." By the turn of the century, however, the YWCA began to rethink its exclusive focus on personal morality and to question the relationship between personal morality and social structures in ways that converged with the concerns of the Social Gospel movement. The Social Gospel movement represented one attempt by liberal Protestants to incorporate the fields of science, sociology, and biblical criticism into their religious worldview and to apply them in concrete ways to the social and political issues of the day. The movement, with its acceptance of Darwinian theory, emphasized progress within the bounds of a corporate vision of society in which individuals at all levels remained interdependent and bound by certain duties and responsibilities. Consequently, Social Gospel advocates deemphasized sin and salvation as endeavors of individuals alone. Walter Rauschenbusch, one of the principal articulators of the Social Gospel, insisted upon the "solidarity of sin," the notion that sin is not only between the individual and God but also may take the form of transgression of God's will with respect to other people. Each person, therefore, had a stake in the salvation of the community. For advocates of the Social Gospel, the progress promised by Darwin's theory of evolution indicated that, just as life-forms progressed toward the human, so society and the individuals in it could progress toward the Kingdom of God. The emphasis on building the Kingdom of God on earth emerged as a constant of the Social Gospel and called upon individual Christians to act, using the model of Jesus' life, in order to effect the social changes required to create the Kingdom. "What would Jesus do?" became the guiding principle of the movement.[46]

The Social Gospel became a guiding philosophy for the YWCA as it moved from a relatively unstructured organization grounded in its local contexts to a national structure that set policy for its constituent groups. The national administration of the YWCA became solidified in 1905 with the merger of two existing umbrella groups, the American Committee of the National Association of Young Women's Christian Associations of the United States, founded in 1866, and the International Conference of Women's Christian Associations, founded in 1877. After years of difficult negotiations, the two united to form the National Board of the YWCAs of the United States of America. The National Board functioned to authorize use of the name "Young Women's Christian Association" for local groups and to provide guidelines for programs and methods, declaring its purpose to be "to seek to bring young women to such a full knowledge of Jesus Christ as Savior and Lord as shall mean for the individual young woman fullness of life and development of character, and shall make the organization as a whole, an effective agency in the bringing in of the Kingdom of God among young women."[47]

Despite the YWCA's professed goal of fostering the growth of evangelical Christianity among all young women in the United States, it was often the case that both national and local white leaders in the movement saw the intended religious experiences as mediated by a number of factors. Clearly, they sought to recognize the ways in which women's religious experiences differed from those of men as a result of the particular constructions of gender in late-nineteenth- and early-twentieth-century America. As we have seen, the YWCA's Bible study program in this period disclosed a class-based approach to fostering the evangelical conversion experience. In addition, as Addie Waites Hunton's and Elizabeth Ross's experiences with the National Board of the YWCA indicate, the white leadership also felt that race mediated religious experience in a way that diluted evangelical Christianity. As a result of this conviction, the YWCA's leadership asserted forcefully its stance that African American women's diminished religious capacity required a relationship of stewardship if they were to remain a part of the movement. Nevertheless, African American women affiliated themselves with the YWCA movement and struggled both to avoid being appropriated by the YWCA in ways that disabled them and to appropriate the YWCA movement in ways that empowered them within their own communities.

African American Women and the National YWCA

African American women first became involved in the YWCA movement in 1893 with the formation of a black association in Dayton, Ohio. In the years following, black women in other cities, including

Philadelphia, Washington, Baltimore, Brooklyn, and New York, gathered to constitute themselves as women's Christian associations. Women in black colleges also became a part of the student component of the national YWCA movement from the 1880s, beginning with Spelman College in 1884, and followed by schools like Wilberforce University, the AME Church's school in Ohio, and Talladega College and Tuskegee Institute in Alabama.[48] African American women created most of these associations independently of white urban or college YWCAs, and the organizations remained independent of white women's activities. By 1912, six African American YWCAs in cities operated as branches of white YWCAs: those in Manhattan, Brooklyn, St. Paul, Poughkeepsie, St. Louis, and Kansas City. Another six—those in Baltimore, Norfolk, Philadelphia, Washington, Dayton, and Charleston—remained independent of white control, refusing to comply with the 1907 policy that sought to attach African American associations to white YWCAs.[49]

In the case of the Washington, D.C., "Colored Young Women's Christian Association," founded in 1905, the internal contradictions of the "branch relationship" policy made the ideology behind it patently clear. This particular YWCA emerged from The Booklovers, a reading club founded in 1894 and consisting of twelve of Washington's black elite women. Although the club engaged primarily in discussions of European literature and culture and maintained a membership of twelve until the late 1930s, some of the members founded a YWCA to engage in work with the community's young working women. White women in Washington did not form a YWCA until one year after African American women founded their organization. The leadership of the African American YWCA—holding to the formal logic of the National Board's 1907 policy—therefore refused to affiliate as a branch of the white YWCA, insisting that the white YWCA should become a branch of their association as the city's original YWCA. Because the leaders of the African American YWCA refused to relent, they eventually forced the National Board to recognize it as an independent association.[50] Such cases served to spotlight the National Board's 1907 policy for subordinating African American YWCAs.[51]

Elizabeth Ross continued to express concern for the future of the relationship between the National Board and black female activists. At the biennial conference of the National Association of Colored Women held in 1910, she sought and gained the endorsement of the NACW for the work of the YWCA in African American communities. She did not retreat from her position on consistency in the use of the YWCA's name and on the methods associations should follow. Ross encouraged those individuals and groups interested in building YWCA organizations to seek training through the National Board in order to undertake such work.[52] In the end, Ross obtained a promise from members of the NACW to withhold judgment on the YWCA with regard to the issues of cooperative work between African American and white women. In addition, she kept at bay any negative judgment of the YWCA as an arena for African American women's work.

And so we return to the question of why some African American women chose to remain with the YWCA in light of their own long and rich tradition of club and church work. Certainly part of the answer to this question lies in an examination of the tradition of organizing in church and club movements. Black women's involvement in the YWCA movement reflects the ongoing willingness to organize in any and all arenas that would prove productive avenues for achieving justice and ameliorating the harshness of African Americans' daily living conditions.

For African American women, then, the YWCA represented merely *one* arena in which to work, and an affiliation that did not supersede other religious, social, or political affiliations. In addition, the YWCA's concern for issues affecting working women commanded the attention of black female activists, since the economic realities of black communities meant that large numbers of black women worked outside their homes. African American YWCA workers saw possibilities in the organization's structure that would allow them to create branches in their communities that could address particular needs while obtaining access to the material resources and international voice of the YWCA. In addition, the national YWCA's emphasis on issues and problems of working women *in cities* proved to be an important attraction for African American female activists who, from the end of the nineteenth century well into the twentieth century, began to see African Americans migrating to southern and northern cities. The YWCA's attention to the urban context provided a base from which black female activists could address changes in African American community life brought on by migration.

Finally, the issue of religious concerns belongs at the center of any framework explaining the links between African American women and the YWCA. While many things separated black and white women in the YWCA at the turn of the century, the common commitment to evangelical Christianity and to its advancement provided a powerful bond. African American women in the YWCA often articulated a dual purpose in forging this union. First, they sought to address their own needs in the context of whatever concerns and approaches arose organically from African American communities. In addition, through the YWCA, black women hoped to become missionaries not only in their own communities but also to white women, preaching that Christianity could build bridges in many directions. As Addie Waites Hunton wrote, she hoped that African American women's work in the YWCA would "awaken to a larger co-operative sympathy all who believe in the democracy of Christianity and who have recognized that the supreme call of the hour is the extension of God's kingdom here on earth."[53]

Nevertheless, it would remain in the domain of African American women at the local level to demonstrate the various ways in which YWCAs in black urban communities could function as productive sites to accomplish this array of goals. New York's African American YWCA proved to be just such an arena in which a group of black women appropriated aspects of the institutional structure and discourse of the YWCA movement in ways that transformed their communities and their own lives, as well as the YWCA movement and the attitudes of many of the white women in the YWCA.

~ 2

"If One Life Shines": African American Women in Networks

*J*ANUARY 26, 1905, marked the first time that African American women in New York City refused to comply with the wishes of the white leadership of the city's YWCA movement. It would not be the last time.

The conflict on that particular January day arose from a dispute over the very terms on which African American women would affiliate with the YWCA. At a meeting held at the Mt. Olivet Baptist Church on January 18, a group of eighty-five African American women formed a Young Women's Christian Association to benefit black women in the city. Carrie T. King, a representative of the group, approached the 15th Street Association,[1] one of New York's major white YWCA organizations, to request the status of an affiliated branch, emphasizing that their primary aim was to gain not financial support but rather a connection with an established YWCA. With a vote of twenty in favor and two opposed, the all-white executive committee of "15th Street" agreed to grant the request for affiliation with two restrictions. First, 15th Street disavowed any financial responsibility for the African American YWCA, and second, it insisted that at some future meeting both groups should work out the details of the formal constitution and bylaws of the new organization.[2]

To the shock of the executive committee of 15th Street, the members of the African American YWCA sent a message that they would not accept affiliation on these terms. In their reply to the committee the following week, a delegation of African American women, led by Lucy A. Robinson, Elisa White, and Edith Leonard, argued that "although they did not intend or propose to become a burden on [the 15th Street Association], they would expect to rely on the Association for help if the need for it arose."[3] After the African American delegates completed their presentation and left the meeting, the executive committee agreed to grant affiliation on the terms laid down by the members of the delegation.

The minutes of 15th Street's executive committee make clear that many of the committee's members harbored serious reservations about the newly constituted African American YWCA. The members of the executive committee, drawn from New York's white elite, felt certain that the African American women who founded the new YWCA did not have the capacity—material, moral, or intellectual—to administer such an institution successfully. The second condition established by 15th Street for an affiliated relationship—that the African American YWCA draw up a constitution and bylaws for approval by 15th Street —sent a clear message to African American women that 15th Street intended to subordinate them and their institution.

Such conflict and contested terrain strongly marked the relationship between black and white women in the New York City YWCA in the years from the founding of the African American YWCA through the end of World War I. Throughout this period, the African American women struggled with the white leadership of the YWCA to become recognized as significant actors in this important women's social reform movement. Given the constant presence of friction, the African American leadership group developed techniques, ranging from direct confrontation to strategic procrastination and silent disregard, through which it achieved its goals. Perhaps the most significant force behind the conflict between African American and white women in the city's YWCA proved to be different visions of leadership and, most important, different modes of authenticating that leadership. For white women in the New York City YWCA, race often emerged as the paramount authenticator of their leadership: the currency of whiteness placed them in a position to "naturally" lead African American women. Certainly, the ways in which their whiteness interacted with their class status—for most of them belonged to the white elite of New York—

should not be underestimated. Among black women in the YWCA, a range of other criteria, such as education, activist experience, religious commitment, and dedication to the cause, all operated as avenues through which leaders could emerge.

Two forces contributed to the ability of African American women in the New York City YWCA to sustain the institution in the years before World War I, years marked by meager financial resources and the racism of many of the white women in the YWCA. During the late nineteenth century, New York emerged as a significant arena for organizational work among African American female activists, both native New Yorkers and more recent migrants from the South. New York's African American female activist network brought together women of varied family and class backgrounds, religious affiliations, political sensibilities, and lifestyles in work that contributed significantly to the lives of all black New Yorkers. Overturning stereotypes of black Christian reformers as elite and elitist political accommodationists, these women represented the full range of life in turn-of-the-century African American communities, and they underscore the degree to which the activism of black women in New York relied on the ability to forge alliances across many lines. In addition to the groundwork set down by nineteenth-century black female activists assisting the women in New York's African American YWCA to sustain the new organization, the resources of the women themselves proved to be of critical importance. A tradition of black women's work in the city combined with the particular talents and energies of the African American women drawn to New York's YWCA movement brought two significant results. This combination of tradition and human commitment allowed African American women to negotiate the tensions evident in relations with white women in the YWCA and to overcome the difficulties engendered by the material poverty of the institution.

Laying an Activist Foundation

The founding and growth of New York City's African American YWCA and a variety of other organizations took place in connection with black churches, a significant locus of community activity among black New Yorkers and, to a large degree, the starting point for interdenominational Christian activism. In W. E. B. Du Bois's estimation in a

1901 study of African Americans in New York City, "the centre of negro life in New York is still the church, although its all-inclusive influence here is less than in a Southern city."[4]

Du Bois and other observers of early-twentieth-century black church life in New York often commented on the class-based nature of church affiliations, among the most commonly remarked-upon characteristics. Du Bois wrote:

> There are thirty or forty churches, large and small, but seven or eight chief ones. They have strongly marked individuality, and stand in many cases for distinct social circles. The older families of well-to-do free negroes who count an unspotted family life for two centuries gather at St. Philip's Episcopal Church . . . The mass of middle-class negroes whose fathers were New Yorkers worship at Mother [African Methodist Episcopal] Zion . . . [A]t Olivet one finds a great Baptist church, with the newer immigrants from Georgia and Virginia, and so through the city.[5]

St. Philip's Episcopal Church provides the most striking example of the ways in which class became inscribed upon African American religious communities in late-nineteenth- and early-twentieth-century New York. An editorial in the *New York Freeman* (one of New York's leading black newspapers at the end of the nineteenth century), addressing the intended move of St. Philip's from Mulberry Street to a location farther uptown (eventually to 25th Street in 1889), underscored the importance of this particular church as an emblem of the strivings and mobility of black Americans. Nevertheless, the *Freeman* criticized its class-based exclusion of some black New Yorkers.

> But in making this change to a more densely populated centre St. Philip's Church will be called upon to lay aside some things peculiar to it, and perhaps dear, if it would attract the people in larger numbers and more democratic condition in life. It will be called upon to divest itself, and that largely, of the reputation for exclusiveness with which it is now correctly or erroneously charged. It can easily do this without abating one jot of its conservative respectability, as a church, and at the same time become a vastly greater educating power among the people.[6]

The abolition of the pew system at St. Philip's, in which members of the congregation purchased the most desirable seats, emerged as chief among the suggestions made in the editorial. Although not all of New York's black churches marked class boundaries so openly, many of them cultivated the reputation of "respectable" churches in contrast to prevalent images of African American religious excess. A white observer in 1911 wrote, "Strangers who visit colored churches to be amused by the vociferations of the preacher and the responses of the congregation will be disappointed in New York."[7] The *Freeman* editorial calls into question, however, the degree to which "respectable" churches functioned sufficiently as motivators for social and political activism, a function that the newspaper editor and many black Christians took to be an integral component of African American Christianity.

Along with the function of New York's black churches as centers of community life came prominence for the pastors of the largest churches. These men, some of them significant national figures in African American political, social, and religious life, dominated the public face of black church life in New York in ways that sometimes obscured the complexities of the internal workings of church communities. The attention accorded certain African American ministers in the city underscored the centrality of both gender and class in the construction of categories of "leadership" in this urban context. Strongly gendered constructions of leadership in New York's black church communities (although certainly not unique to New York, nor to African American communities) obscured not only black women's roles within the churches as articulators of religious convictions but also the work of black Christian women in social service organizations that bridged categories of "religious" and "secular" activities.

Despite the gendering of African American religious leadership as male, African American women in New York City carved out space to develop and gain access to leadership of various sorts. They accomplished this, in part, through black women's traditional means of exerting influence in the churches—church-based women's organizations. These organizations, ranging from international missionary societies to community-based benevolent aid groups, provided an important base of financial support and spiritual guidance for a range of projects undertaken by New York's black churches. The United Tribes, "a company of women of the Mt. Olivet Baptist Church," for example, became a significant fund-raising arm for the Rev. Charles T. Walker, pastor of Mt. Olivet.[8] Significantly, however, a male deacon served as president of the United Tribes, a fact that points to both the potential for productive cooperation between men and women in the churches and, perhaps, the difficulties women sometimes faced in achieving autonomy in organizing.[9]

The churches were not the only arena for women's work, however. In the late nineteenth and early twentieth centuries, African American women in New York City forged a network of activists and organizations that emerged as a significant force both in the city and on the national scene. The work of African American women in these organizations reveals the broad scope of concerns of New York's black Christian activist women.

Unquestionably, Victoria Earle Matthews belongs at the center of this network at the end of the nineteenth century and provides the best example of the ways in which African American women in the city negated simple distinctions between secular and religious work. Matthews, born a slave in Georgia in 1861 and brought to New York by her mother when she was eleven or twelve, attended public schools until being forced by the family's financial difficulties to take a position as a domestic servant. Despite this setback in her formal education, Earle, who married William Matthews in 1879, continued to study and also began to write fiction, some of which she published in periodicals. Over the next years, she wrote for a variety of daily papers in New York and became a correspondent to a number of African American newspapers and journals across the country.[10]

In 1892 Matthews helped to found and became president of the Woman's Loyal Union (WLU) of New York and Brooklyn, an organization that built a national reputation for New York's black activist women.[11] The cross-class membership of this organization, with numbers reaching 150 by 1894, declared in its constitution:

> We, the undersigned, desirous of doing our duty in this our day and generation, believing that if one life shines the next will catch the light.
>
> The object of the Woman's Loyal Union shall be the diffusion of accurate and extensive information relative to the civil and social status of the Afro-American (i.e.) that they may be led to an intelli-

gent assertion of their rights and to a determination to unite in the employment of every lawful and judicious means to secure and to retain the unmolested exercise of the same.

2nd. That the attention of conscientious, conservative, thinking people at large may be directed to the injustice of a practical denial to any class of citizens of that personal liberty and opportunity for happiness which is the unalienable perogative of every human being.[12]

Through the WLU, Matthews and other participants—including such women as school principal Sarah Garnet (widow of Henry Highland Garnet); her sister, Dr. Susan Smith McKinney Steward; teacher and poet H. Cordelia Ray; and Maritcha R. Lyons and S. Elizabeth Frazier, also schoolteachers—pursued their objectives on both the local and national levels. Locally, the WLU took up the issue of employment opportunities for African American women in New York. They called for a "crusade" to gain access to jobs in sales, an area of employment traditionally restricted to white women, and sought ways to ensure that young African American women received training for such positions. Labor questions would remain central to the local work of the WLU, even as its membership looked to address other issues. The WLU also built a treasury for the purpose of conducting various relief campaigns, including the provision of winter clothing for poor children. In the spring of 1894, it applied some of its funds to assist the Cheyenne in South Carolina—demonstrating an understanding of the interconnectedness of the experiences of African Americans, Native Americans, and other minority groups.

Having migrated from the South, Matthews shared with other transplanted southern black women a particular awareness of the links between the past and futures of all African Americans. In July 1894, Matthews circulated a survey among newspaper editors and leaders in the South, "inquiring into the condition and prospects of the people." *The Woman's Era*, the first national African American women's journal, reported, "The circular is . . . designed to gather from the most reliable sources facts as to the mental, moral, and financial position of our people, their relation to their white neighbors, and conclusions as to their probable future, and the possibility of forming Loyal Unions among the women."[13] One month later the WLU held a special meeting, over which Matthews presided, to provide public support of Ida B. Wells's international campaign against lynching. As part of this ongoing campaign, the WLU circulated petitions and organized meetings to urge Congress to pass the Blair Joint Resolution, an anti–"mob law" resolution aimed at bringing lynching under federal jurisdiction. The WLU petition received support from leaders in fourteen states as well as 350 signatories in Canada.[14]

The base established by Matthews and the membership of the WLU, which included chapters in Charleston, Memphis, Philadelphia, and St. Paul,[15] favorably positioned New York's African American female activist network to participate in the building of the national organizational structure of the National Association of Colored Women. Matthews, whose reports from New York to *The Woman's Era* contributed to the paper's ability to develop national sentiment for organizing among African American women, appeared as one of the main speakers at the founding conference (along with Josephine St. Pierre Ruffin, Anna Julia Cooper, T. Thomas Fortune, William Lloyd Garrison, and Margaret Murray Washington, among others), delivering an address on "The Value of Race Literature." Matthews went on to serve as chair of the new organization's executive committee. The WLU also became one of the first constituent organizations of the new national club movement.[16]

Victoria Earle Matthews's participation in the Cotton States and International Exposition, held in Atlanta in 1895, illustrates the broad nature of the concerns of New York's premier African American female activist. Here Matthews—along with a group of organizing officers that included Lucy Thurman and Margaret Murray Washington, both NACW leaders; Frances Ellen Watkins Harper, poet and temperance activist; and Mary V. Cook, professor of Latin and literature at the State University in Louisville, Kentucky, and an active member of the women's movement in the black Baptist church—drafted a series of resolutions against a variety of practices negatively affecting African Americans, including the sale of alcohol at the exposition, the convict lease system (and its "indiscriminate mixing of the sexes"), segregated travel, mob rule, and lynching. The committee also heartily endorsed cooperative work with white southern women, black women's club work, and education in general.[17]

Matthews became best known in New York and nationally through the White Rose Mission and Industrial Association, which she founded in 1897. The White Rose Mission served the dual function of a residential space and neighborhood center, first in a small apartment on East 97th Street and then in a building on East 86th Street. The incorporation statement of 1898 declared, "This Association is incorporated to establish and maintain a Christian, non-sectarian Home for Colored Working Girls and Women where they may be trained in the principles of practical self-help and right living."[18] Temporary lodging and travelers' aid work gave rise to the organization's name, according to Frances Reynolds Keyser, Matthews's longtime assistant at the White Rose and the superintendent following Matthews's death in 1907. Moved by the experiences of a young woman who arrived on a steamer from the South and, in attempting to find her way to her destination, was nearly lured into prostitution, Matthews made rooms available at the 86th Street home. She also arranged for a group of women, under the direction of her sister, Anna Rich, to meet arriving ships in New York and another group to station itself at the docks in Norfolk, Virginia, an important departure point for migrants. Keyser recalled Matthews saying, "Let us call it White Rose and I shall always feel that the girls will think of the meaning—purity, goodness and virtue and strive to live up to our beautiful name." Through the women in New York and those in Norfolk, Matthews emphasized, "a chain of white roses" would be established.[19] Any woman seeking lodging for a period from one night to six weeks had access to the White Rose, and the staff often waived the weekly charge of $1.25 when a lodger could not pay. For annual dues of $1, all members of the Industrial Association could spend a week at the home and have access to the sewing machines.[20]

As a neighborhood center, the White Rose provided a range of services and organized events that drew large attendance and participation. The Mothers' Club provided a venue for adult women to gather informally and sew, talk, listen to music, and read. Matthews's concern for poor, working mothers facilitated the development of a secure support network—practical, emotional, and spiritual—in their struggles to feed and clothe their families. For children, a boys' club and a girls' club not only provided recreation for neighborhood children but also began the process of trade education with sewing instruction for the girls and cobbling, chair caning, and basketry for the boys.[21] Alice Ruth Moore, a club activist and participant at the founding meeting of the NACW, taught kindergarten at the White Rose after relocating from New Orleans. Frances Reynolds Keyser recalled, "The children were truly a varied group, some neat, clean and orderly, giving evidence of careful home training, others sadly neglected, some rude and boisterous, but all learning to love Mrs. Matthews and her faithful helpers and little by little learning important lessons in decency, order, thrift and love for each other."[22] In addition, by 1911 the home offered a Sunday afternoon song service and Bible study conducted by Keyser, which served to bring together the older and younger participants in the work of the White Rose.[23]

The mission also provided a library of materials written by or about African Americans that served as the basis for a class in "race history" taught by Matthews. The *New York Evening Post* reported in 1905 that the library contained such volumes as a second London edition of Phillis Wheatley's poems, an 1859 volume of the *Anglo-African Magazine* containing an account of John Brown's raid on Harper's Ferry and his execution, a first edition of Lydia Maria Child's 1836 *Appeal in Favor of That Class of Americans Called Africans*, a transcript of the Rev. John Jasper's "The Sun Do Move" sermon, and an edition of Harriet Jacobs's (Linda Brent) *Incidents in the Life of a Slave Girl*.[24]

The support mechanism for the White Rose Mission centered on Matthews and her staff but also included other important figures both locally and nationally. Most significantly, the White Rose, among other similar institutions in the city, offered an opportunity for cooperative work between white and black New Yorkers, particularly women. The 1911 and 1912 board of directors included Mary L. Stone, a white reformer; Mrs. S. Elizabeth Wilkerson, also active in the Woman's Loyal Union; the Rev. William H. Brooks of St. Mark's Methodist Episcopal Church; the Rev. Adam Clayton Powell Sr. of the Abyssinian Baptist Church; and the Rev. Florence Randolph, an African Methodist Episcopal Zion minister.[25] Donations and membership subscriptions came from some of New York's most powerful and influential white men, including Andrew Carnegie, Robert C. Ogden, John Wanamaker, Oswald Garrison Villard, and the wives of others, such as Mrs. W. Jay Shieffelin, Mrs. Kiliaen Van Rensselaer, Mrs. Henry Villard, and Mrs. Seth Low. Prominent white female reformers such as Grace H. Dodge and Mary A. Stimson also contributed to the financial maintenance of the White Rose. In addition, nationally renowned black activist figures, including Harriet Tubman, the Rev. Benjamin W. Arnett, and W. E. B.

Du Bois, made donations or were members of the association in 1911 and 1912.[26]

Active participants in Matthews's Woman's Loyal Union and White Rose Mission also involved themselves in other projects that, among other ends, served to underscore the potential of African American Christian female activists to contribute to the life of the city. H. Cordelia Ray, a founding member of the WLU, served as the secretary of the Free Kindergarten Association for Colored Children. The association, founded in 1895 by a number of wealthy white women in New York, first operated in the public school on West 41st Street and then moved to West 60th Street. It remained, throughout, an enterprise dependent on the support and effort of both African American and white figures, including Mr. and Mrs. Henry Villard, Jacob Riis, W. E. B. Du Bois, and Booker T. Washington. The Free Kindergarten sought to provide children a refuge from the streets, an early start on the skills required for school, a free lunch, and warm clothing. It quickly included families in its work. In 1900 Cordelia Ray wrote:

> The teachers find that they have to deal with a different class of children from those previously taught. A great lack of home training is apparent among them, and they have been accustomed to spend their time mostly on the streets. They know no other authority save that of fear, and are governed by blows and hard usage. In view of these facts, it is the aim of the teachers to counteract the evil by making the acquaintance of the mothers.[27]

African American women in New York founded or contributed to a number of other organizations that served young working women, children of working parents, and the elderly. As Dorothy Salem's work demonstrates, concern for both the elderly and children often was the primary motivating factor for African American women to found institutions serving their community. In New York, the Hope Day Nursery, the Colored Mission, and the Colored Orphan Asylum supplemented the services provided by the Free Kindergarten Association. For the elderly, the Lincoln Hospital and Home and the Home for Aged Colored People, both in Brooklyn, drew on the resources of women like Dr. Susan Smith McKinney Steward and Sarah Garnet.[28] The Women's Industrial Club, founded in 1887, assisted young self-supporting women through the Home for Friendless Girls. Mattie Horton, one of the founders, commented: "Now friends, is this not a glorious cause? An institution of our own!"[29]

These institutions constituted a significant force in late-nineteenth- and early-twentieth-century New York through which a network of African American women articulated a sense of urban needs and worked out approaches to these needs, alongside black men and white women and men. Writing in the *New York Age*, Fannie Barrier Williams, an important figure in the national club movement, connected this development with social settlement work in the city. Williams emphasized that the work of institutions like the White Rose Mission, the Free Kindergarten, and the Home for Friendless Girls exhibited things in common with the settlement house movement that serviced European immigrants in urban areas. The neighborhood base of such settlements, the emphasis on the social aspects of poverty rather than individual causes, and services for a multigenerational population are all features that mark the approach of New York's African American community organizations.[30] In drawing upon the philosophy and, at times, the material resources of the settlement house movement, such organizations attempted to overcome the large-scale failure of settlement workers to operate settlements in African American communities. In the process of doing so, however, these institutions established a ground of both cooperation and conflict with white reformers in the city. The cases of the White Rose, the Free Kindergarten, and the Hope Day Nursery underscore the degree to which such enterprises depended on the energies of both African American and white women.

Yet while cooperative work between black and white female activists appears as a significant factor, it was essential to the development of community organizations that African American women develop a strong black women's network. The conflict sometimes engendered by attempts to work alongside white women illuminated for women like Victoria Earle Matthews the continuing need for organizations operated entirely within black communities and by African American New Yorkers. Thus, in the period immediately preceding the founding of New York City's African American YWCA, black female activists had established a foundation in which they articulated Christian-based goals for social reform, formed ties with white reformers, and built an impressive institutional base.

Conflicting Visions

With the establishment of New York's African American YWCA, the founders of the institution built upon the base established by activist women such as Matthews, and they also added new dimensions. Eighty-five people committed to membership at the first meeting, but responsibility for the development and administration of the new organization fell to a volunteer committee of management composed of a mix of native-born New Yorkers and migrants from the South, women of varied religious backgrounds and class positions.[31] Three of the committee's members during this YWCA's earliest years illustrate this variety.

Lucy A. Robinson became one of the principal representatives of the African American YWCA to the city's white YWCA and served as corresponding secretary from 1905 until her death in 1908. She was apparently born in Fayetteville, North Carolina, in 1855, married in 1878, and came to New York after having spent most of her life in the Southeast. Before the Civil War, her family lived in Harper's Ferry, and Lucy's father was killed participating in John Brown's raid on Harper's Ferry. Robinson later studied at Hampton Normal and Agricultural Institute at Hampton, Virginia, and there became one of the Hampton Student Singers. After her marriage, Robinson and her husband settled in Wilson, North Carolina, where she taught school. In 1893 Robinson wrote of this experience for a Hampton Institute anniversary book: "I have taught between two and three hundred children; some of the later ones are hoping to become teachers. I have assisted in Sunday school and temperance work. . . . It seems to be a general custom here, with both rich and poor, white and Negro, to use snuff and liquor, but our work has impressed the young people against these habits."[32] Since teaching, along with her husband's income, could not support the couple and their two children, she did dressmaking work on the side. After moving to New York City, Robinson became a member of the Mt. Olivet Baptist Church and assisted in the founding of New York's African American YMCA in 1899.[33]

Lydia Cuffey Smith, another important member of the early leadership group, became active in the work of this YWCA around 1909, having already established herself in a career as a teacher and journalist. Born the daughter of a minister in Norfolk, Virginia, in 1870, Smith grew up steeped in the work of the African Methodist Episcopal Church. After attending Norfolk Mission College and Hampton Institute, she married journalist Richard T. Smith and taught school; the couple moved to New York in 1893. In New York, Smith left teaching behind and began to work as a reporter for the *Brooklyn Daily Eagle*, distinguishing herself as the only African American woman then employed by a daily paper in the city. During this period, Smith became active in the Equal Suffrage League, serving as secretary for six years, in addition to working with the Howard Colored Orphanage in Brooklyn.[34] Elected to terms as first and second vice-president, Smith became a significant figure for the city's African American YWCA during its early years and went on to become the executive secretary of the African American YWCA in Kansas City, Kansas.[35]

Virginia E. M. Hunt Scott emerged as another figure of significance from the first years of New York's African American YWCA. Scott, a native New Yorker, was born in 1861. Her mother died during Scott's teen years, leaving her to care for her blind father until her marriage in 1889. Despite his disability, Scott's father worked for Trinity Chapel, and Scott, later a member of the Mt. Olivet Baptist Church, accorded the church a place of great importance in her life. Through private instruction as well as study at the New York Conservatory of Music, she became a concert pianist and the organist for Mt. Olivet for twenty-five years. She remained committed to the city's African American YWCA and served as its treasurer from its founding until 1936.

Women like Robinson, Smith, and Scott brought to the founding of the city's African American YWCA a wide range of experience in social service and a lifelong commitment to Christian-based activism. Other women active in the early development of this institution included Frances Reynolds Keyser of the White Rose Mission, the Rev. Florence Randolph of the AMEZ Church, and Edith Leonard, active in the auxiliary of the YMCA and a field agent for the National League for the Protection of Colored Women. Indeed, the women who met on the evening of January 18, 1905, to found an African American YWCA represented an impressive group of activists.

The range of experience of these women completely negates the fears expressed by the white members of the 15th Street Association's executive committee that they would be taking on the burden of an ineffectual group of well-meaning African American women. Nothing could have been further from the truth. As a result of the executive committee's failure to see the pool of resources available in the founding group, missed meanings and conflicts marked the first years of interaction between the two leadership groups. Most significantly, the white members of 15th Street's executive committee failed to put their Christian commitment—the very foundation of the YWCA movement—into play to overcome the division that the American racial system placed between these two groups of women.

The organizational structure established by 15th Street mitigated against a sense of cooperative enterprise between the two organizations. By seeking to affiliate itself with 15th Street, then the center of a small group of affiliated institutions, the African American YWCA acknowledged 15th Street as the preeminent Young Women's Christian Association in the city and sought advice, encouragement, and Christian fellowship from its leaders. But from the outset, 15th Street's executive committee hesitated to include African American women in its decision making. Unlike other affiliated institutions, such as the West Side Settlement, the African American YWCA did not have a representative on 15th Street's executive committee. The executive committee's exclusion of African American women from its deliberations—and even its devotional exercises—sent the message that the leadership of the African American YWCA had nothing to contribute to the affairs of white women.

The executive committee of 15th Street charged a subcommittee of their own members with overseeing the activities of the African American YWCA and appointed a member of this advisory subcommittee to the African American YWCA's committee of management. This representative had "permission to bring a delegate to [the] Executive Committee when necessary."[36] Among the members of the subcommittee in 1905 and 1906 were Grace Mickell Wilson, 15th Street's representative to the African American YWCA's committee of management; Helen Powers Aitken; and Mary A. Stimson. These women—like the other members of 15th Street's executive committee—represented the wealthy and socially prominent New York white elite.[37]

Stimson and Aitken, both members of the Madison Square Presbyterian Church, shared more than membership among the elite and powerful of New York. They were both involved in the work of the Women's Branch of the New York City Mission and Tract Society,

which sought to distinguish itself from the average charity organization. "Charitable societies search out the worthy," one annual report
emphasized, "we the unworthy, in the full belief that the blood of Jesus
will cleanse the foulest, and the Holy Spirit teach and sanctify the most
ignorant and degraded."[38] Thus, alongside their work with the "worthy" young women of the YWCA, Stimson and Aitken held a vision of
the "unworthy" to whom they also felt called to minister.

While Stimson and Aitken extended their interest in YWCA work to
the African American association, Grace Wilson's voice and experience
most often interpreted the African American YWCA to 15th Street in
the beginning. Only on occasion did a representative of the African
American YWCA appear, ushered in to make a report, an inquiry, or a
plea or to receive instructions, and then ushered out before any discussion or decision. By the end of 1905, Wilson declined to continue in
this chair; Mary A. Stimson, "the person most likely, with her knowledge of the colored people, to make this new departure a success,"[39] was
nominated to succeed her. Once again, interaction with the leadership
of the African American YWCA became cast as something for which
white women needed "special" experience and knowledge.

The language of the minutes of 15th Street's committee meetings, as
well as the language found in public annual reports, also reflect an
attempt to subordinate the African American YWCA. The minutes and
reports consistently describe the African American YWCA as in need of
"sympathy," "help," "strength," or "inspiration" or as a "tiny shoot"
when compared with the "hardy vine" of the white YWCA.[40] In addition, the annual reports relegated the African American YWCA to an
inferior position by listing its committee of management under the
names of the white members of the 15th Street "Colored Women's
Branch Committee."[41] For 15th Street, this new YWCA was necessarily hampered in some way by being composed of African American
women and, thus, nothing more than a "colored women's" version of
the YWCA. The African American founders and leaders of this institution, as well as other black New Yorkers, saw it very differently, speaking of their community's YWCA as "the" YWCA.

Struggles between the two leadership groups became most clearly
articulated over financial issues that often masked or stood in for the
attempt on the part of 15th Street's executive committee to subordinate
the African American YWCA. Lucy Robinson, the committee of man-

agement representative who most often visited the 15th Street executive committee meetings in the first year, frequently reported on monies received in collections or donations to the African American YWCA, ranging from $75 in February 1905 to $218.85 in March 1905 and as little as $12.84 in May 1905. As a membership organization, this YWCA collected $1 from each member annually and relied on small contributions for the rest of the operating budget during these first months. Given the precarious nature of finances in African American communities in the early twentieth century, to build an organization relying solely on community resources made for an uncertain future indeed—thus the insistence of Robinson and other representatives of the African American YWCA on a promise of support from the white YWCA (which 15th Street's other affiliated institutions enjoyed).

By March 1905, 15th Street's executive committee came to see the need for additional financial support and—through the intervention of Grace Wilson, as 15th Street's representative to the African American YWCA—agreed to set aside a $500 emergency fund and to appropriate $50 per month "to secure a floor in a desirable location for their work."[42] This appropriation would allow the new YWCA to move from temporary headquarters in the Mt. Olivet Baptist Church, an arrangement made by Virginia Scott, to a more permanent home. Lucy Robinson, summoned to appear at the following executive committee meeting, received a lecture on the firmness of the $50 limit for the rent. The records indicate that the committee of management remained unable to find an appropriate location by May, moving the executive committee to increase the appropriation to $60. In the end, 15th Street's executive committee authorized the rental of an entire house at 169 West 63rd Street for $85 per month. While 15th Street did not increase its contribution, requiring the African American YWCA to make up the balance of the rent by taking in tenants, the committee of management succeeded in obtaining the kind of space that it felt to be appropriate to the work its members were undertaking. The committee also achieved its goals without direct conflict or an overt rejection of 15th Street's plans, an approach that would become routine over the years.

The issue of staffing the institution with paid workers beyond the volunteer committee of management also proved to be an area of some conflict and one through which 15th Street's executive committee emphasized the low standing of the organization relative to other YWCAs in the city. Eva D. Bowles pioneered in this area when she was hired at New York City's African American YWCA in 1907, thus becoming the first paid African American staff worker in a YWCA. Born and educated in Ohio, Bowles came to New York after having taught in various normal schools in the South. She credited Frances Reynolds Keyser with arousing her interest in YWCA work and, by January 1907, had been elected corresponding secretary of the committee of management.[43] In December 1907, in the midst of a period of particular financial difficulties at the African American YWCA, Bowles requested an official appointment from 15th Street's executive committee as "General Secretary thereby giving her a position of greater authority."[44] The committee agreed to engage Bowles as a paid staff member, but the minutes do not reveal the salary at which she was hired. By February 1908, Bowles took a one-month leave of absence due to illness and subsequently gave notice to the executive committee of her intention to leave the position in May and return to Ohio.[45]

Despite Bowles's brief tenure in this position, both the committee of management and 15th Street's executive committee came to see the importance of a full-time staff member for the association. Mary Stimson, then 15th Street's representative to the committee of management, requested permission to hire Addie Waites Hunton of the YWCA's National Board for the summer so that the committee could conduct a search for a permanent secretary. Hunton accepted the position for the duration of the summer at a monthly salary of $40.[46]

Addie Waites Hunton, whose YWCA influence was most profound at the national level, represented a prestigious find for New York's young African American YWCA. Born in Norfolk, Virginia, in 1866 to former slaves, Hunton began her career as a public school teacher in Portsmouth, Virginia, and later became the principal of the State Normal and Agricultural College in Normal, Alabama. From 1905 to 1906, she served as the registrar and accountant at Clark University in Atlanta.[47] In many ways, Hunton's career remained closely tied to that of her husband, William Alphaeus Hunton, until his death in 1916. William Hunton, whom Addie Waites married in 1899, became nationally known as the first African American paid worker in the YMCA when he was hired as the secretary of Norfolk's black YMCA in 1888. In 1891 the YMCA appointed him international secretary for colored work.[48]

Certainly, Addie Hunton's interest in developing opportunities for

African American women in the YWCA had been influenced by her husband's success in building a YMCA movement among African American men. In addition, however, Hunton's later experience at the State Normal College in Alabama (at which African American women founded a YWCA student association in 1900), her participation in the founding of the NACW in 1895, and her service as a board member of the Southern Federation of Colored Women's Clubs must have been equally important in leading her to the national YWCA. For Hunton and many other African American women, the YWCA provided an opportunity to bring together religious concerns and social welfare techniques.

In 1907 Addie Hunton joined the staff of the National Board of the YWCA, based in New York City, to conduct a national survey of YWCA work among African American women. Having moved to Brooklyn, Hunton embarked on a five-month tour of the South and Southwest, returning to the city in March 1908.

Hunton spent the summer of 1908 reorganizing the administrative structure of New York's African American branch and conducting a search for a new full-time, permanent secretary. In addition, she spoke at the meetings of a number of local organizations, including an educational forum at St. Mark's Lyceum and a joint meeting of the Women's Auxiliary of the Afro-American Business League and the Northeast Federation of Women's Clubs. Most important, she served as the national organizer of the Sixth Biennial Convention of the NACW, held in Brooklyn in August 1908. In this capacity, she forged a concrete link between the city's African American YWCA and the officials and members of the NACW.[49]

At the end of the summer, Mamie E. Grandison accepted the offer tendered by 15th Street's executive committee of the position of general secretary at a salary of $50 per month, to be deducted from 15th Street's monthly $60 appropriation to the African American YWCA. Grandison had come to New York after having grown up in Bolton, Mississippi, and graduating from Spelman Seminary in Atlanta; it seems that Hunton recruited her specifically for the position.[50] By January 1909, however, Grandison had left, and Helen Lattimore held the position until September 1909, when she left New York for a job in New Bedford, Massachusetts.[51] Cora Jackson followed Lattimore in the position of general secretary and remained until the spring of 1911. Jackson had grown up in Detroit and was educated at the University of Chicago. After graduating, she taught at the prestigious Baltimore High School for seven years and for one year at Howard University. The *New York Age* commented that, at Howard, "her broad Christian culture, superior intellect, tact and ability in dealing with young women attracted much attention."[52]

Jackson left the position in 1911 in the midst of an intense struggle between the African American committee of management and 15th Street's "Colored Women's Branch Committee," headed by Mary Stimson—a struggle set against a period of a restructuring of the entire New York City YWCA. As early as January 1909, Mary Stimson began recommending to the executive committee that the relationship between the two institutions necessitated a shift in power through which 15th Street could exercise greater control over the African American YWCA. At this point, the membership of the African American YWCA undertook its own restructuring through annual elections of the committee of management. In the January 1909 elections, only Virginia Scott, the treasurer, survived the turnovers. Most importantly for the African American YWCA, the membership elected Emma S. Ransom president of the committee of management and thus put in place a leader with great administrative talents.[53]

Emma Ransom, who grew up in Selma, Ohio, trained and worked as a teacher until her marriage in 1886 to Reverdy Ransom, an African Methodist Episcopal Church minister. For the rest of her life, Emma Ransom moved with her husband to the various cities in which he had pastoral assignments. Her earliest activism, like Hunton's, bridged church and secular work in a variety of ways. In 1895, while Reverdy Ransom pastored a church in Cleveland, Emma Ransom and Lida A. Lowry became the first women in the AME Church to edit and publish a missionary journal for the regional missionary convention they had founded. Through the missionary society and the journal, *Woman's Light and Love for Heathen Africa*, Ransom participated in an important movement among African Americans at the turn of the century in which churches directed a great deal of attention to Christian missionary work in Africa. At the same time, Ransom became involved in the growing national African American women's club movement. In 1895 Sada J. Anderson, the Ohio correspondent for *The Woman's Era* (soon to become the official organ of the NACW), reported, "Mrs. Emma S.

Ransom of Cleveland, one of the editors of 'Woman's Light and Love for Heathen Africa,' one of our missionary periodicals, and the only one published by our women, spent a few days with us. Mrs. Ransom is but to be seen to be loved. Though young in years she is making the world know she is in it."[54] Although she could not attend the founding convention of the National Federation of Afro-American Women in 1895,[55] Emma Ransom and the missionary society for which she served as corresponding secretary sent greetings to the conference partici-pants; this marked the beginning of a connection to the club movement that would remain important to her throughout her life.

Ransom's involvement with the New York City YWCA began when Reverdy Ransom became the pastor of the Bethel AME Church in New York in 1907. Shortly after her arrival in New York, Ransom began to appear as a speaker at meetings of a number of local organizations. One of her most important appearances was before the Equal Suffrage League, a Brooklyn-based club headed by Dr. Verina Morton Jones, one of the city's most prominent African American female activists.[56] In June 1908, when Ransom delivered an address on "Social Service" at the African American YWCA in Manhattan, the notice in the *New York Age* read, "Mrs. Ransom has had large experience along the lines of her address, both as a student and worker, and being an eloquent speaker her address will be well worth hearing."[57] She continued her involve-ment with the YWCA throughout 1908; in January 1909, she was elected president of the branch's volunteer committee of management, a post she held for the next fifteen years.[58]

Upon her election to the presidency of the committee, Ransom un-dertook a campaign to ameliorate the institution's financial difficulties. In the months after assuming the position, Ransom brought consider-able stability to the organization through fund raising.[59] In addition, she sent a message through Mary Stimson, by this time the only channel to 15th Street's executive committee, that 15th Street's level of financial support was inadequate. The executive committee decided to increase its appropriation from $60 to $100 for a period of six months.[60] But Stimson remained dissatisfied with the operation of the institution and initiated a discussion at the November 1910 executive committee meet-ing on the possibility of "dispensing with the number of officers there and bringing the authority here."[61]

While this particular plan never came to fruition, Stimson continued to seek ways to gain control over the African American YWCA. In March 1911, according to 15th Street's executive committee minutes, she "reported the great desire to secure a white woman to act as General Secretary at the Colored Women's Branch for six months."[62] Stimson had already approached Louise Goodrich, a fellow member of the Madison Square Presbyterian Church, about the position, and Goodrich had agreed to accept on condition that she be paid $75 per month, an arrangement that Stimson effected by requesting that the National Board of the YWCA pay Goodrich's salary. Goodrich, whose monthly salary stood at a full $35 more than Addie Waites Hunton's, came to this position having been trained in social work at the New York School of Philanthropy and having taught at Hampton Institute.[63] Goodrich began at the African American YWCA on April 1, 1911, and remained until October 1911, leaving to become superintendent of the New York Colored Mission. Upon departing, Goodrich reported that she "decided that a white secretary is not acceptable to the colored women."[64]

The continuing attempt to wrest control of the African American YWCA from the hands of the women who founded and sustained it took place in the context of negotiations to merge the 15th Street YWCA with the city's other large YWCA, the Harlem Association, founded in 1891.[65] The merger was not finalized until early in 1912, but 15th Street's executive committee abandoned its financial commitment to the African American YWCA in May 1911. Writing to the committee that would become the new Metropolitan Board of the YWCA of the City of New York, Stimson emphasized "the lack of conspicuous success" at the African American YWCA and requested that the Metropolitan Board take immediate responsibility for "the colored branch." The committee agreed to do so and also appropriated $550 for salary expenses for the remainder of the year and $50 for other expenses.[66] At the end of 1911, the Metropolitan Board budgeted $1,800 for the work of the African American YWCA.[67]

The *New York Age* announced that on "January 1 [1912] the Colored Branch of the YWCA severed its connection with the 15th Street branch Y.W.C.A., to become a member of the Metropolitan Association of the City of New York."[68] The very public announcement of the African American YWCA's participation in the restructured organization constituted a potential new beginning through which some of the history of conflict and subordination that characterized the relationship with 15th Street could be overcome. Nevertheless, while the new arrangement provided some benefits to the African American YWCA, particularly in terms of more consistent access to financial resources, the overall structure of subordination remained firmly in place. The new Metropolitan Board continued the practice of denying the leadership of the African American YWCA direct representation on the board. And although the Metropolitan Board's financial support stayed consistent, it was small in comparison to the support granted most of the city's other YWCAs. It would remain for this African American YWCA to forge an identity and support system in large measure independent of the white YWCA structure in New York.

The African American YWCA's leaders were working within the well-established citywide network of black female activists. This network itself made the institution an important force in early-twentieth-century New York despite the inability of white YWCA leaders to recognize the success of the endeavor. In the earliest years of New York City's African American YWCA, it was not financial resources that built and sustained the institution, but rather the energy, experience, and creativity of African American activists. In addition to Lucy Robinson, Virginia Scott, Frances Reynolds Keyser, Addie Waites Hunton, and Emma S. Ransom, a number of other women committed to New York's African American YWCA proved to be significant and representative of the paths of the leadership group in the years through World War I.

Edith Leonard stands out as a figure who devoted enormous energy to this particular YWCA in its early years. Leonard attended the founding meeting in 1905 and appeared before 15th Street's executive committee with Lucy Robinson to negotiate the terms of affiliation. Both Robinson and Leonard came to the founding of the YWCA having been active in the Women's Auxiliary of the city's African American YMCA. From this point on, Leonard often took charge of the weekly meetings, arranged fund-raising concerts and socials, and chaperoned Saturday afternoon outings to parks. Leonard also took a turn as the instructor of the Bible class in 1911. Although she took a position as a paid clerk for the YWCA in 1911, the majority of Leonard's activities remained on a volunteer basis, including work as a field agent for the National Association for the Protection of Colored Women.[69] As with a number of the women who helped to found and develop New York's African American YWCA, Leonard exported her experience when she worked as the general secretary of the African American YWCA in St. Paul, Minnesota, from 1911 until 1914.[70]

Maybelle McAdoo, the chief stenographer of the Afro-American Realty Company (which would become a significant factor in the opening of Harlem to African American residents), also volunteered considerable amounts of time to the African American YWCA. Whereas Edith Leonard never served in an elected position on the committee of management, working instead directly with the membership, McAdoo's involvement with the YWCA remained primarily in the realm of committee work. She also served on the boards of the Hope Day Nursery and the Empire Friendly Shelter. The YWCA's membership first elected McAdoo to the committee of management in 1910, and in 1911 she assumed the chair of the educational committee. On occasion, McAdoo engaged in activities like chaperoning an excursion to Bronx Park or organizing a table from St. Mark's Methodist Episcopal Church at the 1910 YWCA bazaar. Over the years, McAdoo also made her voice public on vital social issues, such as lynching and women's suffrage.[71]

Katie Walters, wife of African Methodist Episcopal Zion bishop Alexander Walters, carved out space for her own activist work at this YWCA. Born and educated in Louisville, Kentucky, Katie Knox married Walters in 1877. She tied her life and work to her husband's career in the AMEZ Church and as a political voice for African Americans, accompanying him to pastorates in Kentucky, California, and Tennessee before moving to New York. Walters's own organizational experience included a term as vice-president of the Woman's Home and Foreign Missionary Society in the California conference of the AMEZ Church. She became an important and regular presence in New York City's African American YWCA, serving as chair of the library committee and organizing a variety of events, some of which involved her husband as speaker.[72]

Finally, Helen M. Curtis, a native of New Orleans and a graduate of Southern University, contributed to New York City's African American YWCA in a number of areas. Trained in Paris in the making of dresses and corsets, Curtis taught dressmaking at the YWCA in 1909, contributing to the trade classes that became central to the identity of the institution after World War I. Elected first vice-president in 1912, Curtis represented the YWCA in a roundtable discussion at that year's National Association of Colored Women's convention. Her most significant contribution to this particular YWCA came with her founding of a Camp Fire Girls club in 1912. With this, Curtis helped develop a constituency among girls under the age of fourteen, who until then were not offered any services tailored to their age group. Curtis left the organization when her husband, attorney James L. Curtis, received an appointment as minister resident and consul general to Liberia in 1915.[73]

An impressive range of organizational experience as well as a high level of education emerge among the most striking features of the leaders of New York's African American YWCA from its founding until World War I. While 15th Street's executive committee had among its members only one college graduate in the years between 1870 and 1900,[74] members of the African American committee of management had degrees from Southern University, Hampton Institute, Norfolk Mission College, the University of Chicago, Avery Normal Institute, Drew Seminary, Spelman Seminary, and Shaw University. Without question, the leadership of New York's African American YWCA had far more impressive credentials in terms of education and practical experience in institution building and social activism than did 15th Street's leadership.

The attempt by the leaders of 15th Street to subordinate the African American YWCA was not based on tangible credentials but rather rested on the conviction that the currency of whiteness always certified them as more capable than any African American woman. This approach becomes most clear in 15th Street's hiring of Louise Goodrich as general secretary of the African American YWCA. The minutes of the executive committee meeting report that Mary Stimson wanted to hire "a white woman" for the position, and Goodrich's most important qualification, in the eyes of white YWCA women, appears to have been just that.[75] No record remains of Goodrich's service at the African American YWCA except for two notices in the *New York Age* concerning YWCA meetings that list her as present.[76] Clearly, she encountered resistance from both the leaders and members of the African American YWCA to the imposition of an overseer whose primary value was her whiteness.[77] That Goodrich had been trained as a social worker and had taught at a black college could not, for the African American leaders, mitigate the insult of this attempt to strip them of control of their own institution.

Despite 15th Street's attempt to subordinate the African American

YWCA, it survived, grew, and became an important and influential institution for black New Yorkers. Although the African American YWCA remained within the structure of the white-dominated New York City YWCA, was excluded from access to the decision-making process of the organization as a whole, and received an unjustly small portion of allocated financial resources, this particular YWCA had access to the stunning human resources of its leaders and members.

An illustration of the degree to which this institution had successfully situated itself within the city's network of black female activists came with a 1910 conference, sponsored by the National League for the Protection of Colored Women, to discuss questions relating to the increasing urbanization of African Americans. An interracial meeting, this conference boasted some of the country's most prominent African American and white voices in the discourse about race in the United States. William J. Schieffelin, Ray Stannard Baker, Frances Kellor, Mary L. Stone, and Robert E. Park were among the white participants, and S. Willie Layten, Major R. R. Moten of Hampton Institute, and Fred R. Moore of the *New York Age* were among the African American participants. In addition, members of the city's African American YWCA constituted a large component of the African American women present, including Emma Ransom, Frances Reynolds Keyser, Cora Jackson, and Lydia C. Smith.[78] Even a cursory reading of the *New York Age*, the city's principal African American newspaper, reveals the degree to which a wide range of enterprises concerned with the welfare of African American people relied on the African American women of the YWCA for their indomitable energies and formidable expertise.

~ 3

"The Home-Made Girl": Constructing a Mobile Private Space

$\mathcal{H}$AD YOU WALKED SOUTH on Sixth Avenue from Central Park South in Manhattan and turned west onto 53rd Street on a Sunday afternoon in 1907, emerging from the shadow and noise cast by the "El"—the elevated train overhead—the street would not have appeared markedly different from any you had passed on the way. As in much of the "Tenderloin" district—from 42nd to 59th Streets on Manhattan's west side—the uninitiated stroller might have been startled by the rapid shifts in the racial and ethnic composition of the area. Changing block by block and sometimes house by house, the Tenderloin housed African American families as well as German, Italian, and Irish immigrants. You would have noticed, however, that 53rd Street residents were predominantly African American.

On that Sunday, you would have seen well-dressed women and men emerging from the three churches located on this street between Sixth and Eighth Avenues. The Mt. Olivet Baptist Church, on the street since 1885 and one of the most influential black Baptist congregations in the nation, commanded a great deal of financial respect, owning property valued at $160,000 in 1907.[1] St. Mark's Methodist Episcopal Church's congregation, championed by its fiercely outspoken pastor, William H. Brooks, often appeared at the center of public struggles for racial justice in the city. Also on 53rd Street was one of the city's inter-racial church communities: St. Benedict the Moor Roman Catholic

Church. Perhaps you might secure an invitation to one of the private clubs lodged along 53rd Street. The Society of Sons of New York, founded in 1884 and known for its annual April ball, owned a building on the street. The group's membership requirements admitted only New York–born men of the most prominent African American families who, in the words of one member of the society, exhibited "the most delicate taste of gentleman-like tone and behavior."[2] The Society of Daughters of New York, founded two years later, followed the Society of Sons in restricting membership to the most "respectable" of native New York women in "band[ing] together for mutual love, protection and elevation."[3]

If visiting from out of town, you could find lodging at the Marshall and Maceo Hotels, which occupied two converted brownstones on 53rd Street. Black clergy and business people tended to stay at the Maceo, while black artists, musicians, dancers, actors, and authors gathered at the Marshall. The Marshall's restaurant, known for its quality fare, also gained a reputation for its Sunday evening orchestra and for the lively gatherings of men and women whose conversation turned, at times, to art or politics or who, at other times, sought the company of prostitutes working out of the hotel.[4]

If you took this stroll in the spring of 1907, you would find New York City's two-year-old African American YWCA at 143 West 53rd Street. At 4 P.M. on Sunday afternoons, the female membership gathered to read the Bible and to pray together and, along with men of the community, to discuss current events, history, politics, or art. Sundays in June 1907 featured lectures on African attitudes toward Christianity, presented by a visiting Liberian scholar; a paper by one of the members on "What Is Required of the Young Negro Women of Today"; and a presentation by Augustus T. Bell, author of *Bell's Ethical Encyclopedia*.[5] The YWCA had leased this building in April 1907 and would remain there for seven years. The organization had been forced to move from its original location at 169 West 63rd Street when its building was bought, along with three others on the block, by the City Mission of the Episcopal Church. Although the move came unexpectedly—the YWCA had a full year left on the 63rd Street lease—and other space possibilities, both temporary and long term, arose for rental, the YWCA spent a great deal of time considering properties before selecting 53rd Street.[6]

The social geography of New York City in the early part of the twentieth century, and of black New York in particular, invested the YWCA's move to West 53rd Street with great significance. With this move the African American YWCA joined individuals and institutions on *the* elite street of black New York. By settling there, the YWCA took up residence among some of the most stable institutions of black New York—churches, the YMCA (founded in 1899), and clubs—and thus declared its intention to become another long-lived New York organization.

～ IN HER EXAMINATION of women in the public sphere in nineteenth-century American cities, Mary Ryan demonstrates some of the ways in which a strictly dichotomized view of the public as gendered masculine and the private as gendered feminine obscures the historically significant and creative ways in which women lived and acted in the public sphere. Recognizing that the public sphere in American history has indeed been constructed in ways that seek to exclude women and to express male power, Ryan examines the presence of women in urban celebrations, in the sex industry, as public consumers, as participants in riots, and as feminist activists. Her work emphasizes the role that class and ethnicity have played in the gendering of public space and in the experiences of women in the public sphere. Contrary to Jürgen Habermas's notion of the public sphere as an arena of rational debate and a unified site in which public opinion is formed, Ryan posits the nineteenth-century urban public sphere as one in which "public life was not enacted in some ideal hall of rational deliberation . . . but on a fluid field of cultural, social, and political mobilization."[7] Most important, Ryan emphasizes that "multiple points of public access" to this process have always existed.

The relationship of black women to public and private space emerged as a central concern of African American women in New York City's YWCA in the period from the institution's founding in 1905 until its move to Harlem in 1913. "Public" and "private" became crucial issues for these women because of the ways in which the public realm in New York became a minefield of tensions of race, gender, class, and sexuality in these years. In addition, the concentration of working black women in domestic service, as well as overcrowded neighborhoods and housing, compromised the ability of black women to create safe and nurturing home environments. The city's African American YWCA's project entailed constructing a private women's space in its building in order to overcome the impact of gendered and racially charged public space on young, working African American women. The "home" of the YWCA functioned both as a safe environment and as a mechanism for instructing women on their domestic duties. This instruction reflected an emerging discourse on the home for African Americans and the philosophy of racial uplift. Through this homosocial space, African American women who came to the YWCA underwent a socialization process to guide them into the proper Christian way of establishing heterosexual family units in the potentially destabilizing context of early-twentieth-century New York.

In addition to emphasizing the construction of family units and Christian home environments, the YWCA used its own space, through holding regular public meetings, in service of the reappropriation of public space. Because it merely approximated a home, the liminal status of the YWCA allowed it to mobilize its private space to invest the public sphere with the Christian energies of its membership. By enlarging the private, this African American YWCA attempted to redeem the public and counter the ways in which the particularly racially charged and gendered atmosphere of early-twentieth-century New York worked against the possibilities of African American women establishing truly safe home environments.

Racially Charged Public Space

In July 1907, two months after New York's African American YWCA opened its new space on West 53rd Street, the *New York Age* published an editorial addressing the relationship between the New York City Police Department and black New York communities.

> Now, it is a fair statement of fact that the New York police force has a greater dislike and nags and persecutes more, the colonized Afro-Americans than they do any of the other sort [immigrant communities]. A kind of war exists between them. Beginning with the San Juan Hill [neighborhood] riots[8] several years ago there has [*sic*] been constant clashes between the two forces. As long as the police regard and treat all Afro-Americans in a colonized district as

if they are suspicious characters and toughs, there will be trouble and plenty of it.[9]

This editorial followed by a few months another *Age* piece aimed at dissuading southern African Americans from adopting an idealized vision of the city and its promises.

> It is impossible for an individual to leave the average Southern State and come into a city like New York and establish himself, all at once, in his new surroundings without, in many cases, suffering greatly. In the large cities of the North competition is severe. Not only is there competition, but there is race prejudice in many of the avenues of life that has to be reckoned with. The cost of living is high and employment not always easy to find. All these considerations lead us to warn our people to think carefully before they decide to pack up and leave their rural homes to come into a large city like New York.[10]

While southern, rural African Americans had long viewed the North, and its cities in particular, as the promised land within the American context, black New Yorkers understood the complexities of life in the urban North and regarded their home with great ambivalence. Certainly, given the systems of slavery, radical segregation, and racial terrorism in the South, the opportunities afforded by life in the North—especially potentially greater access to education, employment outside of agriculture, and some measure of personal security—were undisputed. But these *Age* editorials emphasize the ways in which the city loomed as a highly racially charged environment for black New Yorkers. And the dangers of racial conflict had an impact on politics, economics, religion, and gender relations.

Two race riots, both of which exhibited conflicts of class, gender, race, religion, sexuality, and ethnicity, most dramatically portray the racially charged nature of public space in New York City. For four days in July 1863, mostly working-class Irish men and women rioted against Union Army conscription for the Civil War, a war that they believed held out nothing but economic ruin for themselves. Protesting white laborers in New York, many of them immigrants, saw the loss of male family members' income to the war as an immediate danger. They also had little reason to sympathize with the Union cause: the end of the southern system of racial slavery would ultimately bring unwanted economic competition from black laborers.[11] Targets of the draft riots included the draft office, the homes of prominent Republican politicians, and newspaper offices. In addition, the mob directed much of its rage at African Americans. The attacks against black residents became so fierce that hundreds sought refuge in police stations, although even there they remained vulnerable to attacks. Rioters lynched a dozen African Americans, and many sympathetic whites lost their homes and property.[12]

During this riot, working-class Irish Catholics and upper-class white Protestants played out their conflict on the field of a private institution for black orphans. In burning down the Colored Orphan Asylum, housing two hundred children in a building at Fifth Avenue and 43rd Street, the rioters protested their own exclusion from the category of "worthy" recipients of philanthropic attention from upper-class white New Yorkers. This was a stunning reminder to African American New Yorkers that public space was not safe for them: the attack on the asylum saw orphans fleeing their home as rioters crashed through the doors and ransacked the building before setting it aflame. A bureau heaved out the window struck and killed a ten-year-old resident of the orphanage. Clearly, orphans had nothing directly to do with the political or economic causes of the protest but served primarily as safe and easy stand-ins for a variety of other desired targets, such as the government or wealthy white New Yorkers.[13]

In addition to the attacks on black New Yorkers on the streets and in other public areas, white draft rioters hunted down African Americans in their homes. In various accounts of those arrested, it becomes clear that they broke into and ransacked the homes of people they knew in their neighborhoods. Mary Alexander, an African American woman, testified that she had been ordered by a mob to leave her apartment and that when she returned two days later, she found that much of her property had been stolen or destroyed. Alexander then went downstairs to the apartment of the Shandley family, white neighbors, where one of the sons told her that his mother had most of Alexander's belongings. When Alexander tried to enter the apartment, Mrs. Shandley refused to allow her to, denying that she had anything except a photograph of Alexander's husband. Shandley later insisted that she would not return Alexander's property until she saw what other rioters intended to do with "their" stolen property. This case does not stand alone in accounts of white New Yorkers looting or committing violence on black colleagues or neighbors during the riots.[14]

The attempt to police sexuality perceived as transgressing the hardened categories of race and class also characterized the draft riots. Ann Martin, a white woman, testified that the men who entered her house threatened her precisely because she was married to a black man. Because William Derrickson, an African American, employed a white former prostitute as a maid, William Cruise beat Derrickson and his mother, Ann, who did not survive the beating. Cruise, a neighborhood grocer, had just come from burning down Mary Burke's house. Burke, a white prostitute known for catering to black customers, was among a number of brothel owners and prostitutes, black and white, whose business practices enraged the mobs.[15] Many of the African American men targeted by the rioters were stripped naked in preparation for mutilation and lynching.[16] The rioters who attacked white women like Martin and Burke underscored the ways in which the power and privileges of whiteness could be revoked if one failed to practice white supremacy.

While the memory of the draft riots lingered long in the national memory, another racially charged moment informed the experiences of the women at the city's African American YWCA in its early years. During the summer of 1900, the city again saw rioting and violence aimed at black residents. An encounter between an African American man and a white policeman, with an African American woman at the center, set the stage for a night of rioting during an August heat wave. Sometime in the evening of August 12, Arthur J. Harris, a recent migrant to the city, left the room that he shared with May Enoch[17] on West 43rd Street and went to a local saloon to buy cigars. Enoch went out at 2 a.m. to find Harris and asked him to return home. As she waited for him on the corner of 43rd Street and Eighth Avenue, Robert J. Thorpe, a plainclothes police officer, approached Enoch and charged her with soliciting for the purposes of prostitution. Harris emerged from the saloon as Enoch struggled to break Thorpe's hold on her arm. "The policeman grabbed my girl," Harris later testified. "I didn't know who he was and thought he was a citizen just like myself."[18] A fight ensued between Harris and Thorpe during which, Harris asserted, Thorpe hurled racial epithets and clubbed him. Harris further testified that, in fear for his life, he knifed Thorpe and both he and May Enoch escaped. Thorpe died the next day.

According to newspaper accounts, Thorpe's death did not immediately spark the rioting. Two days after his death, a reported encounter between a black man and two elderly white women outside the house where Thorpe's body lay for viewing sparked the actions of mobs of white New Yorkers. "There is where they are holding the wake for the poor policeman who was killed by a negro," a woman commented to another. Reports indicate that they were overheard by Spencer Walters, a "brawny," drunken black man who aimed a pistol and cursed them. A white man intervened on behalf of the women, and fighting broke out. Other accounts indicate that white men and women on the street attacked Walters without provocation, coming at him with cries of "kill the nigger."[19] A night of rioting followed in which mobs took control of Broadway and Seventh and Eighth Avenues from 34th to 42nd Streets, chasing down and assaulting any African Americans they encountered. Some of the rioters dragged African American men and women from streetcars along the avenues, beat most and shot some. Various mobs also stoned houses that they believed to have black tenants.

Both of the incidents that eventually led to violence on the night of August 15, 1900, illustrate an intricately spun web of gender, race, and class concerns and conflicts in turn-of-the-century New York. First, from the point of view of police officer Robert Thorpe, and the white New Yorkers who engaged in the riot, Thorpe's actions with respect to May Enoch were completely justified. He saw a black woman standing on a street corner in a district thick with sex workers and on a street with more than a dozen houses of prostitution.[20] Like many white New Yorkers and, clearly, many police officers, Thorpe acted on the presumption that African American women who occupied public space were more than likely prostitutes. The newspaper accounts fail to question this assumption and, therefore, allow neither Enoch nor Harris any room to justify their resistance.

On the other hand, in the discourse surrounding the encounter between Spencer Walters and the two white women and their defender, a purpose larger than the "protection" of the women emerges. The *New York Herald* reported: "The women of the region took a prominent part in the riot. They did not attempt, like the fiercer women of the Paris streets, to attack the negroes, but they shrieked vengeance against the negroes and incited the [men] to greater fury. One of these viragoes was heard to say:—'These coons have run this avenue long enough. It is our turn now.'" The following day the *Herald* reported: "Racial animosities long dormant had suddenly burst into a fierce flame. At every street corner white men had gathered, and the general theme of conversation was that the blacks had had too many privileges in this city, that they had abused them, and that the time had come to teach them a lesson. . . . It was asserted on every side that [negroes] had been entirely too bold, and had assumed improper sway in Sixth, Seventh, and Eighth avenues and that the whites must assert themselves."[21] The *Herald* bolstered these assertions by informing its readers that while, on the whole, African American New Yorkers were not criminals, the black population included a sizable portion of the most criminal element of the South. So, control of public space emerged as a salient underlying issue for white New Yorkers who shared this neighborhood with African Americans.

Terror on the part of black residents at the prospect of entering public space characterized the day following the riot. Some residents fled the city, while others took refuge in other neighborhoods. Of those who stayed, most were forced to remain inside. Two days after the riot, *The Sun* reported, "The better class of negroes who kept to their homes after dusk on Friday were out on the streets last night and none of them was molested. The negroes who caused the trouble, the flashily dressed and bediamonded fellows who strut and stand around the Sixth avenue saloons, kept well under cover."[22] "Normalcy," then, would entail a return by black New Yorkers to a mode of moving through public space grounded in an understanding of white control of that space.

Immediately following the riot, information emerged regarding the actions of members of the police department during the height of the violence. African American New Yorkers came forward with accounts that police officers failed to protect victims of mob violence, participated in the rioting, and beat those African Americans taken into custody during the course of the night. A range of city leaders voiced objections in the wake of these revelations. In a Sunday sermon entitled "Perils of a Great City," the Rev. Dean Richmond Babbitt, the white Episcopal rector of a church in Brooklyn, denounced the police.

If one of the policemen in Manhattan was killed in the discharge of his duty, he died a soldier and his murderer should be brought to speedy justice. But what shall we say of one who, sworn to preserve the peace, breaks the peace; and sworn to uphold the law, breaks the law? From him should be stripped his official rank, his badge and his deadly nightstick, and the power to use an office which he has disgraced. The plain fact of the matter, as shown by eyewitnesses, is that the police planned, stimulated, fomented, and practically conducted that riot, and the result of it is that no man nor woman, be they rich or poor is safe under such bluecoated, cowardly bullyism.[23]

In addition to public denunciations by figures such as Babbitt, by newspapers across the country, and by African American organizations like the Young Men's Republican Club, the United Colored Democracy, and the Young People's Christian Association of Sharon Baptist Church, groups formed specifically around issues raised by the riot.[24] One of these groups—a committee headed by the Rev. Charles T. Walker, pastor of the Mt. Olivet Baptist Church—had a diverse membership of men from the community and the support of two African American bishops.[25] This committee began to raise funds, with $1,000 pledged at the first meeting, to obtain counsel to seek the removal of those police officers who had participated in the violence. A more vocal group, the Citizens' Protective League, organized on September 3, 1900, at a meeting called by the Rev. William H. Brooks and held at St. Mark's Methodist Episcopal Church on West 53rd Street, also sought the prosecution of police officers guilty of rioting. T. Thomas Fortune, editor and publisher of the New York Age, the city's leading black newspaper, chaired the league's executive committee.[26] In addition, the league obtained as counsel Frank Moss, former president of the Board of Police, of the City Vigilance League, and of the Society for the Prevention of Crime, and one of the best-known opponents of official corruption in the city.[27]

Newspapers and these committees focused their attention on the actions of Police Chief Devery. The New York Herald, for example, reviewed his record as a captain, inspector, and chief from 1891 through the riots of 1900. Devery's professional history, according to the Herald, disclosed a pattern of repeated charges of protecting brothels and gambling houses, extortion, and accepting money from officers in exchange for desired assignments. Nevertheless, Devery had avoided serving jail time for these offenses—a jury, members of which he was also accused of threatening, had acquitted him of extortion charges in 1896—and continued to advance unimpeded through the ranks of the police department. For his part, Devery answered the charges by saying, "I won't stand for any brutality. It is the business of the police to protect everybody, it don't make any difference whether they are chinks, negroes or what they are. As far as using the club on rioters is concerned, I approve of that . . . [A] policeman doesn't carry his locust to play with or wear as a bouquet."[28]

The two African American organizations that arose in the wake of the riots declared purposes beyond the removal of Devery and the prosecution of police offenders, however. They also revealed a particularly masculinist agenda. The Citizens' Protective League stated its purposes as "first, to afford mutual protection and, second, to prosecute the guilty."[29] In a pamphlet produced by the league (*Story of the Riot*), sworn statements from African American victims of police brutality create a narrative of an epic struggle between African American men and white policemen over the right to "protection." In statement after statement, African American residents of the west side testified that police officers, without provocation, assaulted men of the community.

The larger narrative constructed by the Citizens' Protective League, the newspapers, and other commentators on the riot placed women in a secondary role, marking their presence or absence in relation to men and to public space. May Enoch, the "cause" of the riot, most often goes unnamed in the accounts of the events leading up to Thorpe's death, referred to instead as Harris's "common-law wife," "girlfriend," "wife," or "a negress."[30] Some of the newspapers found it important to emphasize that Enoch, married to someone other than Harris, was merely Harris's "common-law" wife and, therefore, reasonably suspected of soliciting on the street corner. For the Citizens' Protective League, Enoch goes unnamed and is referred to as Harris's "wife." Similarly, almost all of the women who testified for *Story of the Riot* appear in relation to a man who is the primary victim of assault, and, most often, these women are out on the streets accompanied by their husbands. Significantly, women also appear in the booklet as witnesses to attacks on men in the streets—via their windows. Thus, just as part of the masculinist agenda of the league entailed claiming the right of African American men to control "their" public space, it also intended to restrict women to the private realm.

The protest pamphlet produced by the Citizens' Protective League sought to counter many aspects of the newspaper coverage of the riot and events leading up to it. Frank Moss, who compiled the affidavits, emphasized in his introduction that the victims of police brutality who demanded justice represented neither the "dissolute and lawless white persons" who lived in the area nor "the dissolute Negroes who are so often seen lounging about the 'Tenderloin' and its neighborhood," but, rather, "respectable, hard-working men and women."[31] These "respectable" women, who emerge in the pamphlet as adjuncts of men, do not traverse the public space of the Tenderloin and San Juan Hill unaccompanied. And by testifying that their husbands were gainfully employed and had not been drinking, they served as the watchful repositories of wrongs committed against men of the community. Thus, the narrative of the 1900 riot, particularly as put forth by the Citizens' Protective League, sought to subordinate gendered readings of the events to a perspective that emphasized the racially charged nature of the public arena and its effects on African American men.

The draft riots and the riot of 1900 underscore one of the reasons that public space in various New York neighborhoods carried such racially charged meanings. Residential segregation according to race was commonplace and traditional in New York; but the realities of class structures in the city brought poor European immigrants to the same neighborhoods as African Americans. On the other hand, racial boundaries functioned to deny many middle-class black New Yorkers a desired sense of class stratification. A *Harper's Weekly* article on "The Negro in New York," four months after the 1900 riot, explained:

> Property is not rented to Negroes in New York until white people will no longer have it. Then rents are put up from thirty to fifty percent, and Negroes are permitted to take a street or sometimes a neighborhood. There are really not many Negro sections, and all that exist are fearfully crowded. Nor are there good neighborhoods and bad neighborhoods. Into each all classes are compelled to go, and the virtuous and the vicious elbow each other in the closest kind of quarters.[32]

Both segregation and the riots showed that neither public nor private space was safe for African American women and men.

Racialized and Gendered Public Space

The draft riots and the riot of 1900 reveal New York's undercurrent of racially charged attitudes toward public space. They also showcase tensions related to gender, ethnicity, sexuality, class, and religion. All of these tensions complicated black women's access to safe public space, and African American women in the YWCA had to formulate strategies to deal with them. The YWCA's work recognized the interwoven gendering and racializing of public and private space, and the impact of this process on African American women.

A number of demographic realities shaped life for African American women during this YWCA's earliest years. First, New York's black population was primarily an adult one in 1905, with 72 percent of women and 74 percent of men falling between the ages of twenty and fifty-nine. In addition, the population consisted of considerably more women than men from 1900 through 1910. In the age group twenty to twenty-nine, for example, women outnumbered men by 126 to 100 in 1900, 110 to 100 in 1905, and 121 to 100 in 1910.[33] Second, by 1905, New York's black population had been significantly influenced by migration from southern Atlantic states, with migrants from Virginia making up almost three-fourths of the adults in San Juan Hill and the Tenderloin.[34] Herbert Gutman's work on African American families reveals that during this period a significant percentage of African American migrants were single adults rather than family units, which accounts for the predominance of adults in the population. Twenty percent of black women between the ages of twenty-five and forty-four boarded in the homes of people unrelated to them, 3 percent lived alone, and 3 percent boarded with relatives.[35]

Work opportunities for African American women in New York, while not scarce, remained severely restricted in type. The available jobs had a significant impact on the gendering of life in the community. Overwhelmingly, African American women worked as household servants or waitresses (63 percent) and laundresses (20 percent). In addition, compared with white women, a much higher percentage of the city's African American women, both unmarried and married, worked, and they remained employed for more years than white women. The 1900 census figures for New York showed that, of women aged thirty-five to forty-five, 56 percent of black women worked, as opposed to 18 percent of white foreign-born and 19 percent of white U.S.-born women. For women over forty-five, 54 percent of black women worked compared with 14 percent of white foreign-born and 15 percent of white U.S.-born women.[36] African American men's employment range, also quite narrow, showed 86 percent working as unskilled laborers or in personal service.[37]

This demographic sketch reveals a number of significant issues necessary for understanding the African American YWCA's approach to redeeming public and private space and providing African American women with access to power in these realms. Most important, a large percentage of the city's African American women worked as domestics, and many of them lived either in the homes of their employers or as boarders in tenement flats. In their capacity as domestic laborers in the "public" workplace, these women devoted much of their time to helping to maintain the private space of white families while, at the same time, access to their own private space remained severely compromised. As a boarder in a rented flat, a domestic worker might sleep in a front room separated from the other tenants by a curtain, or share a bedroom with other female boarders or children in the family. If she had a room in the household in which she worked, she would be subject to the almost constant scrutiny of her employer. While privacy was certainly hard to come by for many New Yorkers, the contrast between the role that African American domestics played in fashioning the private in white homes and the meanness of their own surroundings in the urban environment certainly made both the public and the private problematic realms for these women.

The public arena also presented difficulties for this large group of African American women. Various African American commentators on black public culture in the Tenderloin and San Juan Hill agreed in certain respects with the complaints of some of the white participants in the riot of 1900 and with discussions in various city newspapers. The bottom line for all of these groups was that there was just too much "public" culture in African American communities. By this they meant that the use of the streets and of other outdoor space by poor African American migrants did not conform to standards set by middle-class and wealthy white and black New Yorkers.

Southern African American migrants tended to use streets, sidewalks, and tenement stoops as common space, in part because of overcrowded housing but also as a result of differing concepts and ordering of public space. Thus, when Mrs. Rosa Lewis, whose testimony appears in *Story of the Riot*, complained that a police officer hit her with a nightstick to remove her from the stoop of her house, the conflict between the two turned, in part, on contrasting notions of the boundaries of public and private. To Lewis, the stoop of her building constituted a reasonable extension of her home space. To the police officer, this incident marked yet another instance of the misuse and appropriation of the public by African Americans. Not surprisingly, the effect of this public culture on young black women emerged as an area of great concern to commentators on the problems of African American neighborhoods. The *Harper's Weekly* analysis of black New York in 1900 argued that overcrowding and the failure of African American residential neighborhoods to reflect class stratification were "a great source of moral contagion, and vice spreads with great rapidity among the women of such quarters."[38]

The theme of "moral contagion" and the role of young women as carriers of "disease" garnered great attention in the discussions about the difficulties of urban spaces for African American communities. For the most part, these narratives about the corrupting influences of the North on migrant women from the South emphasized the inability of African American women to protect themselves from these dangers. Mary White Ovington and Frances A. Kellor, white reformers in New York, made clear connections between the inability to protect oneself and the potential of unprotected women to unleash vice upon the city.[39]

Kellor, one of the founders of the National League for the Protection of Colored Women and the director of the Inter-Municipal Committee on Household Research in New York, warned other reformers about what she saw to be the forces preying on African American women and leading them into vice. Kellor blamed unscrupulous employment agencies that sought to take advantage of the woman "who has left her happy-go-lucky, cheerful life in the South, a splendid cook, a good servant,"[40] in search of a work situation that required as little work as possible. According to Kellor's research, all too often African American female migrants never reached the place of employment promised by the employment agents, either because it never existed or because the women refused to do the amount of work for the low wages they found there. For Kellor, these women, "turned loose upon the city," took a short trip on a straight path to the "hospitals, almshouses, and prisons."[41] Importantly, Kellor placed the real burden of responsibility on the inability of African American female migrants to protect themselves from these agencies. Kellor's writings fostered a sense of "moral panic" concerning the presence of these "unsupervised" women and called for drastic measures by agencies to oversee the trip north, from the employment agent's desk in a southern city to the docks in New York, where female agents of protection societies would assist new arrivals, even to the point of compelling them to see their intended employer before being able to retrieve their luggage at the dock.

Mary White Ovington, one of the founding members of the National Association for the Advancement of Colored People (NAACP) and a longtime supporter of W. E. B. Du Bois's work, published a study of African American life in New York in 1911 that included a chapter focusing particularly on black women. Ovington, whose expertise on black life in New York derived from having lived, for research purposes, for eight months as the only white resident in a model apartment building on West 63rd Street, presented a picture of young working African American women as generating social disorder. Ovington argued that the ratio of women to men in New York's African American community caused the "surplus women" to "play havoc with their neighbors' sons, even with their neighbors' husbands since the lack of men makes marriage impossible for about a fifth of New York's colored girls."[42] While Ovington also found it important to emphasize that some African American women in the city worked hard and expressed ambition beyond the situation in which they found themselves, and while she underscored the discrimination that black women suffered at work and outside of work, she nevertheless saw social disorder and moral contagion as the norm among black women.

Reformers like Kellor and Ovington failed to see the ways in which the gendered and racially charged nature of public space in New York made the prospect of physical or emotional safety profoundly precarious for African American women. The problem becomes clear in one of the cases included in *Story of the Riot*. Nettie Threewitts, a resident of the Tenderloin, testified that at about 10:30 on the night of the 1900 riot her stepfather appeared at her house, bleeding from a gunshot wound. The police followed close behind and dragged her, in her nightgown, down to the stoop of her building, where one of them struck her with his fist and called her a "black bitch." Another officer spat in her face and jabbed her in the eye. She reported that one of the policemen said, "Shut up, you're a whore, the same as the rest of them." The police arrested both Threewitts and her stepfather; she had to post $500 bail for herself.[43]

Even the arena of the YWCA did not necessarily provide a haven from this moral panic. In November 1910, the chair of the education and entertainment committee reported to 15th Street's executive committee that the white participants in a physical culture class at 15th Street had objected to the presence of two African American girls in the class. While the executive committee members expressed surprise that difficulties should have arisen, particularly because black women had occasionally attended other classes at 15th Street, the committee decided to exclude the young women from the physical culture class, saying that it was simply "impossible" for them to remain.[44] African American women in the city's YWCA found, through this episode, that even in an exercise class in a Christian organization, they were seen as carriers of moral and racial contagion.

These layers and layers of conflict and the difficulty African American women had in creating safe home environments and maintaining control over their homes lay at the center of the concerns of this branch of the YWCA. The membership of the city's African American YWCA consisted of young, self-supporting black women, many of whom had migrated from southeastern states to enter domestic service in New York. Once in the city, they found life substantially different from what they had known in the South, but also found that the interpretations of their potential moral effect on the city held much in common with modes of thinking in the white South. In addition, the threat of violence to their persons and their homes remained ever present. In responding to these realities, the African American leadership of the YWCA sought to "throw the strong arms of Christian women" around its membership and make home possible.[45]

At "Home" in New York

Discussions of the meaning of "home" lay at the center of this YWCA's techniques for reinterpreting black women's bodies in the public sphere. And for these women, home remained linked with particular conceptions of marriage and family. As Claudia Tate's work reveals, in African American women's literature in the late nineteenth century, marriage emerges as a means through which African American women exercised and experienced their civil and legal status as free Americans. Tate writes that "for black people, voting and marrying were the signs of the race's ascent to manhood and womanhood. To vote and to marry, then, were two civil responsibilities that nineteenth-century black people elected to perform."[46]

This position is generally read as "conservative" when found in late-nineteenth- and early-twentieth-century black women's political discourse and "sentimental" in black women's fiction of this era. But for these women, it marks instead authority, agency, freedom, and desire. African American women emphasizing marriage as the practice of citizenship did not model their view of marriage and family on the experiences of white women. Fear of racial violence and other concrete consequences of negative images of African American women served as the key distinguishing factor between the ways in which white women and black women in this period defined marriage. The element of fear therefore made the struggle to create safe homes all the more important to the women of New York City's African American YWCA. The work and writings of two women in particular, Addie Waites Hunton and Emma S. Ransom, laid the foundation for how women in this YWCA viewed the importance of the home, marriage, and family.

With her experience as a college administrator, an activist in the black women's club movement, and a public speaker, Addie Waites Hunton proved to be instrumental in formulating an ideological framework that placed home and family at the center of African American women's lives. Two of Hunton's extant pieces of writing in this period speak directly to the question of making "home" possible for African Americans and of the impact of social constructions of race, class, and gender on that work. One was an address she delivered at the Negro Young People's Christian and Educational Congress held in Atlanta in 1902. Hunton's speech, entitled "A Pure Motherhood The Basis of Racial Integrity," came in the context of discussions on "The Colored Woman in the Home and Social Reform." She underscored the achievements of African American women as leaders in the church, in reform movements, and in business but emphasized that "it is in the uplifting and purifying of the home that her greatest work has been wrought, and there rests her greatest responsibility to God and the human race." She continued, "To woman is given the sacred and divine trust of developing the germ of life—it is her peculiar function to sustain, nourish, train and educate the future man."[47] So, here, Hunton sees the home as the arena for women to nurture and build character in men who will serve as the future leaders of the world.

This argument, not unlike those put forth by many other club women, black and white, recognizes women's roles outside the home but calls for renewed attention to the home-based role of mothering. Hunton, however, also addresses the specific charge of moral inferiority of African American women. Her answer puts forth a racially based notion of "pure motherhood" that serves as the salvation of the race. Hunton wrote, "The Briton, Saxon, and Norman mixed their blood to give us the proud Anglo-Saxon. This was accomplished through honorable wedlock, but the Negro woman must tear herself away from the sensual desires of the men of another race who seek only to debase her."[48] For Hunton, "pure" motherhood is both morally and racially pure and must be so because of the history of rape of enslaved African American women by white men and the discourse figuring them as depraved. In addition to avoiding sexual interactions with white men, Hunton cautioned African American women to "wage a warfare against a pestilence of vice within [their] own race." To wage this war, she called for the building of Christian homes.

Hunton elaborated on the theme of the African American Christian home in her contribution to a 1907 symposium in the *Colored American Magazine* on "Woman's Part in the Uplift of the Negro Race." Now, however, we begin to see her moving away from the focus on motherhood to an articulation of a broader vision of womanhood. Hunton here reveals a concern about a construction of African American women's duties that places them exclusively in the home, allowing no role in public life. Her theme, again, is that African American progress depends, in large measure, on the development of "homes where character is molded and life made worth while by refining influences," a work to which women devote themselves. Nevertheless, she emphasizes, a docile motherhood cannot accomplish all that needs to be done. In effect, Hunton argues that the most "womanly woman" goes outside her home to engage in activist work. She writes, "at this period of racial development, the very womanly woman is she who, while seeking ever for the highest and purest ideals for her own home, yet has a heart and an ear for the crying needs of humanity and who is willing to consecrate body and soul as a rock where on the race may build firm and sure."[49]

Like Hunton, Emma Ransom brought to her work in the New York YWCA a concern with constructing "home" for African Americans. One of Ransom's extant pieces of writing, a published version of a speech before the 1905 Boston convention of the Northeast Federation of Women's Clubs, takes up many of the themes that Hunton and other club women saw as deeply important for African American women in this period. The ground that Ransom lays in the speech, titled "The Home-Made Girl," rests on two points. The first is the conviction that one of the most important roles that women play lies in inspiring men to achieve. Ransom wrote, "the type of manhood we shall produce will depend largely upon the character of our womanhood than upon any other cause."[50] The second, and related, point is a profound stress on heterosexual unions and the spiritual power, according to Ransom, they can provide for African American communities.

> [W]e should not permit ourselves to be rescued by the would-be deliverers of our race who would place the upbuilding of our womanhood anywhere outside the sacred precincts of the home . . . The home is the oldest of all institutions. It is the first one that God ever established, and womanhood has no greater title and higher goal than marriage.[51]

In responding to negative characterizations of black family life and of black women in particular in this period, Ransom and other club women posited marriages in which women see as their first duty maintaining the altar of the home. Ransom, like Hunton, emphasized that the human family is composed of individual family units.

Ransom could not rest at this point, however. She was, after all, addressing a convention of African American female activists who, like herself, had built public careers. Ransom presented both encouragement and criticism of women's activist work and of the club movement in particular. Her critique revolved around the ways in which club work sometimes served to make women "restive and dissatisfied" rather than giving them tools to do productive work for African Americans through the arena of the home. Agreeing with Hunton, Ransom had harsh words for African American women who, upon obtaining education or wealth, removed themselves from contact with and concern for other African Americans.

Ransom's prescription for the problems confronting African American women combined this discourse on the home with practical methods of shaping character in young women. First, she emphasized domestic training as fundamental to building character and "culture," because, she wrote, "All the culture clubs in the world cannot make a truly cultivated woman. Culture clubs are made by the amount of culture that each person brings into them" from their home background.[52] In addition, she forcefully advocated contact with the churches and the training provided by higher education. Her approach also sought to expand the boundaries of home: "We must give the girl who has had no [proper home] personal contact with the life of our best homes by bringing our best home life down to them, because they cannot come to us, even if they would. This was Christ's method of helping people."[53] Ransom continued by reassuring those African American women who recoiled at the thought of such contact with poor, uneducated young women that this should prove no threat to their own family structure. "If the home is built right," Ransom wrote, "its foundation will not be shaken by lending its influence to the help of those who are morally and socially needy, any more than the throne of God is overthrown because it is many times let down over against the lives of men and women who, but for its help, would be impotent to rise."[54]

Addie Waites Hunton and Emma S. Ransom, both of whom served as important motivators and guiding figures for black women in New York's YWCA in its early years, helped to shape a discourse on the home that was one of the ways this YWCA addressed public and private space for African American women. This discourse on the home also interacted with a variety of concrete approaches to public and private that both supplemented and conflicted with the discourse.

Performing the Private in Public

The approach taken by the women of New York City's African American YWCA to address the interwoven issues of race, class, gender, sexuality, and public space reveals a complex attempt to make the discourse of the home, as illustrated in Hunton's and Ransom's writings, beneficial for its membership. Both the agenda and the concrete steps taken by the YWCA, however, differed from the masculinist approach exemplified by the Citizens' Protective League. The league sought to ensure the right of African American men to "protect" themselves and "their" women and children (with arms if necessary), an approach that emphasized disciplining public space explicitly through the presence of men. Black women in the YWCA sought instead to redeem public space—to invest public space with the religious energies of the individuals involved in the organization and to expand the boundaries of safe space accessible to African American women.

The first step entailed the establishment of the YWCA's own quarters. The organizational meeting as well as those held during the first nine months took place in the lecture room of the Mt. Olivet Baptist Church on West 53rd Street through the influence of Virginia E. Scott, Mt. Olivet's longtime organist. In October 1905, the branch occupied its own quarters, rented from St. Cyprian's Episcopal Church, at 169 West 63rd Street, between Columbus and Amsterdam Avenues, in the heart of San Juan Hill. After sixteen months there, the branch leased 143 West 53rd Street, between Sixth and Seventh Avenues. These three locations housed the African American YWCA until its move to Harlem in 1913.[55]

The YWCA's multipurpose space served as a residence for a small number of "women with proper references."[56] An announcement concerning rooms at the 63rd Street building read:

> The YWCA provides a safe and comfortable home for young women who come to our city to work and study or visit. The prices are very reasonable and the accommodations are adequate to the needs of busy women. It is the aim of the association to offer to as many young women as the building will hold the home life that is needed in the large city. A special effort is made to have a good dinner on Sunday to accommodate the women who come to the association for dinner in preference to going home after church. The Sunday dinner is served from 2 to 4 at the regular price of 25 cents.[57]

At the same time, the committee of management sought to open the "home" to as many women as possible, keeping the building open from

9:30 A.M. until 9:30 P.M.[58] The goal was to create the atmosphere of a Christian home to which young women could go to find "a safe home and wholesome social life . . . and attractions to offset the allurements of the dance halls and the street." Commenting on the impact of this YWCA on the city, the *New York Age* reported, "The Young Women's Christian Association is filling a long-felt want in the City of New York for the young colored women. It is a very homelike institution, and its cheerful surroundings make it an ideal place to while away a profitable afternoon."[59]

What in particular did women come for, and what did they find at their "home"? As part of constructing the Christian home, this African American YWCA offered two options for women and, sometimes, for men. A weekly Sunday afternoon meeting at the branch served as the foundation of its program. Initially, Bible study and a song service provided the focus of this gathering. But within eleven months of the branch's founding, Bible study became separated from the business of building a home life at the YWCA and appeared instead as a component of the educational programs, along with sewing, cooking, and English grammar, offered usually on Monday or Friday evenings.[60] The Sunday afternoon meeting turned instead to speeches and discussion, framed by brief prayer and supplemented by recitations and musical selections. In March 1909, for example, the YWCA held one of its largest meetings of the pre–World War I era. The correspondent for the *New York Age* reported that the meeting space overflowed with people, causing some to be turned away. As with many of these weekly events, one of the officers of the committee of management, in this case Virginia E. Scott, presided, and Emma Ransom and Alice Scott, the branch's chaplain, offered prayers at the opening and closing of the meeting. The program itself included five recitations by Rosa Green, Nettie Fish Scott, Rhoda Willis, Adelaide Jones, and Harold Simmelly-ier; a paper on the "Influence of the Colored YWCA in Greater New York" by Nellie Wilson; and a variety of musical selections, including vocal solos, a piano solo, and a violin solo.[61] In July 1911, Marie Jackson Stuart, the committee's vice-president, presided over a meeting at which Frances Reynolds Keyser, a former board member and superintendent of the White Rose Mission, spoke on the need to address physical, mental, and spiritual concerns "for a fuller and freer life." In addition, Agnes Adams, a club woman from Boston, addressed the

membership on "Faithfulness." The correspondent described the singing as "appropriate and inspiring."[62]

The YWCA's Sunday meeting served as one of the principal attractions for African American women in the city, as well as many visitors.
Here, over refreshments, one could find interesting companions who
shared one's Christian values. In addition, the speaker of the day might
be an important African American leader in religion, business, or politics, such as T. Thomas Fortune or Fred R. Moore, the editors of the
New York Age during this period; the Rev. Florence Randolph of the
African Methodist Episcopal Zion Church, certainly one of the only
African American female ministers the membership was likely to see;
Grace Campbell, the first African American female parole officer in
New York City and later one of the first five Communist Party members in Harlem; and Emma B. DeLaney, a Spelman graduate and missionary in central Africa.[63] Meetings provided a forum to discuss cur-
rent issues of the day, and the leadership made a great effort to establish
an open and welcoming space for members and visitors alike.

The process of fine-tuning both the format of the meeting and the
role it should play in the construction of a homelike environment at the
YWCA becomes evident in the ambivalent language used to describe
the Sunday afternoon events in the *New York Age* notices.[64] While the
program generally included prayers, music, an address, and discussion,
commentators alternately described the gathering as a "praise service,"
a "song service," a "program," and a "meeting." The difficulty arose,
in part, from the need to distinguish the YWCA Sunday afternoon
activities from church, which the members were supposed to attend in
the morning. Certainly, the ambivalence stems from the fact that the
YWCA was "like" a home but not the actual home of the majority of
women frequenting the branch. What to call the gathering, particularly
given the emphasis placed on the "home-made girl," remained a problem for this liminal place.

In addition to the weekly gathering, a social committee oversaw regular events for the membership and guests, most often held on Thursday evenings. Some of these, usually concerts, functioned as fund-
raisers for the YWCA's work or benefits arranged by organizations
interested in supporting the YWCA. On Valentine's Day in 1908, for
example, the Phillis Wheatley Club held a benefit for the YWCA at the
American Theatre Hall on Eighth Avenue and 42nd Street. A "fluffy

ruffles" contest; a drama called "The Opal Ring," written by Frances Reynolds Keyser; and Deforest, a "female impersonator," were among the advertised attractions. A less raucous benefit, presented by the Willing Workers' Club, featured a lawn social on a Thursday evening. The most poignant benefit event came in 1911 when it became known that Harriet Tubman, ill and impoverished, had been consigned to the home for the elderly that she had founded in Auburn, New York. Adena Minott, a local businesswoman and antilynching activist, hosted a joint benefit for Tubman and the work of the YWCA. In April 1910, the members held a combined fund-raiser and membership drive, billed as a "birthday social" that required each woman "to bring a penny for each year that she has been a Christian."[65] Some gatherings were purely social events for women to relax together or participate in organized activities such as outings to Long Island; a "peanut social," in which prizes were awarded to the woman finding the most hidden peanuts; and a "silent social," in which participants suffered fines for smiling, laughing, or talking. Other events emphasized socializing with men in a controlled environment on nights set aside as "Gentlemen's Night." On occasion, the social and entertainment committee provided "at home" events or open houses for visitors to the city to meet "respectable" people, or to receive holiday visitors during the Christmas and New Year's season.[66]

While building the atmosphere of a Christian home remained at the forefront of the institutional endeavor, a second, and no less crucial, component of the approach of African American women in the YWCA to reconstructing racialized and gendered public space came through the monthly public meetings. No ambivalence concerning language or form intrudes here. These assemblies were public events that actively encouraged attendance by both men and women and through which the YWCA expanded its reach beyond its rented rooms. The monthly public meetings took place primarily at a number of churches, allowing the YWCA to affirm its connections to Protestant churches as well as its commitment to an interdenominational approach. The most important African American Protestant churches in New York served as venues for the public meetings in these years, including Mt. Olivet Baptist, St. Mark's Methodist Episcopal, Abyssinian Baptist, Manhattan Congregational, Baptist Temple, St. James Presbyterian, Mother African Methodist Episcopal Zion, Union Baptist, and St. Paul's Baptist.

The format of the public meeting did not differ greatly from that of the weekly meeting held in the YWCA rooms, generally including a number of speakers and musical selections. But whereas the topics addressed at the weekly meetings usually emphasized Christian concerns, the public meetings often paired a discussion on some aspect of the practical duties of Christians with an address on a more "purely" political, historical, or social topic. Many of those who spoke at the YWCA's monthly meetings were nationally known African American activists. At the June 1906 public meeting at the Abyssinian Baptist Church, Dr. William L. Bulkley, New York's premier African American educator at the time, presented an address on "Sterling Worth vs. Sham," in which he discussed character, education, and business. The YWCA paired his appearance with an address on "Ancient History" by Professor J. E. Maxwell, a teacher in the Baltimore high school for African Americans.[67] In May of that year, W. H. Johnson, M.D., spoke on temperance, and J. Douglas Wetmore, an attorney, discussed the proposed Warner amendment, which dealt with racial discrimination in interstate travel. Other speakers at the public meetings included Mary Church Terrell, Booker T. Washington, and Margaret Murray Washington.[68] Here the YWCA made accessible leading national figures as well as migrants to the city who were successful in their fields and leaders of the city's African American constituencies.

On various occasions, the public meeting became a joint meeting or rally with another organization, as when the YWCA sponsored sessions with the YMCA, one featuring speakers from the AME Church and another focusing on entrepreneurship.[69] Other organizations with which New York's African American YWCA cooperated in hosting public meetings included the Rev. C. T. Walker Club of the Mt. Olivet Baptist Church, the Women's Branch of the Negro Business League, the Silver Spray Circle of St. Mark's Methodist Episcopal Church, and the National League for the Protection of Colored Women.[70]

In all of this work we see the women of this YWCA making the discourse of the home function on behalf of African American women by using the liminality of their institutional space to make it a mobile private space. The discourse of the home generated by women like Addie Hunton and Emma Ransom—an idea that grounded the approach of African American women in the New York City YWCA—arose from and contributed to the "moral panic" of the early twentieth century concerning urban African American women. Frances Kellor and Mary White Ovington, for example, sought to arrest the "contagion" brought about by the presence of large numbers of black women (in excess of the number of black men) in New York City by providing a system of controls. Kellor's remedies included "protecting" black women by providing a structured environment that would effectively discipline their behavior and thus reclaim public space from vice. In the discourse of the home, we find clear evidence of a concern with policing African American women as the first step in racial uplift. As Hazel Carby's work emphasizes, some whites and blacks interpreted black women in the city as "a threat to the progress of the race; as a threat to the establishment of a respectable urban black middle class; as a threat to congenial black and white middle-class relations; and as a threat to the formation of black masculinity in an urban environment."[71] There is no doubt that Emma Ransom and Addie Hunton also participated, through the discourse of the home, in what was in many ways a middle-class project both to emphasize class stratification and to bring the behavior of working-class black women into line with the best of "African American Christian womanhood."

Were we to leave the discussion here, however, we would see little more than, perhaps, a "black version" of the concerns of white reformers. In fact, the mobile private space of New York's African American YWCA represents a creative approach to redeeming public space. The private space of this YWCA, because it was consciously constructed as both safe and Christian, became an arena over which African American women could exercise power and control. In the context of a gendered and racially charged environment, the safe home-like environment had profound value. However, that power and control did not remain limited to the internal space of the YWCA building. In ways similar to African American women's promotion of marriage as a way to exercise and experience the legal status of free American citizens, African American women in this YWCA used its mobile private space as a means of exercising and experiencing their status as citizens of New York City. With limited access to real property ownership or real control over the functioning of city government, the mobile private space of the YWCA functioned to invest the public sphere with the Christian energies of its membership. Through this enlarging of the private, this African American YWCA attempted to redeem the public and counter the ways in which the particularly racially charged and gendered atmosphere of early-twentieth-century New York worked against them. By transporting the mantle of respectability, as engendered in the Christian space of the YWCA, these women sought to overcome the vision of African American women as carriers of moral disease.

The YWCA's mobile private space also allowed African American women to have an impact on public discourse in New York's African American community. The YWCA's public meetings acted as a mechanism for women to construct a space in which men, invited to participate, spoke in ways structured and sanctioned by the leadership of the institution. By providing this arena for discussion, the YWCA was able to shift the balance of discourse by determining who spoke and on what topics. Both men's and women's voices emerged, but men's voices were never allowed to supplant those of women. Through the multiple ways the YWCA interacted with early-twentieth-century black New York, African American women in the institution participated in the ongoing project of constructing African American identities in the American context. Their role in this project would become ever more important toward the end of the first decade of the century as World War I and the emergence of Harlem as the capital of black America raised the stakes once again for African Americans seeking a place in the American community.

~ 4

"We Are It": Building on the Urban Frontier

$\mathcal{T}$HE MAY 1, 1913, issue of the *New York Age* carried a notice concerning New York's African American YWCA that in retrospect appears full of illuminating juxtapositions. First, the paper reported the success of a recent social event, hosted by Sadie Battles, at which "a real Dutch supper was enjoyed by all present." Battles, active in the Women's Mite Missionary Society of the AME Church and chair of the YWCA's house committee, had joined the steady movement of black New Yorkers into Harlem and invited the membership to this fund-raiser at her home at 69 West 132nd Street.[1] The notice also announced that this particular YWCA would be relocating from 143 West 53rd Street to 118 West 131st Street in early May and invited the public to a reception and housewarming that would be advertised in the near future.

As with this YWCA's 1907 move to West 53rd Street, which signaled its arrival as an institution of significance for black New Yorkers, the impending move to Harlem also carried great meaning. The juxtaposition of its announcement with news of the "authentic" Dutch dinner is ironic: the African American women of the YWCA traveled to Battles's home in Harlem, increasingly becoming an important residential section for black New Yorkers, to partake in an "authentic" expression of Harlem's roots as a Dutch settlement. The affair suggests an attempt by these women to romanticize the village roots of Harlem through the consumption of cultural elements of its Dutch community, as well as the degree of naive hope that they placed in the possibilities of Harlem. Not only would their YWCA obtain new space in a less crowded neighborhood of the city, but they would also have the opportunity to experience new cultural adventures as they encountered a different group of ethnic whites than those in the Tenderloin and San Juan Hill. The eagerness with which the women of New York's African American YWCA sought to appropriate aspects of the cultural heritage of their new neighborhood underscores their cosmopolitan stance toward the process of constructing their own identities, communal and individual. As residents of a cosmopolitan city, why would they not celebrate their move to Harlem by participating in Harlem's history?

Truly, the most ironic element of the juxtaposition lay in the fact that, in the end, New York's African American YWCA would *not* take up residence at 118 West 131st Street in May 1913 as planned, precisely because of the opposition of white residents to having an African American institution as a neighbor. Instead, the institution established itself by the end of May at 121–123 West 132nd Street, a space considerably larger than the West 53rd Street location.[2] With this move, New York City's African American YWCA inaugurated an important new phase in its institutional life and began to participate in what would become, during and after World War I, a momentous shift in demographics and in the locus of African American identity construction.

Harlem has come to assume a mythic status, first as the center of black literary activity in the 1920s—the period known as the Harlem Renaissance—and later as the trope for the stifling and constricting inner-city ghetto. Scholarship on Harlem as a center of black cultural production has understood its development in the context of changes brought on by demographic shifts and by domestic consequences of World War I. Nevertheless, the tendency to focus on the 1920s and on the experiences of a small group of writers too often serves to place these developments within a narrative that assumes as a certainty Harlem's emergence as the "Negro Mecca." This interpretation takes its cue from contemporary commentators on developments in Harlem, such as James Weldon Johnson, who wrote, "So here we have Harlem—not merely a colony or a community or a settlement—not at all a 'quarter' or a slum or a fringe—but a black city located in the heart of white Manhattan, and containing more Negroes to the square mile than any other spot on earth. It strikes the uninformed observer as a phenomenon, a miracle straight out of the skies."[3] However, Johnson's perspective overlooks the agency, struggle, and planning of many African Americans and the fear, resistance, and flight of many white Harlemites. His image of a miracle erases the *process* through which Harlem became transformed, as well as the participation of African American women in laying the groundwork for the literary developments of the 1920s by supporting the daily struggle for survival of everyday people.

In the period prior to the Harlem Renaissance, Harlem remained a contested territory that may be thought of as a frontier zone. By modifying Howard Lamar and Leonard Thompson's work and employing a broad definition of a frontier as "a territory or zone of interpenetration between two previously distinct societies,"[4] we can undo the teleological narrative that sees as inevitable the transformation of Harlem from an almost exclusively white neighborhood to the "Negro Mecca." Lamar and Thompson emphasize that this "interpenetration" of "two previously distinct" social groups represents a process with a range of possible outcomes.

> The termination of the process is most clearly indicated by political events—that is to say, when one group establishes political control over the other. Once that has been done, the frontier ceases to exist. This does not mean that the relations between the inhabitants then become static, but rather that a new structural situation has been created and that the ongoing historical process is no longer a frontier process.[5]

While white Harlemites and African American New Yorkers do not represent "distinct societies" in the way that Dutch colonialists meeting the KhoiKhoi at southernmost Africa in the seventeenth century did, for example, the model can nevertheless be quite productive for rendering a more nuanced understanding of the various transformations that Harlem underwent. White Harlemites and African Americans came into contact in the frontier zone of Harlem in a very different way from the previous interactions between African Americans and Irish, Italian, and German residents of the Tenderloin and San Juan Hill. Whites in Harlem saw themselves as in clear possession of the territory and viewed blacks who relocated to the neighborhood as intruders. In addition, class status distinguished white Harlemites from the poor, more recent European immigrants of the west side. In the Tenderloin, African American New Yorkers lived in close proximity to poor European immigrants, many of whom did not yet fully understand or were not positioned to take advantage of the power of whiteness in America. In Harlem, African American New Yorkers for the first time resided in a neighborhood alongside relatively wealthy whites, many of whom had deep roots in the area. Indeed, prior to their meeting on the frontier of Harlem, these two groups had been distinct groups in terms of New York's social geography. On the urban frontier in New York, white residents of Harlem became or chose to become displaced as a result of a long struggle over territory that took a number of years to reach a definitive turning point. Neither African Americans nor white Harlemites were assured success in this process.

Viewing Harlem from the standpoint of the experiences of African American women in the New York City YWCA modifies the narrative of the inevitability of Harlem's emergence as the center of African American life. African American women's experiences in moving to Harlem certainly differed to some extent from those of African American men, given New York's history of racialized and gendered public space. In addition, taking into account the perspective and particular concerns of these women offers new insight into the process of Harlem's transformation. Particularly instructive is the intensity with which they struggled on this urban frontier against a range of antagonists—the white leadership of the YWCA, white supremacists in Harlem, the poverty of their own communities—to stake out and hold territory that would provide a space designed by and for African American women.

"Harlem Rides the Range"[6]

Perhaps more than any other neighborhood in New York City, residents and outsiders have invested Harlem with meanings that speak of both local and national views of race, class, and nation, views that have changed dramatically over time. From its development from a small village to a town and then to a section of the larger city, white Harlemites saw their neighborhood as set apart from the perceived chaos and indiscriminate mixing of the races that, for them, characterized downtown. For white residents, much of Harlem's identity as an enclave for white New Yorkers rested on the ability to maintain both a literal and metaphoric distance from the rest of the city. Harlemites maintained a literal distance as a result of limited access to transportation during the district's early years and maintained a metaphoric distance by viewing Harlem as a white community. Despite the actual presence of African Americans in Harlem from its early days, white residents' discourse on Harlem's identity ignored this population. The increasing visibility of African American and eastern European Jewish residents in the district prompted a hardening of the strategy of distancing through language about boundaries, warfare, and contamination.

An article in the *New York Herald*, a city daily paper, in late 1905 employed the language of warring nations to describe population shifts in the city and the increasing numbers of African American residents in Harlem. Discussing the "untoward circumstance" of visible numbers of African American tenants in buildings on 133rd and 134th Streets between Lenox and Seventh Avenues, the author spoke of these buildings as having been "captured for occupancy" by African Americans. The article continued:

> One Hundred and Thirty-third Street still shows some signs of resistance to the blending of colors in that street, but between Lenox and Seventh Avenues has practically succumbed to the ingress of colored tenants. Nearly all the old dwellings in 134th Street to midway in the block west from Seventh Avenue are occupied by colored tenants, and real estate brokers predict that it is only a matter of time when the entire block, to Eighth Avenue, will be a stronghold of the Negro population.[7]

Emphasizing the negative effect of African American tenants in these buildings on surrounding property values, the article concluded by musing on the inexplicable nature of the development of this "African colony," and, thus, on the inconceivability of positive African American agency in the life of the city. Six years later, as the relocation of African Americans to Harlem increased, the language of warfare and contamination became even more striking. The *Harlem Home News* published a call to arms in 1911, writing, "When will the people of Harlem wake up to the fact that they must organize and maintain a powerful anti-invasion movement if they want to check the progress of the black hordes that are gradually eating through the very heart of Harlem?"[8]

White Harlemites attempted to shore up their borders physically—to use their metaphor of warfare—through the imposition of restrictive covenant agreements by landlords. Gilbert Osofsky points out that landlords on blocks ranging from 129th Street through 141st Street east and west signed agreements affirming that they would not rent or sell their property to African Americans. In a particularly striking example, one agreement asserted that "Each of the parties does hereby covenant and agree [not] to . . . hereafter . . . cause to be suffered, either directly or indirectly, the said premises to be used or occupied in whole or in part by any negro, quadroon, or octoroon of either sex whatsoever."[9] Here the legal language of the covenant as a formal contract between parties also partakes of the religious language of divinely ordained peoplehood. When the Anglo-Saxon Realty Corporation, for example, joined the local property owners as a covenanted people at war against the "black hordes" seeking to "scatter the fortunes" of white residents, the centrality of white Harlem's link to an imagined white sacred destiny is unmistakable. Truly, white supremacists felt themselves under siege.[10]

The March 1914 edition of the NAACP's magazine, The Crisis, edited by W. E. B. Du Bois, called attention to an organization of white Harlemites, founded in 1910, aimed at preventing any further opening of residential property to African Americans. Constituted at a meeting at the white Harlem YMCA, the Harlem Property Owners' Improvement Association (HPOIA) set its sights high, projecting incorporation once community members pledged $100,000 in stock. In a somewhat fearful tone, the Crisis notice concluded that "just what methods will be taken has not yet been stated." One answer to the question of the HPOIA's methods came by the summer of 1914. At a meeting cynically purporting to discuss "Negro Uplift," Du Bois reported, the HPOIA "proposed the colonization of all colored people in New York on the pestilential mud flats of Harlem, where with all the city's crowding no one up to this time has been willing to live."[11]

John G. Taylor, president of the HPOIA, had mentioned the possibility of a literal partitioning of Harlem as early as 1911 but, even then, seemed uncertain of its success. Ever prepared, Taylor had a variety of other strategies to shore up white Harlem's boundaries. When, in 1911, St. Philip's Protestant Episcopal Church, a prominent black congregation, purchased a row of houses on the north side of 135th Street between Lenox and Seventh Avenues—prime real estate on one of Harlem's wide crosstown thoroughfares—Taylor called a meeting of white residents in houses adjacent to these buildings. In an interview in the *Harlem Home News,* Taylor assured the public that the white residents on the south side of 136th Street—that is, those whose rear windows overlooked the buildings now owned by St. Philip's—would remain in their houses and that the HPOIA would assist them in constructing a twenty-four-foot fence in their backyards. This Taylor called the "new dead line," beyond which African Americans would not be allowed to pass.[12]

Taylor, and those who engaged in restrictive covenant agreements, emphasized the degree to which the "invasion" of Harlem by African Americans should be blamed on "white deserters" who rented or sold property to African Americans or who provided financial backing for real estate speculation by African Americans. "The nigger in the Harlem property woodpile is a white man . . . Look deep into this Harlem situation . . . and you will find the unclean hand of the white deserter, the man who backs the Negro saloon on the lower West Side, and the man who breaks up homes in Harlem. He thinks we don't know him, but we do. Our retribution will come when we expose him, and we intend to do so very soon."[13] Taylor's use of terms of contamination, particularly emphasizing the "unclean hands" of those whites who associate with African Americans and the dangers that this alliance poses to Harlem, underscores the importance of the discourse of contamination on the Harlem frontier. In order to maintain the purity of the neighborhood, it was necessary that whites adhere to their whiteness.

One of the most dramatic incidents of a "white renegade" helping to overcome a restrictive covenant agreement came with the 1914 purchase by the Mother Zion AME Church of property on 136th Street owned by the Church of the Redeemer. The Church of the Redeemer had signed a restrictive covenant agreement and yet unwittingly sold the property to Mother Zion, one of the cornerstones of the independent black church movement, through the mediation of Mildred Helm, a white woman from Yonkers.[14] While Helm did not fall into the same category as the saloon owners of whom Taylor spoke, she nevertheless represented the kind of "race traitor" whom he saw as leading to the downfall of white civilization in Harlem. The language of race warfare, combined with a discourse of the contamination brought by blackness, provided the public face of white Harlemites' struggle to defeat the colonizing efforts of African Americans on this urban frontier.

Despite the difficulties presented to African American residents by white denizens of Harlem, from 1910 onward, major institutions and personalities of New York's black communities relocated to Harlem from the Tenderloin and San Juan Hill and began to expand residential options for African Americans. Between 1910 and 1914, the Baptist Temple, St. Philip's Episcopal Church, the Hope Day Nursery, the Salem Methodist Episcopal Church, St. Mark's Methodist Episcopal Church, the Rush Memorial AMEZ Church, the Mother Zion AME Church, the Union Rescue Home, the Bethel AME Church, the National Urban League, and St. James Presbyterian Church all moved to Harlem.[15] W. E. B. Du Bois emphasized the tremendous impact that these relocations would have on quelling the effectiveness of white supremacists in Harlem. Du Bois himself employed a hint of military language.

> Of course the matter of holding property at such strategic points is difficult but possible. If the property of the Negro churches is held and the YMCA really intends to put the building in a decent site in Harlem and the YWCA follows suit, and if the Colored Music School Settlement buys a home—all this and other possible cooperative effort will settle the matter for a long time.[16]

Thus, whereas white Harlemites envisioned the question of territorial control in Harlem as one in which they must maintain complete control and exclude "invaders," Du Bois and other black New Yorkers saw the potential for establishing themselves alongside white residents, despite the very real tensions.

The business of "settling the matter," as Du Bois phrased it, became possible through the work of a number of creative African American realtors, beginning as early as Philip A. Payton Jr.'s founding of the Afro-American Realty Company in 1904. Payton attributed his success in cracking the real estate market in Harlem directly to racism and the contortions to which it moved white New Yorkers. Reflecting on his first big deal, Payton said, "My first opportunity came as a result of a dispute between two landlords in West 134th Street. To 'get even' one of them turned his house over to me to fill with colored tenants. I was successful in renting and managing this house, and after a time I was able to induce other landlords to . . . give me their houses to manage."[17]

In addition to racism as a facilitator of Payton's efforts to expand his business in Harlem, housing development spurred by the extension of public transportation to Harlem in the period from 1891 to 1904 became important. As Osofsky and others have noted, developers invested in new, luxurious apartment buildings in Harlem with the expectation that transportation access would attract new residents. The overabundance of housing and a real estate bust by 1905 left developers with buildings standing empty. Some turned to black realtors like Payton, John E. Nail, and Henry C. Parker to find African American tenants for their buildings; others rented to eastern European Jewish immigrants who sought to move uptown from the Lower East Side.[18] Thus, unlike any other African American urban district, Harlem offered to African Americans the very height of urban luxury in newly constructed buildings. Under unique circumstances brought about by real estate speculation that failed to bring in white residents, black New Yorkers and recent migrants to the city had the opportunity to occupy new construction that had been intended for affluent whites, instead of being extended access to this housing only after white residents no longer had need of it.[19]

The increasing numbers of African Americans in Harlem, as well as the relocation of black institutions to the neighborhood, often sparked punitive actions by predominantly white institutions that had previously serviced Harlem's small black population. Perhaps the most striking example of this came with the 1913 expulsion of African American children from a Sunday school by a priest at St. Luke's Episcopal Church in Harlem. The priest's action came after he had asked the children's parents to withdraw from this predominantly white church and begin attending St. Philip's, the newly arrived black congregation. The *New York Age* remarked that such incidents were becoming common in Harlem, and as was often the case, denominational religious bonds between whites and blacks could not overcome the larger racial struggle.[20]

In the spring of 1911, the African American branch of New York's

YMCA announced its plans to move to Harlem "within the next two years." Its branch chair, the prominent doctor E. P. Roberts (whose wife Ruth Logan Roberts would become an important member of the YWCA's committee of management in the 1920s), emphasized the intention to move, as well as the plan to construct a new building for the organization's work at a cost of $300,000. The *Age* article, profiling this YMCA and its plans, reminded readers that the African American YMCA—in stark contrast to the situation of the African American YWCA—"is self sustaining to a marked degree. Its building at 252 W. 53rd Street is paid for and is valued at $500,000. Financial aid is only asked at intervals to meet certain exigencies that arise."[21] Circumstances dictated, however, that the much more financially impoverished YWCA would move to Harlem before the YMCA.

Toward a "Room" of Their Own

In making the move to Harlem, the African American YWCA entered into the struggle particular to that frontier zone and, at the same time, inaugurated a new phase in its relationship with the exclusively white governing structure of the New York City YWCA. Frontier contact in Harlem concerned a struggle over territory and control of geography, and the ongoing conflict between African American and white women in the YWCA involved a struggle over the very identity of the city's YWCA. Just as white Harlemites refused to envision the potential of the neighborhood as an integrated one that benefited from the presence of a diverse group of people, the YWCA in New York had become deeply invested in an identity that rested on whiteness, purity, and firm boundaries. The Metropolitan Board structure, which afforded representation to every YWCA branch affiliate in the city except the African American branch, remained the starkest representation of the boundary of whiteness that the white leaders had constructed. Beginning with the African American YWCA's move to Harlem, the African American leaders challenged the boundaries and identity of the YWCA as a white institution in a variety of ways, and the white leaders resisted. Fund raising, the distribution of funds, and the choice of location for the African American YWCA emerged as the most significant arenas in which these two groups struggled during this period. Despite the ongoing difficulties and, indeed, the escalation of tensions in the relationship between white and African American women in the city's YWCA, the African American YWCA's leaders saw this period as one in which they gained ground, both literal ground in Harlem and ground in terms of agency and power within the YWCA.

Two forces converged, along with the opening of Harlem to African Americans, to facilitate the relocation of New York's African American YWCA to Harlem. First, the decision to move took place because the lease on the 53rd Street house expired as of May 1, 1913. Second, by this time 53rd Street was no longer the undisputed center of black New York life, and Harlem, as one of the neighborhoods in which black New Yorkers increasingly set down roots, presented possibilities for providing services.

The search for a new home presented greater difficulties than either the African American committee of management or the exclusively white Metropolitan Board anticipated. What transpired in May 1913 gives one indication of the difficulties. At the May 12 meeting of the Metropolitan Board of the New York City YWCA, a board member made a report concerning the opposition of "a portion of the Harlem community" (obviously white residents) to the plan of the African American YWCA to move to 118 West 131st Street. The Metropolitan Board summarily resolved "That the Board of Directors feels strongly that it is for the good of the whole that the Colored Women's Branch give up the house in question, and that an expression of great appreciation be sent to them if they make this generous sacrifice."[22] As with the national YWCA's capitulation to southern white women's "comfort" through the subordination of African American YWCAs to white YWCAs, the New York City YWCA constructed the "whole," for whose good black women were to sacrifice, as a white body. The board's minutes do not indicate what form this "expression of great appreciation" took—indeed, the African American YWCA does not appear in the minutes for many months following this incident—but in this instance the committee of management did comply.

Having given up the West 131st Street location, the members of the committee of management explored new options. Fortunately, they had access to the very realtors who had assisted in the process of opening Harlem to black residents. Mrs. J. C. Thomas, chair of the YWCA finance committee in 1912 and elected to the committee of management in 1914, was married to James C. Thomas, a prominent undertaker and former president of Philip A. Payton's Afro-American Realty Company. In addition, committee of management member Maybelle McAdoo worked as the chief stenographer at the Afro-American Realty Company.[23] The experience of Thomas and McAdoo seems to have served the organization well in securing an alternate location to the one they had been forced to abandon. At the spring closing exercises of a girls' group meeting, Helen Curtis "announced to the assembled girls and their friends that her prayers had been answered . . . and that . . . the Young Women's Christian Association had almost within the hour closed a deal for two houses at numbers 121 and 123 West 132nd street, where suitable alterations were to be made." A contribution of $1,000 from Grace H. Dodge enabled the African American YWCA to sign the lease and make the move on such short notice.[24] It seems likely that this location—two adjacent buildings on the north side of the street between Lenox and Seventh Avenues—would provide even better facilities than the 131st Street location. Nevertheless, taking full and productive possession of the building required renovations to connect the houses and convert the two rear yards into one.

New York City's African American YWCA moved into its new home in July 1913 and boasted that the renovations of the buildings had been undertaken by a firm of African American architects and an African American electrical contractor. This had been effected through a campaign conducted with the Metropolitan Board by the industrial committee of the National League on Urban Conditions Among Negroes.[25] The Metropolitan Board contributed $50 per month for the salary of the secretary, at that time Gertrude James, and $75 for rent; the board increased this appropriation by $35 per month in October 1914.[26] Despite the fanfare with which the African American YWCA made the move to 132nd Street, it was clear by the time of the move that 132nd Street would only serve as a temporary home. An impending $4-million joint New York City YMCA and YWCA campaign promised this YWCA a newly constructed building, most probably somewhere in Harlem.

The joint campaign was a result of the YMCA's role in the 1911 merger of the various YWCA institutions in New York. Because of mounting debts incurred by 15th Street and its affiliates, the institution's YMCA advisers strongly encouraged the merger and promised YWCA participation in the planned financial campaign as an incentive.

Thus, as a reward for consolidation and the formation of the YWCA of the City of New York—an agreement negotiated with the mediation of Grace H. Dodge—the YWCA was to receive $3 million of the $4 million expected to be raised.[27] How that $3 million would be apportioned, however, became an issue of great concern to the women of the African American YWCA, who expected due consideration.

When it came to the negotiations to determine what portion of the money raised the African American YWCA would receive, Emma Ransom negotiated with Grace Dodge, vice-chair of the campaign committee and president of the YWCA's National Board. Years later, Ransom's husband, Reverdy, recalled the events of the negotiations, writing that Dodge "sent for Mrs. Ransom and offered to appropriate $10,000 for the benefit of the Colored Women's Branch, at which Mrs. Ransom, on behalf of her board flatly refused to accept, informing Miss Dodge that she could raise $10,000 herself and would consider nothing less than $100,000, as a share for her branch out of the one million dollar campaign."[28] In the final stages of the negotiations, Reverdy Ransom recalled, Emma Ransom met with Dodge and

> squarely faced her with the un-Christ-like and cowardly attitude her Board was assuming and insisted that they would be satisfied with nothing less than adequate facilities for the activities of the Colored Women's Branch in that area. Miss Dodge was so agitated over the matter, she suggested to Mrs. Ransom that they get down on their knees and pray over the matter. This they did, Mrs. Ransom doing the praying and Miss Dodge doing the crying, but after prayers and tears, she finally got the pledge from Miss Dodge that they would get the $100,000 sought.[29]

As Reverdy Ransom constructed the situation in his memoirs, Emma Ransom, a powerful personality, utilized the drama and spectacle of the highly charged context of prayer to break the white leadership's resolve to make themselves comfortable at the expense of African American women. His account emphasizes the degree to which Emma Ransom, as president of the committee of management, was required to remind the white leadership of the YWCA of the purported Christian basis of the association's work. Through her performance, Ransom emotionally affected the generally intractable white leaders of the YWCA and foiled the attempt to maintain a racialized identity for the YWCA through a financial erasure of African American women.

The African American women did, indeed, receive the $100,000 appropriation, although when compared with the money allocated for the YWCA's other new buildings, the amount still seems shamefully small. With its $3 million, the YWCA planned to construct six new buildings, in addition to the one for the African American YWCA, each costing from $400,000 to $800,000. These new construction projects included the National Board building at 52nd Street and Lexington Avenue, the New York City YWCA's Central Branch (formerly the 15th Street Association) building that still stands on Lexington Avenue at 53rd Street, and a building for the white Harlem YWCA at 124th Street and Lenox Avenue.[30] Without question, the apportionment of funds positioned the African American YWCA as the poor and undeserving sister of the branches of the New York City YWCA that served white New Yorkers.

The joint YMCA/YWCA fund-raising campaign received a great deal of attention in New York's press, black and white, and the *New York Age* alerted African American New Yorkers to the campaign, scheduled to take place between November 10 and 26. The YMCA and YWCA appointed Dr. Jesse E. Moorland, international secretary of the Colored Men's Department of the YMCAs of North America, to take charge of the fund raising among African Americans. Moorland had proven to be an extremely effective fund-raiser, having already conducted YMCA building campaigns in Chicago, Philadelphia, Atlanta, Washington, Los Angeles, Indianapolis, Baltimore, Kansas City, and Cincinnati, and boasted a total of $1 million raised.[31] The *Age* and African American participants in the drive pointed out that this fundraising effort—an extremely public event in the life of the city's YWCA and YMCA—represented a significant display of inclusion of African Americans in the movement. The first *Age* article covering the plans for fund raising commented: "Recognition of the worth of the colored citizens of New York has been accorded by the Joint Campaign Committee of the Young Women's and Young Men's Christian Association in the city."[32]

In addition to the recognition it would bring to Christian activist work by African Americans, the financial benefits of the fund-raising effort—made manifest in two newly constructed buildings (one for the African American YWCA and one for the African American YMCA)—

became a source of pride for many black New Yorkers. A writer in the *Age* looked ahead to assess the impact of this development for the African American YWCA, writing:

> The colored women of this city are to have a YWCA branch in Harlem that will be miles ahead of their present home. It will be fitted out with due regard to their special needs as well as to the general requirements of the association work. They are to be rewarded for their unremitting endeavor by seeing the women under their charge established in a position of comfort such as they have desired these many months.[33]

The African American women of the YWCA saw the possibilities of their own building, "the first model YWCA building for colored women in the world," for pointing African Americans toward the future. In addition, a permanent home in their own building moved African American women in the YWCA one step closer to participating in the movement on an equal footing, even though achievement of this remained many years in the future.

The African American YWCA and YMCA in New York announced the upcoming campaign and the intended uses of the funds raised during a meeting held at the Abyssinian Baptist Church on West 40th Street on October 26, 1913. The Rev. Adam Clayton Powell, pastor of the church, presided. Those gathered heard addresses by Reverdy C. Ransom, then editor of the *A.M.E. Church Review*; Dr. C. T. Walker, former pastor of the Mt. Olivet Baptist Church and one of the founders of the African American YMCA in New York; and Jesse E. Moorland. The following Sunday interested parties met at the Mt. Olivet Baptist Church, the first home of the African American YWCA, where speakers included Emma Ransom, Eva Bowles (then at the National Board of the YWCA), and Bishop Alexander Walters of the AMEZ Church, whose wife chaired the library committee. Moorland stressed an approach to fund raising that focused on bringing contributions from African Americans to the highest level possible. Moorland showed great pride in the fact that, of the $1 million he had raised in the two years prior to the New York campaign, one-third had been contributed by African Americans. He challenged New York City to do as well as other cities had in this respect.

In addition to the high priority assigned to fund raising among African Americans, the leaders of the campaign would devote attention to obtaining contributions from white donors in the city and elsewhere. This aspect of the work had been given national attention through a challenge grant made by Chicago's Julius Rosenwald, president of Sears Roebuck. Rosenwald guaranteed $25,000 for any YMCA that could raise $75,000 for an African American branch. New York City's YMCA was therefore eligible, but for the first time, Rosenwald included the YWCA, pledging an additional $25,000 for New York City's African American YWCA. According to a report that Addie Hunton made to the National Board of the YWCA in 1913, Rosenwald's interest in the YWCA had been sparked in a meeting between Hunton and Rosenwald sometime before the start of the financial campaign in New York.[34] Rosenwald's letter to the white leaders of the joint campaign committee confirming his offer underscored his particular concern with the development of YMCA and YWCA work among African Americans.

> My primary interest in the campaign, as evidenced by my contribution, lies in the hope that funds will be provided for a Y.M.C.A. building for colored men and a Y.W.C.A. building for colored women. I believe the colored as well as the white people of New York will seize this rare opportunity to be helpful to one another and thus united make the campaign a success.[35]

Throughout the two weeks leading up to the commencement of the campaign, Moorland conducted meetings at the YMCA building on 53rd Street for the volunteers, and he appointed captains for the twenty-five fund-raising teams, each comprised of ten members. Ten of the twenty-five teams came from among the YWCA group. Each volunteer pledged five of his or her own dollars and made a commitment to canvass for funds for the two weeks of the campaign, with white volunteers following much the same procedure.[36] The *New York Age* announced to African American New Yorkers that they could monitor the progress of the entire financial campaign on "the monster clock"—on which amounts, rather than hours, would be posted—placed above the regular clock on the Metropolitan Life Insurance Company's fifty-story tower at Madison Avenue and 23rd Street and "visible from all parts of the city." Lafayette Hall in the basement of the Lafayette Theatre on Seventh Avenue at 132nd Street, formerly a segregated theater and recently opened by new owners to African Americans, served as the headquarters throughout the two weeks. Gertrude James, secretary of the African American YWCA, and T. J. Bell, secretary of the African American YMCA, along with five stenographers and two assistants staffed the headquarters.[37]

The campaign among black New Yorkers opened with 250 workers gathered for dinner at Lafayette Hall. Whereas the white fund-raisers met for lunch each day, the African American volunteers, more likely to have full-time employment outside of YWCA or YMCA work, met for dinner each evening to assess the day's results. Moorland and the other organizers, including Emma Ransom, employed current technology, as well as secular ritual and symbols, to arouse interest in the work and to excite an emotional response of dedication and pride in the campaign. At the opening banquet, the workers sat at their tables singing "songs in the dark," with the words projected on a screen, in order to create a sense of community among the volunteers. Moorland's addresses to the volunteer workers and to other interested members of New York's African American communities often included stereopticon projections of photographs of YMCA buildings around the country whose construction had been facilitated by Moorland's involvement. The *New York Age* supported Moorland's display of African American progress by printing an illustration in one of its issues as the campaign neared its end. The illustration shows a dark-skinned African American man dressed in formal attire holding a sign reading, "It is Your Duty to Help Your Race by Contributing to the Colored Y.M.C.A. and Y.W.C.A. Building Fund."[38]

Once the campaign was underway, the fund-raising teams participated in a daily ritual in which they competed for a banner reading "We Are It," awarded at the evening dinner to the team bringing in the highest daily total of pledges. The contest for the banner quickly became a dramatic rivalry between the men and the women, and the victorious team hung the banner each night on either the men's or women's side of the Lafayette Hall headquarters.[39] Their spirited competition underscores the tension inherent in cooperative work between the YWCA and the YMCA, and clearly, African American men and women invested themselves in the separate, gendered identities of their respective organizations.

Contributions from African American New Yorkers ranged from less

than $1 up to $1,000. The majority of donations and pledges, as re-
corded in a list of subscribers to the campaign printed in the *New York
Age*, were between $5 and $25. Among the contributors regularly associated with this YWCA, most donated only slightly more than the
average. Helen Curtis donated $100, Gertrude James, $50, and Madame Virginia Scott, $25, for example. Within the first four days, Afri-
can Americans in New York pledged almost $11,000, of which $3,175
was in cash.[40]

The most spectacular development during the first week came as the
result of a presentation that Emma Ransom made to Judge McLean, a
white resident of Harlem, on behalf of the YWCA's building fund.
While it is not clear whether McLean made a contribution to the fund,
his African American butler, Squire Garnett, pledged $1,000 for the
YWCA building. This episode underscored the degree to which hard-
working African Americans like Garnett, clearly dedicated to saving
money for his future, were willing to donate that money to the cause of
New York's African American YWCA. The approach to fund raising
clearly linked the future of individual African Americans to the destiny
of community institutions like the YWCA branch. There is some irony
in the dissonance between the fund-raising expectation—that this African American institution relied in some measure on donations from
white philanthropists—and the result: a large donation from a working-
class African American man.

Garnett's response to Ransom's appeal to a wealthy white man con-
founded some of the expectations of white YWCA leaders regarding
approaches to fund raising. It seems clear that they felt the approach to
appealing for funds from African American donors differed somehow
from the approach aimed at white donors. Garnett, however, heard the
appeal directed at his employer only because he stood in the room in his
role as butler. According to newspaper accounts, he inquired—of Ransom or of McLean we do not know—whether he too could make a
contribution. When told that he could, he notified Grace Dodge of his
intention. That Garnett made his pledge to Grace Dodge indicates
that Ransom's presentation was specifically directed toward a potential
white donor. It was common practice in the campaign that African
American contributors made pledges or actual donations directly to
African American volunteers. White donors whose pledges (for work by
African American or white women) were obtained by either white or

black campaign workers always made their contributions directly to the white leadership. Garnett's donation, the largest from a black donor (along with E. P. Roberts's), created a great sensation among African Americans. He was the only African American donor mentioned in the *New York Times* coverage of the joint financial campaign.[41]

Even a cursory examination of the patterns of donations reveals the vast disparity between the financial resources of white and African American New Yorkers. The daily totals for white campaign workers as reported in the *New York Times* ranged from a low of $33,640 to a high of $186,369. One team brought in a one-day total of $52,744, aided by a donation of $50,000 by J. P. Morgan and Company. Other large donations included $350,000 from John D. Rockefeller; $500,000 from Grace Dodge's brother Cleveland and his wife, Pauline Morgan Dodge; and $2,500 from tobacco king Benjamin Duke.[42] Julius Rosenwald specifically designated his donation of $50,000 to be divided between the African American YWCA and YMCA. The Phelps Stokes Fund, which donated $2,500, earmarked its gift for the African American YWCA alone. With the exception of these two wealthy white donors—with Julius Rosenwald and Ruth Pastor Stokes being two of three Jewish contributors (the New York City Young Men's Hebrew Association also made a donation)—the African American YWCA did not have access to the kinds of funds that white campaign workers could mobilize. While the white members of the campaign committee emphasized in their public statements that their effort remained at the grassroots level and did not rely on large donations, it seems that the white campaign workers' perception of large and small donations differed considerably from that of black workers. On one day of the campaign, for example, the white Harlem YWCA received $1,139 in pledges from fifty individuals, and the African American campaign committee, $1,856 from 235 individuals.[43] The final report of the campaign committee counted 298 pledges by white donors of more than $1,000, compared with two such donations by African Americans. In addition, 1,274 whites donated funds in the range of $100 and $1,000.[44] Despite access to such a large pool of money, the *New York Times* reported, campaign workers failed to meet the $4 million goal by $226,498, although by the time of the final report in 1917, records indicated a total of $4,053,119.43.[45]

Jesse E. Moorland and his committee of workers also fell short of their $50,000 goal. The *New York Age* reported that the African American workers collected pledges and cash donations in the amount of $40,931.32.[46] The final campaign report figure differs—it records a total of $37,114.63—primarily because the white campaign committee meticulously distinguished between "pledges from white people" and "pledges from colored people." The African American campaign workers considered all the funds they raised, whether from white or black donors, to be part of their campaign total, while the white workers appropriated all white donations for the "general" fund. This distinction lay at the root of the conflict that would later develop between African American women and white women in the New York City YWCA over the distribution of the funds. In making the distinction between "white" and "colored" money, the white leaders of the city's YWCA made a claim to racialized territory in the fund-raising process and prevented the mingling of money that came through the hands of white and black donors.

The atmosphere in the New York City YWCA just prior to the campaign, during the fund raising, and in the period of pledge payments following the campaign underscored the frontier mentality of clear racialized boundaries in the YWCA. The atmosphere created a great deal of confusion for African American YWCA women concerning their place in the organization as a whole, confusion that became manifest most strikingly in a YWCA event just prior to the fund-raising campaign. On November 7, 1913, the city YWCA held a pageant called "The Ministering of the Gift," in which 1,500 young women participated. Attended by Jesse Wilson, the daughter of President Woodrow Wilson, and her fiancé, the event merited a long article in the *New York Times* the next day. It began with a procession led by five young women, daughters of wealthy white New Yorkers prominent in the YWCA and YMCA movements, dressed in blue gowns with "royal purple" trains. "The first scene of the pageant introduced the spirit of 'Friendship,' Miss Christine Shutz, a member of the Studio Club of the YWCA. 'They seek me,' said the Spirit of the association, 'but are separated by caste.' Then Friendship brings the groups together, and joining hands they form one large ring, and gradually still holding hands pass into the background."[47]

Without any irony, the pageant included in a later segment "a big group of little colored children," according to the reporter, singing "Swing Low, Sweet Chariot" and "Let My People Go." In this moment of public ritual in the YWCA, then, the participants engaged in a statement against "caste" division yet underscored the practice of segregation within the organization by relegating the African American young women to a separate portion of the program. Dorothy Perkins, daughter of George Perkins (chair of the joint campaign's executive committee), underscored the reading of caste as "ethnicity," "nationality," or "class," excluding race as a potential interpretation. Perkins found the pageant "a beautiful sight." "What struck me particularly about it was the spirit of democracy among New York girls which it demonstrates."

Despite the impact of African Americans in the YWCA on black New Yorkers, the contradiction between "democracy" and segregation often brought a spotlight of criticism to the YWCA. *The Crisis* took note of segregation at the YWCA pageant by comparing it to one held in Brooklyn in which African American women took part "not as a special feature, but along with the other girls."[48] Mixed reviews in *The Crisis*, for example, of the YMCA's record in particular helped to create an atmosphere in which YWCA and YMCA workers experienced some difficulty in collecting on the pledges made by black New Yorkers during the two-week campaign. Early in 1914 Du Bois published a stinging critique of the YMCA's racial policies, emphasizing that the white leadership of the organization never gave African Americans anything other than second best, particularly in the area of facilities. He cautioned people to remember that "it is an unchristian and unjust and dangerous procedure which segregates colored people in the YMCA movement. However much we may be glad of the colored YMCA movement on the one hand, on the other hand we must never for a single moment fail to recognize the injustice which has made it an unfortunate necessity."[49] In a letter to the editor of the *New York Age*, Hubert Hamilton, a black New Yorker, echoed Du Bois's concerns about separate facilities in the YMCA. How could northern African Americans support a segregated institution, he asked, when "ten millions of colored people even in the South are agitating and fighting segregation, both in letter and in spirit."[50]

In addition to the issues raised by criticism of the segregated YMCA and YWCA movements, other realities impeded collecting the pledges. As any fund-raiser knows, once the excitement of the campaign drive ends, one must invest additional energy to convert pledges into cash.

The *Age* reported that, as of May 5, 1914, only $12,512.19 had been received, leaving $17,805.58 in unpaid pledges; most significantly, almost half of the $12,512.19 collected were donations from white New Yorkers.[51] As late as January 1917, the joint campaign committee report counted only $10,131.13 collected on pledges made by African Americans, as opposed to $3,905,046.32 from white donors.[52]

Given the joint campaign committee's meticulous reporting of donations by people according to race, its recommendation in April 1915 to withhold the promised $100,000 from the African American YWCA is not surprising. In its discussions with the Metropolitan Board, the campaign committee argued that since the rate of payment on pledges by African Americans had been so low, the plans for the building should not proceed until they could find some way of increasing the percentage of pledges converted to cash. According to the minutes of the Metropolitan Board, the white leadership of the city's YWCA clearly did not approve of this approach because it would delay moving forward on the building plans; however, the board accepted the joint committee's decision and constituted a special committee to explore the issue, particularly Emma Ransom's claim that most of the unpaid pledges had been made by African American men.[53]

The joint campaign committee's actions in this matter were, however, dishonest and dangerous to the long-term financial health of the YWCA. While the drama of the two-week fund-raising campaign required the excitement of the revelation of large pledges, like John D. Rockefeller Jr.'s $350,000 pledge at the opening of the campaign, the drama was, in reality, staged. Rockefeller's donation did not constitute a pledge made as a result of vigorous fund-raising efforts by the joint campaign committee, but had been negotiated between the committee and Rockefeller more than four months prior to the start of the campaign. Rockefeller pledged $250,000 of his total to the YWCA and attached a number of conditions to that pledge. He required that the campaign bring in "satisfactory valid pledges" of $4 million by March 31, 1914. Certainly the roughly $27,000 deficit in the African American campaign endangered the receipt of Rockefeller's promised funds. However, the conditions placed on the YWCA in particular required that the YWCA use his fund for one or more of four of its building projects—the Central Branch, the Harlem Branch, the West Side Branch, and the African American YWCA—and that all four projects must be completed.[54] By separating so rigidly donations according to race, the joint campaign committee punished and humiliated black New Yorkers for their financial poverty relative to white New Yorkers and again put in place a mechanism to subordinate African American women in the YWCA.

It was not until the end of 1915 that the Metropolitan Board asserted itself vis-à-vis the campaign committee and on behalf of the African American YWCA. Throughout 1915, various members of the board had emphasized that the African American YWCA needed additional space and financial support in order to maintain the services it provided to black New Yorkers. In November 1915, Emma Ransom made a special appearance at a meeting of the Metropolitan Board, saying, according to the minutes, "that new life would be given to the members if any hope was held out" for a new building.[55] In December, the committee appointed to investigate and make recommendations regarding the new building reported on the issue. Rather than speak in their own voices in assessing the situation, the white members of the committee merely presented a statement from the leaders of the African American YWCA to the entire Metropolitan Board. The statement reads as another cry on the part of African American women in the YWCA for recognition of their work, their successes, their needs, and, indeed, their very being. The statement reads:

Whereas the Colored Women's Branch is so limited in its present dormitory accommodations that young women have to be constantly turned away;

Whereas it cannot with its present gymnasium condemned, offer any opportunities whatever for athletic work to young women, and is forced to refuse constant appeals for such opportunities;

Whereas it is, though at present free from debt, obliged to curtail its work in instructive, social and recreational lines, in order to meet the heavy expenses incurred by constant repairs on the buildings and by a heavy rent;

Whereas it has already outgrown the present accommodations and has a constantly increasing membership;

Whereas there is a lack of any such opportunities in the community as might be offered, if there were adequate equipment, by the Colored Women's Branch of the YWCA.[56]

The African American women's statement employs a number of rhe-
torical strategies that had become standard for them in attempting to be
heard by the Metropolitan Board. While these women rarely referred
to their organization as "the colored women's branch"—the only title
that the white leaders used—here it functioned as an effective opening strategy, not to place themselves in a subordinate position vis-à-vis
the Metropolitan Board, but rather to articulate their identity as one
branch in a unified YWCA. Once again, the leaders of the African
American YWCA refused to accept the identity of the YWCA as a
white institution, an identity construction that always left them on the
margins.

The committee recommended that the Metropolitan Board authorize the leaders of the African American YWCA to search for a site for a
new building. The minutes concluded: "After much discussion about
the optimism of the colored people and references to the difficulty of
collecting the pledges made at the time of the campaign, this resolution
and recommendation were accepted."[57] By March 1915, Ransom and
the committee of management had found a lot at 137th Street between
Lenox and Seventh Avenues, and in December 1916, Vera Scott Cushman, president of the Metropolitan Board, purchased the property for
$13,000.[58]

The purchase of this lot in the heart of Harlem represented significant movement toward the attainment of one of the primary goals of
the leaders of the city's African American YWCA. Yet the property was
not ideal—as a comparison with the African American YMCA's purchase that fall reveals. The YMCA had secured a desirable location for
their new building on 135th Street, a wide and much-used thorough-
fare between Lenox and Seventh Avenues. The site was very close to
the 135th Street station on the Lenox Avenue train line and across the
street from the public library. The African American YWCA's situation
turned out quite different. Unlike the YMCA, which purchased three
existing buildings to create a site for a new building, the YWCA bought
a vacant lot on the north side of West 137th Street. While this would
serve the African American YWCA well in the future by providing
room for expansion, at the time it meant building on a narrow residential street where fully one-third of the lots were empty.[59] Indeed, this
represented a frontier of sorts, as Harlem was still a developing neighborhood in many ways.

Internal Frontiers

In moving to Harlem, New York City's African American YWCA engaged a number of frontier boundaries in interacting with white residents of Harlem and with the white leaders of the YWCA. The struggle with both of these groups turned on questions of racialized identities— of the neighborhood and of the YWCA—and in both cases, African American women in the YWCA demanded an inclusive construction of these identities. Arguing for positive agency for the African American YWCA in both the city's YWCA and in Harlem, the African American leaders insisted that by embracing its interracial identity, the YWCA would not change its essential nature as a Christian institution. On the contrary, such a move would serve to sharpen and make manifest its Christianity.

At the same time that New York's African American YWCA worked to reconstruct the YWCA's and Harlem's identity, it had to confront its own internal frontiers, particularly those of class and regional conflict. With the move from the close and poor quarters of the Tenderloin and San Juan Hill to the relative luxury and potential of Harlem, the women of this YWCA found themselves in changing class circumstances. The fear that the troubles of the Tenderloin and San Juan Hill, such as crime and vice, would follow them uptown led many African Americans to draw sharper class distinctions among themselves. Where would the YWCA stand on these questions? As an institution whose membership and leaders crossed class boundaries freely, the African American YWCA's response became crucial in the period just following the move to Harlem. Cecelia Holloway Cabaniss Saunders, who in 1914 assumed the position of executive secretary of the African American YWCA, proved to be a pivotal figure in the institution's struggle with its identity in this period.

Cecelia Holloway came to work in New York City's African American YWCA after having spent two years as a field organizer for the National Board of the YWCA, along with Addie Waites Hunton and Elizabeth Ross. Unlike the majority of the leaders of this particular YWCA, Holloway emerged from the cradle of America's black aristocracy and boasted a family pedigree of four generations of free blacks. Born in Charleston, South Carolina, in 1883, Holloway grew up in a family deeply connected with the class and social privileges that light skin accorded African Americans, particularly in Charleston. Indeed, the Holloway men were among the founders of the Brown Fellowship Society, whose membership had been limited at the time of charter to "fifty free men of color of good character." Her father, James H. Holloway, benefited from the wealth of his family's business, a harness and carpenter's shop founded in the late eighteenth century, but also worked in a variety of other fields. During Reconstruction, James H. Holloway and Harriet Hampton Holloway, Cecelia's mother, worked as schoolteachers for the newly freed slaves under the American Missionary Association administrator in Charleston, Francis Cardoza. Later, James Holloway received an appointment as postmaster of Marion, South Carolina.[60]

Cecelia Holloway went on to attend Fisk University, which educated many of America's black elite. There her classmates included Elizabeth Ross, who would be her connection to the National Board of the YWCA, and George Edmund Haynes, Ross's future husband and a sociologist and Christian activist. Graduating fourth in her class at Fisk, Holloway worked as a teacher at South Carolina State College before moving to New York and the National Board of the YWCA in 1910.[61] In 1912 Holloway married James E. Cabaniss, a graduate of the New York Dental College, who died one year later.[62] She left her position at the National Board of the YWCA following her marriage but continued to be active in the city. In 1913 Cabaniss served as a featured speaker at the Conference of Workers Among Boys and Girls, addressing those assembled on some aspect of "Housing Conditions Among the Colored People in Greater New York." Cabaniss had become so well known in New York for her work on local issues and with the national YWCA that in 1912 the Harriet Tubman Neighborhood Club elected her to honorary membership, along with Margaret Murray Washington, Frances Reynolds Keyser, Addie Waites Hunton, Nannie Helen Burroughs, and Mary McLeod Bethune—impressive company indeed.[63]

In January 1914, Gertrude James resigned as the branch general secretary in order to become the secretary of the African American YWCA in Norfolk, Virginia, and Cecelia Holloway Cabaniss accepted the position.[64] Within a year of becoming the general secretary, Cabaniss married John D. Saunders, a real estate agent in New York.[65] From the outset of her tenure at the New York City YWCA, Cecelia Cabaniss

Saunders focused her energies on making the African American branch an institution that could provide the best possible service to black residents of Harlem. This entailed continuing those programs already in place, but in addition, Saunders became involved in building other local institutions, such as the community center located at Public School 89 at 134th Street and Lenox Avenue. This community center put the children of the neighborhood at the forefront of its work, planning programs and services that included "Mothers' Meetings," films, musical programs, "clean and graceful" dances, lectures on health, and a public forum for discussions. Josephine Pinyon, then a secretary at the National Board of the YWCA, was to be in charge of an afterschool playground on 138th Street between Lenox and Seventh Avenues, closed to traffic between 2:00 and 6:00 P.M. Saunders worked on the board of the community center from its founding along with other New York activists, including James Weldon Johnson, Grace Nail Johnson's husband and field secretary for the NAACP; Eugene K. Jones of the Urban League; and George W. Allen, vice-chairman of the African American YMCA.

Although Saunders quickly became an important and much appreciated figure in New York's African American YWCA, one of her first public moments came in the midst of a controversy that revealed the potential class, color, regional, and religious conflicts in the functioning of an institution like this YWCA. The July 16, 1914, issue of the *New York Age* greeted its readers with a two-column article carrying a "charge of inhospitality against [the] YWCA" made by Nannie Helen Burroughs, a well-known Baptist activist and founder of the National Training School in Washington, D.C. Burroughs had made these charges public at a meeting in Brooklyn, also attended by Cabaniss, of the Empire State Federation of Women's Clubs, an organization with close ties to the YWCA. Burroughs told the story of having arrived in New York at midnight with two of her young students, all three drenched in a downpour. She continued, "As you approach the building no. 121 West 132nd street, you see by the brilliant light 'Y.W.C.A.' This is the place. How glad you are to get in—wet, bedraggled, tired." Burroughs asserted that when she asked to speak with the secretary, Cecelia Cabaniss greeted her "clad in a kimono" and informed her that there was no room to take the three women in; instead, Cabaniss offered to send them to the Home for Working Girls. Burroughs then attempted to telephone a friend to see if they could stay with his family, but the friend was out of town. In the office where the telephone was located, she said that she had been "entertained" by a group of the young female lodgers at the YWCA, "holding High Court" and engaged in a discussion of "hair." Burroughs and her two companions then left the YWCA and spent the night in the Pennsylvania Railroad station.

In Burroughs's complaint before the women's club, she underscored her understanding of the incident as having ramifications beyond her individual situation, and she relied on a class analysis to do so. Burroughs concluded her published statement by saying,

> My friends, I write not to express any personal grievance; people of that type are objects of prayer and missions, but I write to warn young women against going to this place after dark, seeking shelter, and expecting to find even in the air, the spirit of cordiality, hospitality, and Christian welcome. It is not there and never will be until they get women filled with the spirit of the Lowly Nazarene. Personally, I entertain no feeling against any one. I speak for a Cause. I would give my life for the girls of my race, not in words, but in deeds.
>
> Yours for the highest development of Christian womanhood.[66]

Burroughs railed against a growing class of African American social workers who entered the profession only for personal gain. "They go into the work to get a decent salary, certain social ambitions and to feed 'the humble' with a long spoon, at other people's weak expense. God forbid that poor, green girls should fall into the hands of one of these faddists," Burroughs wrote. She insisted that had she gone with her two young charges to a house of prostitution, they would have been given a place for the night. Burroughs questioned, through the lens of class, the Christian capacity of the YWCA leaders. How could Cabaniss represent "the highest development of Christian womanhood" dressed so casually and suggestively in a kimono? How sincere could the Christian uplift of the organization be when its residents engaged in a frivolous discussion of hair? Burroughs's experience of Cabaniss and the city's African American YWCA revealed it to be an institution led by insufficiently Christian, elitist women who sought to contain and, ultimately, distance themselves from the poor masses of black folk through "missionary work."

Cecelia Cabaniss responded to the charges at the Empire State Federation meeting; in the following week's issue of the *Age*, Emma Ransom and Cecelia Cabaniss also replied in writing. Ransom underscored some of the points that Cabaniss made at the meeting, chiefly, that the dormitory capacity of this particular YWCA was a meager nineteen beds and that, on the night Burroughs arrived, eighteen of the beds had been taken. But just as Burroughs relied on class distinctions as a factor in determining "true Christian womanhood," so did Ransom and Cabaniss in their response. Ransom maintained that Burroughs had pursued a personal grievance against Cabaniss, in whom, she wrote, "we have every confidence in the capacity, integrity, and Christian spirit." But Ransom continued, attacking Burroughs.

> We are surprised that a woman like Miss Burroughs, who, we would suppose, is brought in frequent contact with people of gentle manners and good breeding, would not mistake the greeting of a woman of culture for the 'indifferent, sneery, telling-you-to-move-on air.'[67]

In fact, Ransom charged Burroughs with expecting special treatment because of her "high standing and prominence" as a leader of the women's movement in the black Baptist church.

The Burroughs incident highlights the difficulties that the city's African American YWCA faced in seeking to establish itself as a Christian institution on the rapidly changing frontier of Harlem. The conflict between Burroughs and Cabaniss emerged from a range of boundaries internal to African Americans in the early part of the twentieth century. The dark-skinned Burroughs regularly put forth a strong critique of the privileges accorded light-skinned African Americans like Cabaniss, and accused light-skinned African Americans of complicity in systems of racism that injured darker African Americans. Burroughs, a southerner, also privileged the experiences of poor, southern, rural African Americans, the majority within the black population at that time. Cabaniss, a southern-born migrant to New York, along with the other African American women of the city's YWCA, committed themselves to serving African Americans in a northern urban context.

In addition, Burroughs's critique of Cabaniss's attire reveals the contours of a debate over the boundaries of African American communal identity. In the same way that the members of the African American YWCA sampled Dutch cuisine as one way of expressing themselves as sophisticated New Yorkers, Cabaniss's kimono spoke of the cosmopolitanism she valued. For Burroughs, this cosmopolitanism represented a worldliness that, as a serious Baptist woman, she repudiated, but also a worldliness that threatened traditional community boundaries. The conflict between the two women took place at a significant juncture in an ongoing process of structuring African American identity. In a nation poised on the threshold of massive population shifts among African Americans, of urbanization, and of participation in a world war, Burroughs and Cabaniss represented two different yet overlapping viewpoints. Burroughs remained committed to a communal identity based in the experiences of the southern black working class and clothed in a Baptist sensibility. As Burroughs announced at a convention of black Baptist women:

> The common people of whom God has made more than of the other kind, are shouting the tidings of salvation as they dig the trenches and throw up the breastwork for battle. . . . God is going to line up the common people . . . and crush . . . all the avarice, the secular spirit, worldly schemes, ignorance, and practical indifference.[68]

While Cecilia Cabaniss Saunders and other African American women in the New York City YWCA saw their work as grounded in Christian commitment and focused on cross-class cooperation, they did not appeal to the apocalyptic language so characteristic of Burroughs. For these women, the end time would not come through an obliteration of the cosmopolitan and commercial possibilities of the northern cities. Indeed, for them the city represented the hope of fashioning the African American identity into a cosmopolitan modern American one that understood the particularities of African American experiences but also participated in the world. This stance of the women of New York City's African American YWCA set the stage for their participation in U.S. involvement in the war in Europe, as well as for their work during Harlem's zenith in the 1920s.

~ 5

"Interwoven Destinies":
Wars at Home and Abroad

$\mathcal{I}$N SEPTEMBER 1919, as the United States emerged from World War I, the bishops of the African Methodist Episcopal and the African Methodist Episcopal Zion Churches separately published petitions to Congress and other white political leaders. These petitions, on behalf of large constituencies of African American Christians, expressed the hopes and frustrations that many black Americans felt in this period of intense and rapid changes in American life. In their concluding paragraphs, the AME bishops called for a bold new relationship between African Americans and the nation in light of the common experience of the war. They wrote:

> Our claim to an equitable ownership of this country is attested by three centuries of toil for its development and expansion, as well as by heroic deeds and sacrifices in its defense of the fields of sanguinary conflict from Bunker Hill to Metz. We are here, and here to stay—not as aliens or pariahs, but as a bona fide and integral part of the body politic. Our supreme desire is to be allowed to exercise our inalienable rights without let or hindrance, to prove a strong prop in the support of American institutions, and to continue a helpful factor in the development of American industry.[1]

The AMEZ bishops presented a more tempered petition but warned that African Americans would no longer "submit without organized protest to the injustices practiced" against their communities in various parts of the country.[2]

The war era precipitated significant changes in American social, political, and economic life, and African American communities in particular experienced the monumental transformations of the Great Migration. Scholars have estimated that, between 1916 and 1921, one half million southern African Americans migrated to northern cities, spurred by a combination of cotton crops decimated by boll weevil infestations in the South and war-related labor shortages in the North. New York, for example, experienced an increase of 66.3 percent in its African American population between 1910 and 1920. James Weldon Johnson has described this period by noting that "for the Negroes of the South this was the happy blending of desire with opportunity."[3] In light of wartime rhetoric of the American commitment to expanding access to democracy for all the world's citizens, as well as expanding economic opportunities in northern cities, many African Americans felt heightened hope for their collective future. This hope was tempered, however, by realities like those described in the bishops' petition. After years of commitment to the United States, African Americans felt the frustration of being denied full access to the rights of citizens.

Black and white women in the national and New York City YWCAs approached the combined opportunities and frustrations of the period through means that sometimes converged but often diverged. Publicity became a central focus for both groups of women. During the war, the National Board of the YWCA developed a large propaganda machine through pamphlets, posters, and a weekly paper, the *War Work Bulletin*, all of which advertised its role in dealing with labor issues at home and with war issues abroad. In one discussion in the *War Work Bulletin* on the topic "When Publicity Is Education," the YWCA emphasized that "Educational publicity must turn the uninterested portion of the public into believers. Statements of accomplishments must demonstrate that YWCA work does what it is intended to do."[4] Through its publicity campaigns, the YWCA emphasized its role in generating patriotic sentiment, providing services to white soldiers abroad, and assisting women engaged in war-related work at home. In one poster depicting three white soldiers, each in a different branch of the military, the YWCA's caption read, "Keep them smiling . . . This home is helping our boys over there." Another poster presented a drawing of a white woman wearing overalls and holding an airplane in one hand and ammunition in the other. The caption reads, "For every fighter a woman worker . . . Care for her through the YWCA."[5]

YWCA publicity during the war focused on presenting American women and their contributions to the nation's war effort, in effect, portraying a particularly gendered Americanness. An examination of the ways in which the YWCA constructed Americanness reveals the degree to which its sense of national identity remained grounded in whiteness. The national YWCA excluded African American women in a number of ways as visible participants in its publicity campaigns on patriotism. The organization never included visual images of black women in its "general" pamphlets and posters, relegating them instead to brochures and articles—typically directed at a white readership—that depicted the separate category of "colored work." Often, white members of the YWCA's publicity committee produced these images and stories with very little sense of African American women's perspectives on their own work with the YWCA. For the YWCA, "*the* American woman" remained essentially a white woman.

Within the separate group of pamphlets and articles that portrayed African American women—bearing titles like "The Colored Girl Gets Her Chance," "The Colored Girl a National Asset," and "Colored Women Make Good"—the National Board of the YWCA revealed the quandary facing black women as loyal supporters of the American project and, at the same time, as members of a group suffering from racism and discrimination. The YWCA's publicity campaign to promote black women, for the first time in the YWCA's history, as "Colored *Americans*" reflects the hopeful tone of the era. The article "Colored Women Make Good" begins with an anecdote that presents African American women as valuable and loyal supporters of the war effort. "'What are you colored women going to do for the war?' a colored factory worker was asked a year ago. 'Whatever our leader, Mr. Wilson, wants us to do,' was the quiet reply. They have made good on that promise."[6] The construction of the black woman in this story as a "quiet" follower of "our leader" served the YWCA's ultimate purpose of casting black women as a loyal constituent group within the American people. The caption to a photograph of white and black women doing factory work, used in the pamphlet "The Colored Girl a National Asset," put it bluntly. "Wartime emergency gave the colored girls a chance to show that they are as good Americans as white girls."[7]

At the same time, however, the YWCA promoted the notion that

African American women inherently posed dangers to the country, which the YWCA, if supported, could help to contain. The long-term threat that African American women presented to white laborers, as a result of new employment areas opened by the war, emerged as perhaps the most significant danger imagined by white YWCA women. Through the publicity department, the YWCA emphasized to its white audience that it had ways of containing the economic challenge that African American women made to white workers. In addition, the YWCA's publicity department assured white Americans that it had formulated plans to control the perceived chaos resulting from the increasing numbers of African Americans moving to America's cities. The caption to another photograph in "The Colored Girl a National Asset" asserts that "wholesome fun, provided by the Y.W.C.A., makes the colored girl a better woman, a better worker, a better citizen of her country."

African American women in New York's YWCA and in YWCAs across the nation also placed publicity at the center of their wartime work with the organization. In this time of heightened democratic rhetoric and new discussions of civic responsibility, African American women in the YWCA saw the war era as a critical moment for black Americans to make themselves felt as "a national asset" in order to make a yet stronger claim to the rights of citizenship. They placed the need for particular kinds of representations of themselves—as Americans, as laborers, as members of families, and as leaders—at the heart of the story of their service to the nation. In addition, they consciously linked their own projected image with the question of how African American men in the military were portrayed. Indeed, the period of World War I was one in which black YWCA women most publicly addressed men's issues. In this project of representing themselves and black men, African American women in the YWCA found common ground with white YWCA women but often clashed with them in significant ways.

The Crisis of the World

In the period leading up to the formal entrance of the United States into the war in Europe, culminating in the declaration of war on April 6, 1917, African Americans discussed the meaning and impact of the war on their communities of oppressed Americans. Should black men fight in this war even though the government consistently failed to protect their rights as citizens? Would the shedding of the blood of African American men in defense of "democracy" convince whites to relinquish exclusive control of the category of "American"? What would be the consequences if African Americans failed to participate in the war? The participation of African American men as soldiers in this war, a war the president insisted would "make the world safe for democracy," proved a difficult debate for black Americans and brought about a crisis for many white Americans for whom "white" and "American" were synonymous. The call for African Americans to support the war and show themselves as patriots profoundly challenged the exclusion of blacks from the category of "American" implicit in systems of racism throughout the United States. "Support" of the war took on gendered meanings that called on black men to render military service and black women to labor on the homefront. Although engaging in different activities, black women and men both faced the disparity between the rhetoric and realities of the period.

James Weldon Johnson, then editorial page editor of the *New York Age*, anticipated the official declaration of war with a reflection on the danger of African Americans being viewed as unpatriotic. He wrote, in part:

> The bald truth is the Negro cannot afford to be rated as a disloyal element in the nation. Imagine the results if he should for an instant arouse against himself the sentiment which is now directed against the pro-German element. But there are other reasons besides selfish ones. The Negro should not do anything to mar his splendid record from the Boston Massacre to the slaughter of Carrizal. For in spite of all, this America is our country.[8]

Outlining the history of African American military exploits from the death of Crispus Attucks in 1770 to the defeat of the 10th Cavalry regiment of black troops in the U.S. campaign against Pancho Villa following the Mexican Revolution, Johnson's editorial underscores the traditional fixation on manhood and citizenship as tied to participation in military campaigns. However, Johnson and other African Americans who supported participation in the war tempered that support by insisting on the reciprocity implicit in the relationships among manhood, citizenship, and military service. The call by African Americans for citizenship rights, according to Johnson, has been grounded in a history of loyalty to the nation, a loyalty that should ultimately lead to the full extension of civil rights. The emphasis on reciprocity served as the basis for W. E. B. Du Bois's famous call for support in *The Crisis*.

> We of the colored race have no ordinary interest in the outcome. That which the German power represents today spells death to the aspirations of Negroes and all darker races for equality, freedom and democracy. Let us not hesitate. Let us, while this war lasts, forget our special grievances and close our ranks shoulder to shoulder with our white fellow citizens and the allied nations that are fighting for democracy. We make no ordinary sacrifice, but we make it gladly and willingly with our eyes lifted to the hills.[9]

Other African American voices, however, opposed African American support of U.S. involvement in the European conflict. A. Philip Randolph and Chandler Owen, editors of the New York–based radical newspaper *The Messenger*, wrote, for example, "We would rather fight to make Georgia safe for the Negro," and Randolph suffered arrest in Cleveland in 1917 as a result of his opposition to the war.[10] This was a view shared at all levels of society in African American communities. James Weldon Johnson reported a lively debate about the war that took place in a Harlem barbershop. When a patron was asked if he intended to "join the Army and fight the Germans, he replied amidst roars of laughter: 'The Germans ain't done nothin' to me, and if they have, I forgive 'em.'"[11] Whether they embraced the opportunity to fight for their country or whether they resisted supporting the war effort, African American men who debated the question all saw the profound double bind created by the question of fighting a war for a country that denied African Americans full access to the rights of citizens.

The women of the Woman's Convention of the National Baptist Convention remained divided on the question of supporting the war. They agreed that the failure of the federal government to address the problems of lynching and segregation severely compromised the rhetoric that upheld the war as a battle to spread democracy throughout the world. They did not, however, agree on whether participation or boycott of the war effort would be the best approach to highlighting this inconsistency. S. Willie Layten, president of the Woman's Convention in 1918, encouraged support of the war effort as an investment in the national future of African Americans. Nannie Helen Burroughs, secretary of the convention, disagreed. Attacking President Woodrow Wilson as a hypocrite, Burroughs told the members of the convention,

> He likes to write—he likes to say things. He has used up all the adverbs and adjectives trying to make clear what he means by democracy. He realizes and the country realizes that unless he begins to apply the doctrine, representatives of our nation would be hissed out of court when the world gets ready to make up the case against Germany and to try her for her sins.[12]

Burroughs's vocal opposition to the war brought the force of the machinery of government down on her: the War Department placed her on a list of individuals who posed a threat to the country and monitored her travels, correspondence, and contacts with other people.[13]

Despite the conflation of patriotism and military service, the history of blacks as American soldiers had proven profoundly complicated. Military leaders had generally evaluated the performance of black soldiers as excellent, and as Arthur E. Barbeau and Florette Henri have written, "tales of black military service remained one of the glories of black history, becoming more glorious in the retelling. The battles black troops had fought were symbols of equal citizenship that could not be erased by Jim Crow or disfranchisement."[14] Yet these soldiers lived with the profound fear that white Americans harbored of armed black men, and with discrimination within the military and from white civilians.

These conflicts came to a dramatic head in August 1917 when an African American battalion of the 24th Infantry Regiment, stationed at Camp Logan near Houston, became involved in a highly publicized incident. The episode began when an African American soldier attempted to stop a white police officer from beating a black woman on the streets of Houston. The police arrested and beat the soldier, as well as a superior officer who had gone to search for him. Later that night more than one hundred soldiers from the battalion marched into Houston and eventually began shooting. In the end, sixteen white men, five of whom were police officers, and two black civilians had been killed along with four members of the battalion. The military officially labeled the incident a mutiny; the soldiers involved underwent secret courts-martial. From among the first group tried, thirteen men received death sentences. The military hanged them three days later, denying their right to appeal. Sixty-seven soldiers received prison sentences, many of these life terms; sixteen others were sentenced to death. Eventually, President Wilson commuted the death sentences of ten soldiers, placing the total number of men executed at nineteen.

While the white public chose to view the "Houston mutiny" as another instance of the inability of black men to control themselves, and certainly of the danger of entrusting them with weapons, African American commentators, some white supporters, and even a War Department investigator viewed the situation differently. The investigator reported:

> The ultimate cause of the riot were [*sic*] racial. Certain men of the 24th Infantry apparently resolved to assert what they believed were their rights as American citizens and United States soldiers . . . On the other hand, the Police Department and many citizens of Houston resented the presence of colored soldiers and resented on the negro the badge of authority of the United States uniform. It is my belief that the tension had reached that point where any unusual occurrence would have brought on trouble.[15]

The investigator's delineation of the layers of tension in Houston illustrates the quagmire in which African American soldiers and African Americans in general found themselves concerning the question of military service and citizenship.

African Americans knew full well the context that contributed to the explosive nature of racial tensions and to the events in Houston in August 1917. One month earlier, East St. Louis, Illinois, had erupted in four days of bloody violence between white and black residents. Labor issues in East St. Louis fanned the already smoldering fire of racial animosity as union leaders threatened to use black workers in the meatpacking houses and metalworking plants should white workers fail to support the unions. Indeed, the insistence of these very unions on remaining exclusively white created a situation in which employers knew that some black workers would be willing to work as strikebreakers, as had happened in 1916. In the spring and summer of 1917, as African Americans from the rural South migrated to places like East St. Louis in search of employment, white residents perceived an increasing threat to their own jobs. White workers demanded that African American migrants be kept out of the town, and on two days in May, a mob of three thousand hunted for an African American man rumored to have killed a white man. Tensions escalated until, in July, a group of African American men fired on a car full of white men driving through their neighborhood, whom they believed to be drive-by shooters. In the rioting that ensued, whites burned and looted the homes of black residents and shot or burned over a hundred people. In subsequent days, the Mississippi revealed the gruesome results of the violence as bodies floated down the river.[16]

In the three months following Woodrow Wilson's declaration of war, as many African Americans began to look for ways to facilitate their country's participation in a war that the president characterized as "the most terrible and disastrous of all wars," the events in East St. Louis and Houston called into question once again the relationship of African Americans to the nation. In response to the violence in East St. Louis, the NAACP organized a protest march on July 28, 1917, and James Weldon Johnson took charge of the planning stages. On that Saturday morning, ten thousand black New Yorkers silently marched down Fifth Avenue with drummers leading the group. The women, among them a large contingent of YWCA women, and the children participating in the march dressed in white, and the men, in dark suits with straw hats. They carried signs that read, "Mr. President, Why Not Make America Safe For Democracy?" "Treat Us so that We May Love Our Country," "Patriotism and Loyalty Presuppose Protection and Liberty," and "We Are Maligned As Lazy And Murdered When We Work."[17] A group of Boy Scouts circulated leaflets outlining "Why We March" that declared:

> We march because we are thoroughly opposed to Jim-Crow Cars, Segregation, Discrimination, Disfranchisement, LYNCHING, and the host of evils that are forced on us. It is time that the Spirit of Christ should be manifested in the making and execution of laws . . . We march in memory of the honest toilers who were removing the reproach of laziness and thriftlessness hurled at the

entire race. They died to prove our worthiness to live. We live in spite of death shadowing us and ours.[18]

East St. Louis, Houston, and the NAACP march all contributed to the atmosphere in which African Americans raised voices both in support of and in opposition to the participation of African American men as soldiers in the war. By the time the United States entered the war, the regular army segregated African American soldiers into four regiments, the 24th and 25th Infantry and the 9th and 10th Cavalry. In addition, the National Guard had eight units of African American soldiers. Following the events in Houston, the army decided not to make use of any of the "Colored Regulars" in the war, because of the perceived potential of these soldiers to create difficulties, but did plan to use black men in the National Guard and those who came into the new National Army under the draft.[19] In this way, the military felt it could bring in black men less accustomed to military service and who would, therefore, be easily assigned to labor details. In their study of African American soldiers in World War I, Arthur Barbeau and Florette Henri estimate that 80 percent of all African American men in the military at this time engaged in labor.[20] Here the military skillfully made use of black men's abilities in support of the war and yet, by restricting their access to military combat, remained able to withhold the benefits of military service from them.

African American soldiers in both combat and labor units trained in various camps throughout the United States, many of them in the especially hostile South. The odyssey of New York's 15th Regiment of the National Guard—from its training to its ultimate transformation into the 369th Infantry Regiment of the 93rd Division, a combat division—illustrates the difficulties African American soldiers faced at home and abroad. Under the command of a white New Yorker, Colonel William Hayward, and with the Rev. William H. Brooks of St. Mark's Methodist Episcopal Church as chaplain, the almost 1,500 men of the 15th Regiment attempted to prepare for the most technologically brutal and horrifying war the world had seen up to that point. Denied the full support of the National Guard, this regiment had no access to an armory and, lacking sufficient arms and uniforms, was forced to train in the streets of New York, substituting sticks for weapons. Ironically, this regiment became well known for its spectacular band, led by James Reese Europe and drum major Noble Sissle, both celebrated composers and performers. The National Guard would not fund the soldiers but found a separate source of money for the band.[21]

The 15th Regiment received some additional training at Camp Whitman near Peekskill, New York, and, eventually, at Camp Wadsworth near Spartanburg, South Carolina. The regiment remained only twelve days at Wadsworth because of the hostilities of local whites. The mayor of Spartanburg prepared for the regiment's arrival with a speech before the Chamber of Commerce, declaring, "[T]hey will probably expect to be treated like white men. I can say right now that they will not be treated as anything except negroes. We shall treat them exactly as we treat our resident negroes."[22] Despite Colonel Hayward's attempts to defuse tensions through such means as public performances by the regiment's band, and the spirited defense of the 15th Regiment by New York's white regiments stationed at the camp, the army relocated the 15th to Camp Merrit, New Jersey, before sending it overseas in December 1917. The regiment had had a total of three weeks of training.[23]

After initially using the regiment as laborers in France, the army eventually transferred the 369th Infantry (formerly the 15th Regiment of the New York National Guard), along with the rest of the 93rd Division, to the French army, which eventually used the 369th in combat. Fighting with the French, the 369th distinguished itself in all its battles. Two of its members received particular attention when they singlehandedly fought off a German raiding party of almost forty men. Sergeant Henry Johnson, one of the two, became the first American soldier to be awarded the Croix de Guerre.[24] The French went on to award the Croix de Guerre and Distinguished Service Medals to many other soldiers of the 369th.

Even though the American Expeditionary Forces relinquished control and responsibility for the 369th and other units of the 93rd Division to the U.S. military worked to maintain the hold of white supremacy and segregation over African American soldiers fighting alongside the French. The U.S. military produced a document called "Secret Information Concerning Black American Troops" and distributed it to French officers to guide their interactions with African American men. The document read, in part:

We may be courteous and amiable with [black officers], but we cannot deal with them on the same plane as with the white American officers without deeply wounding the latter. We must not eat with them, must not shake hands or seek to talk or meet with them outside of the requirements of the military service.

We must not commend too highly the black American troops, particularly in the presence of [white] Americans. Make a point of keeping the native cantonment population from "spoiling" the Negroes. [White] Americans become greatly incensed at any public expression of intimacy between white women and black men.[25]

The authors of "Secret Information" placed its instructions in the context of the urgent threat, from the point of view of white Americans, of racial contamination from black Americans. Rather than revealing "secret information" about black soldiers, this document instead revealed much more about the fragility of the white soldiers in the face of the success and self-confidence of African American men.

While the military abroad exhibited tremendous fear that relaxed interactions between French and African American soldiers threatened the ability of white Americans to subjugate African Americans, the propaganda machine at home took another approach. The Committee on Public Information (CPI), a governmental committee, sought to reassure white Americans that African American participation in the war would not threaten the racial status quo. CPI films, such as *Our Colored Fighters*, seemingly directed at African American viewers, can be read as an attempt to defuse whites' fear of armed black men in a number of ways. One of the films portrayed four African American men tap-dancing, with the commentary that "they had 'rhythm' in France no less than under the southern sun."[26] Instead of an image of armed black men confidently fighting side by side and socializing with French soldiers, the CPI film returned familiar images of happy darkies.

Yet at the same time that the committee sought to assuage the fears of white Americans, it sought to make use of African Americans' hopes for greater access to the benefits of American society by holding out the promise that "a result of this war will be a wonderful amalgamation of the races within America."[27] However, for most African American consumers of CPI propaganda, the fantasy of this unspecified type of "amalgamation" would not have been an adequate substitute for equal rights. African Americans remained invested in the reciprocal relationship between the practice of citizenship, which sometimes entailed military service, and the extension of the full rights of citizens.

"The Girl You Leave Behind"

While wartime service for American men became conflated with military service, service for American women remained tied to the domestic sphere of the individual household, as well as the national sphere of the "homefront." Given the racialized contours of American self-definition, African American women's formulation of service on the homefront necessarily took on questions of race and representation. How best to support African American men in their participation in the war occupied many African American YWCA women in New York City and across the nation.

By this time, the National Board of the YWCA recognized thirteen African American YWCAs that served urban populations. These city associations, along with the National Board's Colored Work Committee under the direction of Eva D. Bowles, former secretary at New York City's African American YWCA, undertook to define the means of supporting soldiers and participating in the war effort.[28] The National Board of the YWCA appointed Bowles "Secretary for Colored Work" in 1912, and by the time the United States entered the war, she had established a bureaucratic structure to address the issues and problems raised by the war as they affected African American women and men. In staffing her committee, Bowles drew on a number of women who had been involved in urban associations, such as May B. Belcher, the secretary of the St. Louis African American YWCA, whom Bowles assigned to oversee the South Central Field of war work among African Americans. In addition to bringing experienced African American YWCA workers to the New York headquarters of the Colored Work Committee, Bowles also appointed a large group of local YWCA women to serve as "war workers." Helen Curtis, Sarah C. Battles, Addie Waites Hunton, Florida Ruffin Ridley, Ethel Kindle, and Marie Peek Johnson were among the New Yorkers associated with the African American YWCA who joined the ranks of the Colored Work Committee.

Bowles and her committee would serve as the central avenue through which African American women participated in "war work." The National Board organized a War Work Council in June 1917 that focused its work on young women affected by the war, leaving most of the direct work with men to the YMCA and other men's organizations.[29] Here the YWCA did not see itself as abdicating a responsibility to men, primarily because it joined with the YMCA, the National Catholic War Council, the Jewish Welfare Board, the War Camp Community Service, the Salvation Army, and the American Library Association to form the United War Work Council, and the YWCA did direct some of its literature to men. The YWCA's War Work Council determined that the need for work with women appeared greatest in areas near army training camps, as well as in cities where women had moved for employment purposes. In addition, the YWCA provided assistance to women in England, France, and Russia during the period of U.S. involvement in the war. Finally, the YWCA examined women's labor issues and aided women entering the labor market for the first time or moving into new kinds of work made accessible by the war.

The YWCA anchored its war work to its concern with "social morality," a category encompassing questions of sexually transmitted diseases, sex education, and moral education according to a particular understanding of Christian standards. The National Board of the YWCA had established a Commission on Social Morality from the Christian Standpoint in 1913, which outlined the purpose and method for conducting social morality lectures for young women. In the commission's 1913 report at the YWCA's biennial convention, its members emphasized that straightforward education in the science of reproduction could not accomplish the goal of helping young people to "withstand the temptations that assail from within and without," but also requested "that the formative power of spiritual forces . . . be fully enlisted."[30] This investigatory commission evolved into the formal Social Morality Committee.

The YWCA's Social Morality Committee did not originate the emphasis on a Christian moral component to sex education. Manuals of the period typically stressed the moral implications of sex education, most particularly for women. On the first page of one such manual, William J. Robinson, a physician, boldly took up the question of "the paramount need of sex knowledge for girls and women" as compared with men. He wrote,

> The first reason why sex instruction is even more important for girls than it is for boys is because a misstep in a girl has much more disastrous consequences than it has in a boy. The disastrous results of a misstep in a boy are only physical in character; the results of the *same* misstep in a girl may be physical, moral, social and eco-

nomic. To speak more plainly. If a boy, through ignorance, rashly indulges in illicit sexual relations, the worst consequence to him may be infection with a venereal disease. But he is not considered immoral, he is not despised, he is not ostracized, he does not lose his social standing in the slightest degree.[31]

In the end, the author threatened, the girl in such a situation "must remain a lonely wanderer to the end of her days."[32] In addition to the great moral, social, and physical consequences of illicit sex for young women, Robinson argued that sex education was important for young women because "essentially woman is made for love. Not exclusively, but essentially, and a woman who has had no love in her life has been a failure."[33] Richard C. Cabot, a physician whom the YWCA engaged for a series of three lectures on "The Consecration of the Affections," emphasized desire but placed it in a more thoroughly Christian context than did Robinson. Regarding desire, Cabot told a conference of YWCA workers, "The fundamental longing, then, in human body and mind is the longing for God. Sex, so-called, is one aspect of that longing, patriotism is another, and the reaching out after science and truth and beauty are others, but none of these is any more fundamental than the others."[34]

To this end, the YWCA's Social Morality Committee recommended a program for girls up to age sixteen that emphasized the place of romantic love in women's lives and framed it in a context of a sacred history of whites. The report stated:

> The material to be presented should tend to develop a healthy sense of romance, by means of poetry (such as the story of the Holy Grail), pageantry, heraldry, Old World folk lore, hero tales; to modernize this sense of romance by study of national or community customs and local color, "Knights and Ladies of Today"— their manners and customs; to spiritualize the laws of life, by means, for example, of the Christmas story; to lead to discussion of the fundamental laws of ethics—truthfulness, honor, faithfulness, right and wrong, helpfulness.[35]

Thus, the YWCA's program, specifically designed for young white women, encouraged these girls to think of themselves as perpetuating the racial line of the European Old World. While the program for young women above the age of sixteen did not entail such romantic methods, it too stressed a connection between health and social morality.

In addressing young women on the homefront on the issue of sexuality, YWCA materials told these women that the desire to suspend "common conventions" could be understood during wartime, but that for the sake of American men fighting abroad, they could not do this. In a *War Work Bulletin* article on "The Girl Side of the Case," young women read that sex was not a proper way to express their patriotic sentiment. "Girls, too, are eager to share in patriotic service. It is inevitable that when they are not in line for recognition they will go in search of adventure. The lure of the army uniform is very real. The uniform symbolizes both sacrifice and gallantry,—qualities which make a great appeal to the imagination. Therein lies the danger."[36] The article concluded with a call for young women to reaffirm their individual moral standards and to engage in a broader campaign for social morality.

In addition to broad, gendered moral issues, the YWCA's social morality program also addressed the public health issue of sexually transmitted diseases. One of the Social Morality Committee's wartime pamphlets spoke directly to white men abroad. In "The Girl You Leave Behind," white soldiers saw a drawing of a young white girl and read a warning against supporting prostitution in France.

> It would never do for the avengers of women's wrongs to profit by the degradation and debasement of womanhood. Every hardened prostitute who offers herself to you was a young girl once, till some man ruined her. If you accept her, you are shaming all girlhood. Above all, you are shaming and insulting the girl you hope to marry some day, and who is waiting for you at home, whether you know her yet or not.[37]

As part of its attention to the sexual health of white American soldiers stationed in Europe, the YWCA's War Work program also provided canteen services staffed by white women. Through the canteens, the YWCA sought to provide an ongoing connection for soldiers to models of "the girls left behind" as well as a homelike environment in which they could relax and socialize instead of frequenting prostitutes. The YWCA engaged no African American women to go to Europe as part of the program, nor did it provide services for black soldiers. Addie Waites Hunton and Helen Curtis, both associated with the African American YWCA in New York, along with a number of other black women, went to France through the YMCA in order to work with black soldiers.[38] The YWCA remained relatively unconcerned with this group of men and did not address any of its health literature to them.

The question of sexually transmitted disease rested in a gendered context and, importantly, in a racialized context. A pamphlet on syphilis produced by the American Social Hygiene Association argued that the disease represented "the chief enemy of the white race" and therefore required particular attention by medical specialists.[39] Although concerned about the impact of venereal disease on white Americans, health experts, to a large extent, reached the conclusion by the early part of the twentieth century that, as James H. Jones phrased it, syphilis was "the quintessential black disease."[40] White doctors tended to argue that the inherent immorality of African Americans made this the case. One southern white doctor wrote, "Virtue in the negro race is like 'angels' visits—few and far between. . . . I have never examined a virgin over fourteen years of age." And another wrote that the disease was "so prevalent among the men, one can imagine what it was among the women, who had no virtue or chastity to protect them."[41] The medical interpretation of African Americans as naturally inclined to carry venereal diseases, as well as the assumption that it affected blacks and whites differently, led to varied approaches by physicians over the years, which generally resulted in inattention to the disease in black communities.[42] And the YWCA's view of the public health issue of syphilis—as with the general recommendations on social morality—remained largely focused on white women and men.

Beginning in 1913, the National Board of the YWCA sought lecturers to carry out its social morality program, as well as funding for lecturers' salaries. While he insisted that his involvement remain a secret, John D. Rockefeller Jr. both funded the program and participated in the selection of lecturers. The earliest YWCA work of conducting social morality lectures clearly focused on white women, with lectures taking place only in white student or city YWCAs. In the spring of 1917, Dr. Max J. Exner of the YMCA, an adviser to the YWCA's Social

Morality Committee, corresponded with Rockefeller about expanding the YWCA's lecture program to include "social morality work among the Indians." Rockefeller declined to fund the expansion on the conflicting grounds (according to Exner's understanding of Rockefeller's rejection) that, first, he supported an approach to the lectures that included "women of all races and creeds" and that, second, they should hold off on expanding the work to include Native Americans "until social morality workers for women are more sure of their ground in work among our own women."[43] In many ways, Rockefeller's reaction to this proposal and the contradictory nature of his reasoning mirrored the YWCA's own approach to its sense of identity. As a national organization, the YWCA maintained that it developed programs and provided services to women regardless of race. At the same time, it insisted on the segregation of African American women into separate "branches" that underscored the white leaders' sense of the "special needs" of black women.

The emphasis on racially separate local branches became particularly pronounced in the national YWCA's work during World War I, through the development of the Colored Work Committee. The secretary of the committee, Eva D. Bowles, administered a budget of $200,000, allotted by the War Work Council from its $5 million total budget. Although the YWCA established the War Work Council in June 1917, it did not include black women in its original vision and did not appropriate a budget for African American women until January 1918. Eventually, the War Work Council increased the Colored Work Committee's budget to $400,000, a total that included a $4,000 donation from Theodore Roosevelt's Nobel Peace Prize award money. And the members of the Colored Work Committee informed the War Work Council that besides the appropriation for their general budget, they also expected to receive a share of the council's budget for social morality lectures, publicity, and emergency housing for African American women who moved to cities seeking employment.[44]

The YWCA's already existing Social Morality Committee did incorporate African American women into its work, hiring two black female physicians to travel and conduct lectures. Dr. Sara W. Brown and Dr. Ionia Rollin Whipper, both based in Washington, D.C., lectured at black colleges and at city YWCA organizations for African American women. In March and April 1919, for example, Whipper worked at a frenzied pace, delivering fifty-six lectures at eight colleges in six states, speaking to over twelve thousand people.[45]

The Colored Work Committee focused much of its energy and budget on hostess houses, supervised recreation centers for women visiting soldiers at training camps. While the War Work Council administered hostess houses for white women and left the Colored Work Committee to supervise those for African American women, the white women of the War Work Council employed images of African American women as a hypersexualized threat to white society in order to raise funds for its work. In a YWCA brochure that John D. Rockefeller Jr. used as part of his own fund-raising campaign for the YWCA's war work, the YWCA discussed "work in colored communities affected by the war" almost exclusively in terms of the moral threat posed by black women. The pamphlet asserted, "A large number of our cantonments are in the section dense in colored population. The colored American girl is subject to every strain and temptation in war times that is put upon her white sister. The very safeguard thrown about white girls makes the menace of the colored girl more real."[46]

The Colored Work Committee's concern with establishing hostess houses in camps where black soldiers trained did not rest primarily with containing black women's sexuality but rather with protecting African American men and women from real physical danger, particularly in camps in the South. Hostess Houses provided a calm and safe haven for African American women, some of whom had suffered the danger and indignities of segregated travel to reach the camps to visit their male relatives and friends. The Colored Work Committee's first Hostess House, at Camp Upton, Long Island, opened in November 1917 in temporary quarters and in April 1918 in a new house under the supervision of Lugenia Burns Hope of Atlanta's Neighborhood Union.[47] By the end of the war, the Colored Work Committee had established sixteen Hostess Houses, with Upton serving as the training center for women assigned as "hostesses" at other camps.[48] Hope described her arrival at the new house at Camp Upton in April 1918 and her surprise and joy at the quality of the house and the volume of use by soldiers in the evenings after their visitors had left the camp.

> When we entered a little lady rose from her seat amidst a group of soldiers and came forward to meet us. The spacious room was full

of soldiers. Every chair and space at all tables were taken and some men were standing. Some were writing, others reading, playing games and talking. In one corner apart two of the hostesses were guiding the great hands of the men in copy-book exercises. Officers and many men spend the evening in an effort to teach these soldiers, but so many wanted to learn that the hostesses volunteered also. Every one in the room seemed to be enjoying himself in his own way, yet it was quiet and restful; there was no smoking, no loud talk, yet men, men of all conditions and nationalities were there.[49]

Although the YWCA's Hostess House work remained segregated, Hope's description of life at Camp Upton, as well as other accounts of her time there, point to the importance of African American women's Hostess House work to Jewish soldiers and their families and friends. Hope described Jewish men relaxing in the African American Hostess House, as well as services that she and other hostesses at Upton provided to mothers and wives of Jewish soldiers. While the white women of the War Work Council boasted that, because of the existence of the Colored Work Committee, the Council provided equal services to whites and blacks, Lugenia Hope and other women in the Colored Work Committee pointed out that, in the most concrete terms, they alone really provided services to everyone who came to them.

Many African American women involved in the wartime work of the YWCA emphasized the importance that a new and more public service role for black women would have in mitigating the impact of racism and sexism on their communities. Therefore, representations of African American women emerged as an issue of profound significance for black YWCA workers, and the Colored Work Committee took it on in terms of policy, practice, and publicity. One of the earliest decisions that Bowles and the committee made concerned the representation of African American women in YWCA publicity material. Eva Bowles read to the committee a story released by the publicity department and written by a white YWCA worker clearly for a white audience. The story described the African American Hostess House at Camp Funston, Kansas. As with much of the YWCA's wartime publicity concerning African American women, the article declares that "the behavior in the colored hostess houses is just the same as in the white." The author did not, however, present African American men and women as "just the same" as white men and women, but as merely sufficiently controlled in their behavior through the presence of the hostess house.

In fact, the presentation rests on the assumption of fundamental differences between blacks and whites and on the hypersexuality of African Americans. Describing the soldiers and women who used this hostess house, the author wrote almost incredulously that "some of these are most attractive and several of the colored officers, themselves fine looking men, have very attractive and ladylike looking wives; there are no more loud voices, there are no more demonstrations of affection in the barrack in the camp than in the house on the hill."[50] Fortunately, the author concluded, the hostess houses solved "what was threatening to become a most difficult problem," that is, that some of the African American officers' wives waited for their husbands on the porch and in "public" view, an unacceptable situation for white onlookers. Thus, the YWCA's publicity department boasted that its programs successfully contained the sexuality of black women who, although "ladylike looking," threatened to contaminate the entire camp. Bowles and the Colored Work Committee demanded, as a result of this particular article, that the publicity department remove parts of articles that did not "conform with the spirit and policies of this movement."[51]

The Colored Work Committee's struggle with the War Work Council's publicity committee over representations of African Americans proved a difficult one, as the *War Work Bulletin* often recycled familiar stereotypes, while at the same time attempting to make blacks appear as "American" as everyone else. In two striking illustrations in the *War Work Bulletin*, the conflict becomes clear. In one issue, the caption to a photograph of a nursery at a white Hostess House reads, "Mother and all the family have a happy day at camp when the YWCA Hostess House has a nursery like this." The photograph shows two white children attended by an African American woman in a domestic's uniform.[52] This African American woman, excluded by the caption from the category of "mother," assumes the familiar role of the caretaker of white families, giving white readers the message that although the YWCA helped to provide expanded employment opportunities for black women, they should not fear the loss of their domestic servants.

In another issue of the *War Work Bulletin*, which discussed white American soldiers in France and their war brides, one photograph shows a group of black soldiers standing with a white woman in a YWCA uniform. The caption reads, "If you wanted to give a foreigner a typically American dish, whom would you select to cook it? Wouldn't you choose a colored chef? The selection of a colored force in the kitchen of Debarkation Camp No. 1 at St. Nazaire, France, seems specially fitting, for it is in this camp the little French brides, on their way to America, get their first taste of American hospitality and cooking."[53] As one of the very few instances in which African American men appear in the YWCA's *War Work Bulletin*, this photograph and text work to make invisible or inconsequential the military experience of black soldiers in France.

In addition to the struggle of the Colored Work Committee against problematic representations of African American women by white YWCA women, the committee also confronted perceived adversaries within African American communities, particularly when it came to questions of "respectable behavior." Florida Ruffin Ridley—a journalist and YWCA war worker, and the daughter of Josephine St. Pierre Ruffin, a founder of the black women's club movement—set out a particular standard for black women's behavior in YWCA Hostess Houses in an article in the *New York Age*. Ridley wrote that the great significance of the Hostess House rested on its "being used as a training center for future homes and . . . attracting to itself representative colored women from all sections of the country, who are responding with enthusiasm and intelligence to this opportunity, not only to become part of the great war, but also to prove to the men that colored women are ready, willing and able to stand shoulder to shoulder with white women in rendering service."[54] Like many other African American women in this period, Ridley saw the service that they could offer the country as having broad ramifications. Significantly, here she underscores the impact she hoped such service would have on gender relations in African American communities and on the ability of black men to see black women as their allies in struggle. For Ridley, the Hostess Houses served the broad and ongoing purpose of teaching young black women how to create "respectable" homes that met the same standard as white homes.

Because African American women in the YWCA invested their wartime service with such deep significance, their representations of themselves held an important place, as Ridley's emphasis on "representative women" illustrates. In practice, this sometimes meant a strict and narrow application of standards of respectability. Lester Walton, entertainment critic for the *New York Age*, published a scathing piece in June 1918 about a group of black women who went to Upton to perform in the camp's theater and suffered from that narrow standard. According to Walton's account, the YWCA hostesses denied the performers overnight accommodations, not because of any actions on their part, but merely on the presumption that, as actresses and singers, they were necessarily immoral women. Walton wrote,

> Turning young women performers out into the cold and denying them the right of sleeping quarters does not speak well for Christians whose duty it is to extend a helping hand to those needing assistance. Is the hostess house to be conducted as an exclusive club or is it to serve the public? It seems to me that this is a most unfair and inconsistent point of view for Christians engaged in the work of administering spiritual guidance to take.[55]

While the Colored Work Committee seems to have made no formal response to Walton's charges, its adherence to hard-line standards in representing African Americans provides an answer. Its members pursued their goal of presenting "positive" images of African Americans, whether that meant struggling against the publicity committee of the national YWCA's exclusively white War Work Council, or against internal community threats to such "positive" images.

An Urban Homefront

African American women in the New York City YWCA became very involved in a variety of campaigns in support of the war and of African American soldiers in particular. As soon as it became clear that New York's 15th Regiment of the National Guard would be called up, the Woman's Loyal Union called on black women in New York to support the men of the 15th. Within a month of the declaration of war, black women in the city had formed a Woman's Auxiliary to the 15th Regiment and set about collecting reading materials and other items for the "comfort bags" they eventually provided for the soldiers of the regiment. A special "committee on tobacco" saw to it that the soldiers' requests for cigarettes and other tobacco products were met. In addition, members of the Woman's Auxiliary, a group of almost four hundred women, met at churches and regularly visited the homes of soldiers with dependents to determine what services they could provide.[56] In addition to participating in the Woman's Auxiliary, black YWCA women in New York supported the work of the Circle for Negro War Relief, organized in November 1917. The Circle collected goods to package as comfort kits for soldiers and also provided educational materials for black soldiers in training camps. Through various large fundraising events, the Circle for Negro War Relief in New York raised over $2,000 to purchase an ambulance, which it donated to Camp Upton for black soldiers' use.[57]

The medical care of black soldiers also became an issue as African American women of New York joined with African Americans across the country in demanding that black nurses be included in the work of the Red Cross. Adah B. Thoms, president of the National Association of Graduate Colored Nurses from 1916 until 1923 and assistant superintendent of nurses at New York's Lincoln Hospital, led the campaign. Thoms, active in New York's YWCA and elected to the African American YWCA's committee of management in 1921, spoke before the 1917 meeting of the National Medical Association, the major professional organization for African American physicians, and underscored the promise African Americans felt inhered in the particular historical moment of the war. Thoms told her audience that "whether [President Wilson] meant to include us or not makes no difference. We are included, and there is no power outside of ourselves that can keep us from sharing with the rest of mankind the liberty and freedom for which democracy stands."[58]

The Woman's Auxiliary of the 15th Regiment, which had participated in fund raising for the Red Cross and of which Thoms was an important member, became affiliated with the Red Cross. At the same time, the auxiliary assisted Thoms and other African American nurses in challenging the Red Cross's policy of denying black nurses access to the Army Nursing Corps. In January 1918, Thoms wrote a letter of protest to Jane A. Delano, chair of the Red Cross, in which she questioned the failure of the organization to include trained and qualified black nurses. Thoms wrote, in part,

I don't understand how the Red Cross, being international in scope, can fail to recognize intelligent, competent American women who, prompted by a spirit of unselfishness, are willing to serve and die if necessary for their country. How an association as great as the Red Cross and with such noble ideals as it represents, can take time to make a distinction in color, a thing over which we have no control, and for which we are not responsible, is beyond my comprehension.[59]

Despite the difficulties that black nurses experienced with the organization, African American women in New York's YWCA formed a chapter of the Red Cross while at the same time supporting the struggle of black nurses to receive appointments through the Red Cross. In the December 8, 1917 issue of the *Age*, the African American YWCA announced that it had requested all branches to form chapters of the Red Cross and that, in compliance with that request, black New Yorkers could affiliate with their new chapter.[60] The difficulties that African American women in New York experienced with the Red Cross reveals some of the contours of the dilemma of representation during this period. Calling on the Red Cross to recognize their skill and their patriotic commitment, black nurses understood the potential implications of being excluded from opportunities for service at this moment. In the same way, African American YWCA women in New York answered the call to form a chapter quickly and publicly in order to claim ground from which to promote particular images of themselves as supporters of the war effort.

In addition to forming a Red Cross chapter in support of the war, African American women in the New York City YWCA participated in a number of programs encouraged by the government. In preparation for the draft, New York State conducted a state military census, and black YWCA women in the city assisted in that project. This YWCA also took an active role in the government's food conservation program, conducting food substitute demonstrations at its Harlem building. With the guidance of a special committee chaired by Ruth Logan Roberts, the women helped to sell war bonds through the Liberty Loan program, and the African American YWCA functioned as an authorized agency for the sale of Thrift Stamps.[61]

The leaders of New York's African American YWCA also enlisted young members of the YWCA in the Patriotic Service League, an avenue for young girls to "express [their] patriotism" in "simple ways" on the homefront. In a *War Work Bulletin* article on the league, girls

read of the imperative of the patriotic girl "to put more 'pep,' enthusiasm and energy into study, athletics, housework or whatever her daily
work may be. Not to do things in an ordinary, but in an extra ordinary way."[62] In October 1917, a representative of the Patriotic Service
League visited New York's African American YWCA and addressed a
group of sixty girls interested in forming a league; by November, this
group had undertaken a knitting project to supply soldiers.[63] Addie
Waites Hunton devoted a great deal of time to the Patriotic Service
League during part of 1917 and 1918 and undertook the responsibility
of working with African American girls in Brooklyn and Manhattan
before leaving to work for the YMCA in France.[64]

With the assistance of the National Board's Colored Work Committee and New York City's Metropolitan Board, the African American
YWCA in Harlem expanded its commitment to war work by opening
a War Service Center. Emma Ransom approached the Metropolitan
Board in March 1918 with the idea of providing a center for African
American soldiers and their relatives and friends, as well as a recreation
center for African Americans in Harlem. The Metropolitan Board appropriated $2,000 for this work; the center, located at 127 West 136th
Street, opened on July 4, 1918. To administer the center, the YWCA
appointed Ruth A. Fisher, a graduate of Oberlin College and a former
instructor at Tuskegee Institute. The center's first floor housed the
canteen for soldiers with a library supplied by the American Library
Association. In addition, it served as a venue for club meetings, dramatic performances, and public lectures, including a series of vocational
lectures by W. E. B. Du Bois. The center also hosted a special exhibit of
sculpture by African American artist May Howard Jackson. In the summer of 1919, the workers at the recreation center began a program of
community singing, endorsed by the national YWCA as a means of
"bringing people of every type, age and race together."[65]

In addition to organizing activities directly supporting African American soldiers and U.S. involvement in the war, the women of New
York's African American YWCA faced an enormous task in dealing with
the housing and employment issues facing the large numbers of African
American women and men who had migrated to New York in search of
greater opportunities. In order to serve this population's particular employment needs, the city's African American YWCA established a new
standing committee on employment and immigration. The leaders of

this YWCA and of other organizations serving African Americans in New York understood the changes in employment opportunities for African Americans in this period as representing a significant turning point that required delicate handling. Early in 1917 the Urban League and the Russell Sage Foundation sponsored a conference on "negro migration," through which the Urban League and cooperating organizations, including the African American YWCA, urged southern black migrants to present a "positive" and professional image. The conference's published report focused on this question, asserting the necessity of instructing new arrivals

> as to the dress, habits, and methods of living necessary to withstand the rigors of the Northern climate; as to the efficiency, regularity and application demanded of workers in the North; as to the danger of dealing or going with unscrupulous or vicious persons and of frequenting questionable resorts; as to the opportunities offered by the towns and cities of the North in schools, hospitals, police protection and employment; as to facilities offered by the church, YMCA and YWCA and other organizations.[66]

Following up on this, an Urban League study of employers who hired both white and African American workers found that African American workers indeed made a favorable impression on their employers.[67]

The African American YWCA concerned itself with issues relating to African American women in particular. Its employment bureau, licensed since 1906, served as an intermediary agency between employers and women seeking positions. From early on in the war, the employment bureau began to experience an increase in requests from employers seeking African American women, as well as the beginnings of a shift in the kinds of employment requests handled. In September 1917, the African American YWCA announced openings in the areas of "high class millinery and dressmaking establishments, power workers of all kinds, feather work, hemstitching, scalloping, printing, multigraphing and mailing."[68] The employment bureau assisted in training women to take the civil service examination for postal clerk positions in New York, resulting in the first such appointment of an African American woman, and facilitated the placement of the first African American telephone operator at Grand Central Station. The employment bureau also placed African American women in positions as clerical, stock-room, elevator, bookkeeping, stenographic, and wrapping workers, all positions in areas not traditionally open to African American female workers in New York City.[69]

To alert African American women in the city to new employment possibilities, this YWCA presented a variety of vocational training sessions and lecture series on labor opportunities, including a lecture by W. E. B. Du Bois on trades and housework; a lecture by Madame C. J. Walker, the creator of an extremely successful beauty business, on "The Business Woman"; and a series by local professionals on dentistry, journalism, social work, nursing, stenography, and millinery.[70] By the end of 1918, the city's African American YWCA had handled 3,355 requests from employers and had placed 1,609 women in positions.[71]

Both the Colored Work Committee and the War Work Council devoted considerable attention to labor issues affecting African American women during the war. Indeed, the primary image of African American women one finds in War Work Council literature is as workers who had been afforded unprecedented opportunities in this period. Literature from the National Board of the YWCA dealing with black women and labor emphasized the newness of African American women working in factories, as well as their record of productivity in these lines of work. In the article "The Colored Girl Gets Her Chance," the YWCA tells readers that "for the first time in history the colored woman has become a real factor in the labor world. . . . They work under the handicaps of lack of organization and lack of training, yet, where they have been given a fair test, they have more than made good." The organization asserted that "the YWCA, in its work among colored industrial girls claims for them equal standards with all other employed girls,"[72] truly a bold claim in that historical moment.

While the national YWCA was attempting to interpret African American women to white America and to present them as "a national asset" in the labor force, the reality was that YWCA work remained strictly segregated. Eva Bowles's claim that the YWCA worked with all women in the same manner because it provided separate and similar services remains a charitable interpretation of a segregated system in which black women in the YWCA received inequitable financial and institutional support. The realities of the YWCA's approach to black women's labor issues, as well as these women's working realities, mitigated the boldness of both the assertion of equal treatment within the YWCA and the YWCA's call for an equal chance for black women in the working world.

The YWCA's publicity gave great attention to the women who entered professions from which they had been previously excluded and which constituted a substantial improvement over traditional jobs as domestics, laundresses, and agricultural workers. However, a 1918 study of working conditions for African American women in New York City highlighted the compromised nature of the new labor opportunities, indicating that black and white YWCA leaders recognized at least some significant difficulties and inequities. The study, sponsored by the YWCA, the Russell Sage Foundation, the New York Urban League, the Women's Trade Union League, and the Committee on Colored Workers of the Manhattan Trade School, involved a survey of 242 employers in New York, 214 of which employed African American women. Gertrude Elsie Johnson MacDougald, a native New Yorker, member of the African American YWCA's committee of management, and employee of the U.S. Department of Labor, conducted the survey.[73]

The results of the study were written up by Mary E. Jackson, a Rhode Islander working as the industrial secretary on Bowles's Colored Work Committee. Analyzing the experiences of 175 black women working in New York, MacDougald and Jackson found that 72 percent of their sample had migrated from the South and that 75 percent were under the age of twenty-six. These workers had a higher level of education than the average white female worker in the city—over half had completed elementary school, a significant number had completed high school, and some were college graduates. Despite the relatively high level of education, these women remained untrained in the industries they entered during the war because discrimination had forced most of them into domestic service. Although migrating to the North during the war presented new employment possibilities, these women nevertheless experienced a great deal of hardship in their work lives, earning substantially less than white women when performing the same labor. In summarizing the study, Jane Olcott, a YWCA historian, wrote, "Colored women were the marginal workers of industry during the war, releasing white women for more skilled work and replacing the unskilled and semi-skilled men."[74] Thus, during the war, African American female workers in New York entered professions that had previously been closed to them, but they did not have access to the same jobs that white women did. In addition, the study found, African American women were the first to be released once men began returning to the positions they held before the war.[75] And finally, these women experienced considerable mistreatment at the hands of white coworkers.

As part of the project of representing African American women in new ways during the war, Bowles and the Colored Work Committee emphasized that black and white female workers had responsibilities to one another. In an interview published in the *War Work Bulletin*, Bowles pressed the idea that "unconsciously the destiny of the colored girl has been so interwoven with that of the white girl that the two can never be separated." As the executive of the Colored Work Committee, Bowles told black and white women in the YWCA that the labor changes brought on by the war should be seen as permanent marks of progress for all Americans. Directing herself to white women who now faced the prospect of working alongside African American women, Bowles outlined the adjustments that black female workers would be required to make in entering into new employment arenas. She argued that only when white female laborers understood and embraced their responsibilities to black women would all parties emerge from the war period with favorable prospects. Bowles told white readers of the paper that "unless the white girl sees her responsibility to the colored girl and helps her to understand the standards of work and wages, much that has been accomplished will be undone, and the white girl herself will suffer. It is to the same standard that is set for the white girl that we are trying to bring the colored girl, and we are emphasizing to her the importance of not working for smaller wages than the white girl."[76] Here Bowles attempted to assure white female workers that African American women's access to new arenas of labor need not debase white women, economically or socially. Bowles asserted that the changes on the labor scene would be permanent and would, indeed, bring an end to the "wages of whiteness"—the tangible and intangible benefits accruing to white workers.[77] At the same time, she insisted that only white women could assure that they would not be reduced to the level of black workers prior to the war.

As with labor issues, the approach of African American YWCA women, at both the national and local level, to urban housing issues balanced questions of public representation and the specific needs of black women. With significant numbers of African American women and men migrating to New York City in search of employment opportunities and to escape Jim Crow, a housing shortage developed among black New Yorkers. Harlem, which had represented the first opportunity for black New Yorkers to feel some breathing room in terms of housing, now began to become quite crowded. In addition, relatively high rents meant that a single young woman arriving in the city could not afford to take an apartment on her own. She would also find few residences for single women in which she could rent a room. For example, the African American YWCA at this time had only nineteen beds for short-term residents. Neither the White Rose Mission and the Empire Friendly Shelter, both long-established New York institutions, nor the more recently organized Sojourner Truth Home, under the auspices of the New York Urban League, had the capacity to address such large numbers of women seeking housing.[78]

As a preliminary means of dealing with this growing problem, as well as in an attempt to find lodgings for black women visiting soldiers about to embark for Europe, the African American YWCA expanded its already established rooms registry. This entailed members of the committee of management visiting homes of black New Yorkers interested in renting to boarders referred by the YWCA. Once the home had been "investigated," the African American YWCA entered it into the registry. The housing crisis brought on by the stress of the war years moved the African American YWCA to appoint a full-time worker to expand the small registry. In December 1917, the committee of management hired Vivienne Ward-Stokes, a native of Raleigh, North Carolina, who had previously worked for the National Urban League and the Woman's Bureau of the Department of Labor, to oversee the housing effort. While the Metropolitan Board recognized the need for such a service at the African American YWCA, it did not appropriate funds for Stokes's salary, which the National Board ultimately absorbed. Because of her success developing a local rooms registry and the Colored Work Committee's belief that the issue of housing for single working African American women required national attention, the Colored Work Committee hired Stokes to become the national rooms registry organizer. New York's African American YWCA then turned to Marie Peek Johnson to replace Stokes.[79]

The registry of rooms held by the African American YWCA ultimately did not meet the needs of black women in New York, as the number of requests far exceeded the organization's ability to provide rooms. They could not look to their new building to help in the crisis: the land for the new building had been purchased in November 1916, but conflict over payment of pledges as well as U.S. entry into the war had delayed the project. As an interim measure, the committee of management selected a building at 137th Street and Seventh Avenue, whose purchase the Colored Work Committee facilitated. The building, 200 West 137th Street, was owned by Lillian Dean Harris, a popular Harlem figure. Known as "Pig Foot Mary," Dean had amassed a fortune selling pigs' feet, fried chicken, and corn on the streets of Harlem and had invested her profits in real estate. According to lore, she paid for this building in full in cash.[80] The War Work Council provided $9,000 of the $10,000 down-payment and $14,000 for furnishings and equipment. The Metropolitan Board bore much of the cost of renovations. In November 1919, the African American YWCA opened the Blue Triangle Residence, with a capacity of eighty-eight women, and the committee of management hired Harriet Edwards as director of the residence. Edwards, who had served as secretary and bookkeeper for the Circle for Negro War Relief before spending time working in France under the auspices of the YMCA, had lived in New York's African American YWCA for two years and was therefore familiar with the issues facing such a residence.[81] The opening of this residence allowed the leaders of this YWCA to make their best effort to address the effects of changing demographics on young, self-supporting African American women.

∿ NEW YORK CITY'S African American YWCA emerged from the war period with new energy and powerful material means through which to have a strong impact on the community of African Americans in Harlem. White leaders at the National Board of the YWCA engaged in a program of representing black women as "colored American girls" rather than as "colored girls," an approach that brought an important new spotlight to the participation of African American women in the YWCA. The Colored Work Committee also took up this project of wartime representation, and African American women welcomed an opportunity to present themselves as patriotic Americans. However, both white and black women in the YWCA approached the issue of representing African American women in ways that relied on older images. Bowles and the Colored Work Committee held fast to standards of "respectability" for African American women that, in many ways, embraced traditional images of black women as morally dangerous and potentially morally contagious.

White leaders in the national YWCA retreated rather quickly from the wartime emphasis on the Americanness of African American women. In the first issue of the *Blue Triangle News*, formerly the *War Work Bulletin*, the National Board assessed itself and its work at the end of the war. In discussing "colored work," the author emphasized the growth in membership among African Americans during the war years, as well as the general growth of the work "to dignified proportions." Following this section, however, the YWCA eviscerated the message of the dignity of black women's work with a photograph of four black children in a rural setting. The caption reads, "Happy-go-lucky and content with a minimum amount of miscellaneous clothing, these colored children of the rural districts of Alabama are nevertheless potential citizens under the Stars and Stripes."[82]

In addition to withdrawing Americanness from black women and replacing it with "potential citizenship," the national YWCA increasingly turned to international issues in ways that made African American women's YWCA work invisible. In one striking example, the YWCA's Department for Work with Foreign Born Women provided a *Handbook of Racial and Nationality Backgrounds* that discussed cultural differences among national groups, prefaced by a table that presented "a simple racial classification." The table lists, in painstaking detail, peoples who fall under the "racial" categories of Teutonic, Keltic [*sic*], Italic, Helleno-Illyric, Lettic, Indo-Iranic, Chaldean, Tartaric, Slavic, Finn-Tartaric, Chinese, Japanese, Korean, and Filipino. Africans and people of African descent are notably absent in this "simple racial classification."[83] Thus, while the YWCA used the moment of the war to include black women as Americans, the interwar period saw a retreat from this stance and, in many ways, an attempt to deny the presence of African American women in the organization.

At the same time, however, the Colored Work Committee, transformed after the war into the Bureau of Colored Work, gave local YWCA organizations, like the African American YWCA in Harlem, a powerful anchor for their work. Through the work of the Colored

Work Committee, the number of paid black staff in local YWCAs increased from nine in 1915 to 112 after the war, and the national black membership rose to twelve thousand.[84] In her final report before the War Work Council, Bowles emphasized her commitment to the Bureau of Colored Work, as well as its importance to black women in local YWCAs, saying, "The time has passed for white leadership for colored people; as white and colored women we must understand each other; we must think and act and plan together, for upon all of us rests the responsibility of the girlhood of all nations."[85] The financial support of the Colored Work Committee had assisted New York's African American YWCA in acquiring new staff, a recreation center, and a residence. And the connection with this increasingly powerful committee within the national YWCA helped to overcome the turn of the National Board's attention elsewhere, as well as the ongoing conflicts with the Metropolitan Board of the New York City YWCA.

Two particular developments after the war helped the African American YWCA in New York to emerge with greater prominence and a more confident sense of its identity. The January 3, 1920, edition of the New York Age reported on both. In one article, the Age described the physical plant of the African American YWCA's recently completed building, located at 179 West 137th Street. Boasting a cafeteria with a capacity of one hundred, an information desk, reception rooms, offices, meeting rooms, classrooms, a gymnasium, a pool, and shower and locker rooms, this YWCA became the best-equipped African American YWCA in the country.

In another notice, the paper reported that Emma Ransom had been elected to a seat on the previously all-white Metropolitan Board. Dr. Fanny Cook Gates, who became general secretary of the YWCA of the City of New York in May 1918, first broached the question of permanent representation for the African American YWCA in January 1918 but received a cold reception from the Metropolitan Board. Repeatedly over the course of the next year, the board discussed and tabled the proposal, and Gates failed to accomplish this particular goal before her resignation in May 1919. Finally, in December 1919 the Metropolitan Board voted to appoint Ransom, although not in the context of equal representation for all branches of the New York City YWCA. The board's minutes record that its members elected Ransom "to fill a vacancy made by a recent resignation."[86] Nevertheless, Ransom's position on the Metropolitan Board represented a significant milestone for African American women in the YWCA in New York and across the country. Her presence as a leader on the Metropolitan Board served as recognition of fourteen years of work by black women in the city's YWCA, and as an affirmation of the value of the investment that these women had made in the YWCA as an important avenue for African American women to serve themselves and others. This new sense of self and purpose, as well as the material gains of the imposing new physical plant, positioned New York City's African American YWCA to assist black New Yorkers through the economically and politically turbulent years following the war.

~ 6

"A Grand Place": Black America's Community Center

$\mathcal{I}_N$ 1940 the Harmon Foundation, an important source of support for black artists and writers in Harlem in the interwar period, funded the production of an eleven-minute film profile of New York's African American YWCA. The short film, made by two black filmmakers not directly involved with the YWCA, uses the frame of a young woman's letter home from her room in the YWCA residence to introduce various aspects of life within the YWCA complex. She begins: "My first week here has been most thrilling. The 'Y' is a grand place to live—lovely rooms and excellent meals in our cafeteria." The scene shifts to the cafeteria, where we see well-dressed men and women lined up to be served hot meals. The young woman then describes various courses she is taking, including secretarial training and dressmaking, and tells of the attraction of the clubs, swimming pool, and athletic activities. She continues excitedly: "Some people think that the 'Y' turns out old maids, but it isn't so mother. We have parties and dances all the time and the loveliest 'Beau Parlors' where we may entertain." We then see the parlor, where a young woman waits and watches as men and women pass through the room. Finally, a man arrives and the woman greets him. The two sit down together and talk. He takes her hand. The letter concludes: "There are so many things to do and every one is so nice to me that I haven't had time to be homesick. Best wishes to all. Lovingly. . . ."[1]

   This fictionalized vision of the YWCA in Harlem promotes the organization as a community center that embraces all of Harlem and welcomes African Americans from across the nation and blacks from around the world. One aspect of the film's portrayal of New York's African American YWCA is particularly striking. The film contains no reference to the Christian origins and grounding of the YWCA, so the organization appears as one entirely lacking in religious emphasis. Although the text that introduces the film speaks of the YWCA in Harlem as bringing "'the more abundant life' to Negro girls through its activities," the emphasis the filmmakers place on activities removes the branch's motto from its original Christian context. The highlight on romance also serves to diminish the religious element. In the film, "religious women" and "old maids" become conflated, and the concern with members' access to romance betrays a certain fear of an imagined "lifestyle" of Christian African American women. The producers of the Harmon Foundation film, however, did not seek to create a fiction but rather portrayed the institution they saw. Upon visiting, they found an organization that, at this point in its history, constructed its image as a community center rather than a Christian home, and as a vehicle for educating African Americans in civic responsibilities rather than solely for church membership.

   How did this institution reach the point where outsiders describing it made no mention of its religious orientation and concerns? An examination of the activities and services the branch offered, and of the ways in which the organization served to foster leadership skills in young women, reveals that its leaders did not, in fact, abandon the Christian component of their work. Instead, the leaders of this YWCA expanded their vision of the boundaries of Christian concerns to embrace a range of "secular" issues. Rather than undergoing a clear process of secularization in which it set aside religious emphases, New York's African American YWCA reformulated its Christian vision through attention to the widest possible range of issues confronting African Americans.

   In shifting from overtly religious programs such as Bible study to an almost exclusive focus on activities that seem viscerally to have no religious basis, New York's African American YWCA, along with the YWCA as a whole, participated in a process that had been underway since shortly before World War I. Increasingly, the YWCA moved toward an emphasis on the Social Gospel, seeking to regenerate the social order through the activist intervention of individuals and churches. Influenced by Walter Rauschenbusch, a major articulator of the Social Gospel and a sometime speaker at national YWCA conventions, the YWCA embraced the idea that humans could solve the problems of society and assist it in progressing toward the Kingdom of God. And, as with Rauschenbusch and other proponents of the Social Gospel, the YWCA felt strongly that America and its democracy would play a particular role in bringing about the Kingdom of God.[2]

One of the most significant stages in the YWCA's movement toward the Social Gospel came with the adoption, at the national YWCA's convention in 1920, of the Federal Council of Churches' 1912 statement on the "Social Ideals of the Churches." This statement, largely concerned with labor issues, affirmed as its fundamental principle that "the churches stand for equal rights and justice for all men in all stations of life." In addition to addressing such issues as collective bargaining, minimum wage, occupational safety, and equal political and economic rights for women, the Federal Council of Churches' statement asserted that "the teachings of Jesus are those of essential democracy and express themselves through brotherhood and the cooperation of all groups."[3] Upon adopting this statement, the national YWCA added a number of recommendations for its own use, including one that encouraged the YWCA to "use its resources to further the preparation of women for responsible citizenship and to direct their energies toward the achievement of social righteousness."[4]

During the interwar period, the national YWCA, as well as the women of the YWCA in Harlem, employed language that equated the essence of Christian teaching with "democracy." For these women, American democracy presented the greatest possibility for constructing the most truly Christian society, one that recognized the value of all its members. Without letting go of their own Protestant commitments, the women of the YWCA realized that America's future included people from a variety of backgrounds and that this reality required new approaches. As rhetoric about "democracy" and "social justice" replaced discussions about Christianity and personal morality, the religious grounding seems to have disappeared in the way the organization represented its purpose. In some respects, the YWCA now sought to move individuals to convert to democracy rather than to particular forms of evangelical Christianity. However, rather than discard its

Christian origins, the YWCA embraced the language of democracy in order to express its sense of self in new ways. Ironically, the YWCA moved toward this language at a time when the denial of full participation to African Americans within the organization and without appeared prominently in the public eye and, in many ways, became more fully entrenched. White America continued to withhold the full benefits of citizenship from African Americans despite their service to the nation in World War I.

African American women in the New York City YWCA supported the YWCA's commitment to the Social Gospel but also sought additional emphases that spoke to their concerns for racial justice. The Social Gospel's insistence on examining both personal morality and the social sources of sin had a corollary tradition within African American Christianity. African American Christians had long emphasized the responsibility of all Christians to deal with social ills as a necessary component of Christian commitment, with racism representing the most significant American malady. In adopting the "Social Ideals of the Churches," the YWCA very publicly pledged itself to improving economic and labor conditions for American workers but did not, at this point in its history, explicitly focus on racism as a major social evil. While African American women in the YWCA indeed viewed American democracy as a manifestation of Christianity, the nation's failure to extend democracy to African Americans made it an imperfect democracy. In the New York City YWCA, African American women pointed out that the shift to a language of Christian democracy carried different meanings for them than it apparently did for white women.

The Harlem Renaissance and significant religious and political developments in the interwar period also constitute an important backdrop for shifts in the emphasis that New York's African American YWCA placed on its religious roots. The concentration of black writers, artists, and musicians in New York City in the 1920s brought international attention to Harlem as the center of a new and affirming culture that bound blacks together, not because they saw themselves as representing a common problem, but because they had "a life in common."[5] Alongside this cultural renaissance, Harlemites also saw a new political culture take hold in their neighborhood. Black socialists, communists, nationalists, and separatists found vibrant constituencies in Harlem and made it, in Jervis Anderson's words, "the most militant community in the black world."[6] With these additional avenues for support and succor, black churches no longer represented the primary refuge for black Americans, nor the principal means of mounting political lobbying campaigns on behalf of African Americans.

In terms of religious life in Harlem in the interwar period, two significant developments deserve attention. First, the population boom that had begun during World War I led to a corresponding proliferation in the number of churches. Some commentators saw the growth in the number of churches as far out of proportion to the population growth, however. For example, in 1930 James Weldon Johnson observed, "There are something like one hundred and sixty colored churches in Harlem. A hundred of these could be closed and there would be left a sufficient number to supply the religious needs of the community."[7] Many of the new churches, as Johnson noted, belonged to either new denominations or no denomination, were housed in storefronts, and often constituted an ephemeral part of the Harlem landscape. In addition, Harlem also saw the development of a significant number of new religions (many of these non-Christian and generally termed "sects" and "cults") that often revolved around a charismatic individual. The neighborhood's most spectacular leaders of new religions—Father Divine, Daddy Grace, and Sufi Abdul Hamid—flourished in this period.[8] The fracturing of Harlem's Christian communities resulted in a certain sense of religious dislocation for some residents who now felt a loss of the sense of connectedness they had found in the years when Harlem was a smaller place. With all of these changes, new options, and exciting developments, institutions like the YWCA in Harlem felt pressed to keep up with the times and market itself in new ways.

In her 1937 annual report, Cecelia Cabaniss Saunders discussed her vision of the religious values underlying the work of the city's African American YWCA in ways typical of the YWCA as a whole in this period. She began by posing the question, "How, if at all, in this Branch have we 'interpreted our Christian faith in living terms?'" Saunders responded in two ways. First, she wrote, "we have refused to consider any girl's problem as outside the sphere of the YWCA and have made an honest effort to help every single individual who has looked to us." Her second response underscores the commitment to living Christian democracy. "The second answer lies in the harmonious relationship of individuals in the Branch—a group representing a complete cross section of Negro American life. These individuals are committee members, staff members, girl members, older members, Branch employees. A completely unconscious attitude of fraternity exists between all. There is neither an attitude of superiority from the administrative group nor of inferiority from employees."[9] Saunders's emphasis on the various activities and services that this YWCA offered as its means of interpreting Christianity in "living terms" provides an important key to understanding the work of the branch in the interwar period. A number of factors and functions—including the new building, finances, unemployment during the depression, trade education, food services, and camp activities for girls—emerge as central to the daily life of this African American YWCA and as its basis for interacting with the surrounding community.

A Community Center

The establishment of a permanent physical plant in Harlem constituted a crucial step in the African American YWCA's development in the interwar period. The new administration building, and the residence and annex that would eventually sit adjacent to the main building, made the city's African American YWCA a community center in ways that had been impossible in its previous smaller accommodations. As a center open to the entire community and to groups and individuals from around the world, this YWCA connected a variety of constituencies. Olivia Pearl Stokes, who grew up in Harlem, belonged to the Abyssinian Baptist Church, and worked at the YWCA for some time, underscored this function of the YWCA in her reminiscences of Harlem in the 1930s. She recalled, "Right around the corner was the YWCA. So we had the combination of the Y, the church, and then those two organizations were linked to the world. The Y was linked to the world, our church was affiliated with the Protestant Council of the City of New York. So that as we grew up, in leadership, we were linked to the whole world."[10] Moreover, because the YWCA required those who used the facilities to become members, the new building in Harlem brought into the YWCA people who might not otherwise have interacted with it or been exposed to its philosophy.

Early in 1920, after many years' delay, the newly constructed building at 197 West 137th Street finally opened to serve New York's African American residents. Because of the delay and the intervening war, the cost of the building, originally estimated at $100,000, reached a total of $153,632.92 for the lot, title, taxes, construction, equipment, and furnishings. In April 1920, the Metropolitan Board found itself with a $69,694 deficit on the building, to which it applied $20,000 in interest from the 1913 fund-raising campaign. In addition, the African American YWCA took a $50,000 mortgage to cover the deficit. By the spring of 1921, however, the burden of the mortgage had been relieved to a large degree by John D. Rockefeller Jr.'s contribution of $12,000 intended to meet the first mortgage payment.[11]

To celebrate the opening of the building, the African American YWCA scheduled a weeklong series of events and invited branch members, community residents, and interested parties to a variety of programs. The formal opening celebration, attended by prominent African American New Yorkers as well as white supporters (including Corinne Roosevelt, Theodore Roosevelt's sister), featured speeches and a concert by Paul Robeson.[12] The new five-story brick building, with two front entrances, was located on the north side of 137th Street between Lenox and Seventh Avenues. Sitting closer to Seventh Avenue, it had empty lots on its east, west, and north sides when it first opened. Near the east entrance was a large, U-shaped information desk, which the branch staffed from 7:00 A.M. until 10:00 P.M. Cecelia Cabaniss Saunders viewed the information desk as the entry point for visitors and members, not only to the work of the African American YWCA but also to the life of the city. Olivia Pearl Stokes, who worked as a staff member at the information desk in 1935, gave a sense of Saunders's vision for the broad function of the desk. In an interview, Stokes recalled:

> That marvelous person who hired me when I was eighteen years of age, Mrs. Cecelia Saunders, executive at the YW[CA]. She was a great lady; she was an older woman then. . . . Mrs. Saunders had a marvelous way of working with her staff. For instance, I was director of the information desk. There were two telephones on it. Mrs. Saunders had a theory that anybody who came to that information desk should have the information she wanted, about anything in the world, in five minutes. Mrs. Saunders and her husband

would come by and test you. One day they came by and asked me, "Where do you buy an alligator in New York?" And I said, "At the zoo." That was the correct answer. You had the *New York Times* every morning and you were supposed to peruse it, and anything that anybody called about, you were supposed to know how to find the answer. If one was asked about the U.S. Office of Education, you had to know where a person could reach that to get further information. So I became very skilled and specific and information conscious.[13]

In the basement of the building, the branch operated a cafeteria with a capacity of one hundred; the cafeteria also provided a venue for community gatherings of various sorts. Many who ate there on a regular basis remarked on the high quality of the food, a quality that drew a range of people. Jean Blackwell Hutson, director of the Schomburg Branch of the New York Public Library for thirty-two years, recalled, "You know, people . . . who could have eaten almost any place would come and have Sunday dinner there." On the main floor, the lobby proved an important gathering place for men and women of the neighborhood and a relaxed venue to meet new people. Hutson reminisced, "I wish I could convey, or maybe you already know, how busy a place it was and how sociable and influential it was . . . I remember the friendships and marriages that developed in the lobby."[14] Olivia Pearl Stokes also emphasized the liveliness of the Harlem YWCA, where as a young woman she first met many influential African American intellectuals and political leaders.

In addition to the information desk and the lobby on the main floor, the new building contained various rooms for meetings, conferences, and parties. In the first few years of the building's operation, hundreds of clubs and organizations not affiliated with the YWCA met there. In 1921, for example, a Lutheran Mission; the Howard, Fisk, Morehouse, and Spelman Alumni Clubs; the Bermudian Benevolent Association; the Antillean Holding Company; the Women's Non-Partisan Political League; the Debutantes' Social Club; and the Delta Sigma Fraternity all used the YWCA's facilities.[15] The National Nurses' Headquarters and Registry, founded in 1917 by Adah B. Thoms, president of the National Association of Graduate Colored Nurses from 1916 until 1923, was one of the organizations that found a first home at Harlem's

YWCA. Thoms sought to provide the best registry of African American registered nurses for doctors and public consumers. When she had no place to house the new venture, she approached Cecelia Saunders and Emma Ransom about the use of a room at the YWCA, a request they quickly granted. Viola Chapman, the membership secretary at the African American YWCA, loaned the registry a desk, two chairs, a table, and a card file. In later reminiscences, Thoms credited the YWCA with giving her work invaluable support.[16]

The main building also functioned as the site for a range of YWCA club meetings and other activities. In 1934, for example, 8,263 adults participated in dancing and stretching classes, bridge lessons, singing groups, basketball, dramatics, rollerskating, swimming, tennis, and volleyball, and made use of a game room with a Ping-Pong table and other games.[17] The branch opened organized club activities to all members of the YWCA and also provided recreational services to nonmembers in the community. Lectures and discussion groups constituted an important category of these open events, much as the monthly public meetings in churches in the Tenderloin helped the YWCA women to touch base with residents. In 1937 the African American YWCA offered "Negro History" study groups and a series of lectures on "The Negro in . . ." literature, music, science, drama, and athletics. Other groups meeting in the building that year discussed a range of topics: international politics ("Sino-Japanese Conflict" and "What Can We Do for Peace"), national politics ("How to Erase the Negro Stereotype" and "Significance of Re-Election of President Roosevelt"), career issues ("How to Behave in an Office"), and interpersonal questions ("Boy-Girl Relationships," "Personality and Charm," and "What Price Petting").[18]

With the opening of the new building and the steady growth of the African American population in Harlem, the African American YWCA experienced a steady growth in membership. At the beginning of 1918, Harlem's YWCA had 229 members, 43 of whom were under the age of eighteen; by the end of the year, the membership total had reached 1,156, including 187 girls. The available membership figures indicate a steady rise over the following decades, with an approximate total of 2,000 members in 1928, a reported total of 4,447 in 1938, 4,744 in 1942, and more than 5,000 in 1944.[19] Only with the construction of a new building, designed specifically for multipurpose use and accommodation of large numbers of people, could New York's African American

YWCA expand in this manner. Anna Arnold Hedgeman, the branch membership secretary from 1927 to 1933, wrote in her autobiography that she was initially attracted to the YWCA in Harlem because of the possibilities its impressive physical plant presented. "Our branch also had an impact on the entire nation," she wrote, "for it was the best equipped facility available to Negroes in the United States."[20]

The Harlem YWCA maintained connections to the writers and artists of the Harlem Renaissance as well as to prominent black leaders, and their presence made the branch a lively place. Both Anna Arnold Hedgeman and Dorothy Height recalled that Langston Hughes and Countee Cullen, among others, viewed the branch as a cultural center and "came to greet Harlem residents and guests from all over the world."[21] Florence Ellis Dickerson remembered meeting Alain Locke, Bill "Bojangles" Robinson, Lester Granger, W. E. B. Du Bois, and Countee Cullen at the YWCA.[22]

In terms of its capacity to meet requests for residence, however, the African American YWCA remained strapped for space even after the opening of the new building. Since the main building at 179 West 137th Street did not include rooms for long- or short-term residents as the old buildings had, the YWCA continued to rely on the residential building it had purchased during the war. The residence, located at 200 West 137th Street just across Seventh Avenue from the new building, had a capacity of eighty-eight women, still falling far short of the level of service the leaders wished to provide to the community and to black women from around the world who visited New York. At the end of 1923, the New York City YWCA sold 200 West 137th Street to an African American undertaker for $72,000 and began to look for other options for housing.[23] The committee of management felt that the construction of a new building on the empty lots adjoining the branch building would provide the best possible solution.

In March 1924, the Metropolitan Board contacted John D. Rockefeller Jr. for assistance in building this new residence. Writing for the Metropolitan Board, Mrs. William Rossiter described the board's view of the situation to one of Rockefeller's secretaries. She wrote of the "deplorable conditions confronting Colored girls and women in Harlem" and pointed out that "aside from rooms in private homes, only 36 beds are known to be available for public demand for Colored girls or women, in a population of nearly 200,000. When private homes are not available, these girls are 'on the street.' Low types of white men add nightly to the dangers of young, untrained, irresponsible girls. The results are beyond words."[24] While the leaders of the African American YWCA might not have chosen the danger of interracial sexual contact as the primary motivation for seeking a residence, they welcomed Rossiter's fund-raising success. Rossiter called attention to the empty lots adjacent to the 137th Street YWCA and estimated that a new building would cost between $225,000 and $230,000. She asked for a donation from the Laura Spelman Memorial Fund, a fund named for Rockefeller's mother and through which he had made many donations to the New York City YWCA in the past. Through W. S. Richardson, another secretary, Rockefeller declined to contribute to the new project, citing his desire to see other YWCA projects he was funding through to completion before beginning anything new.[25]

Almost one year later, Richardson presented the situation to Rockefeller again, emphasizing Harlem's need for such a residence, and also pointed to the additional political implications of failing to act. In his memo to Rockefeller, Richardson said: "Urgency of situation lies in great need of proper homes for colored girls in district. Almost impossible to find them. Furthermore, colored people in Harlem urge action and incline to criticize daily. Some unfortunate attitudes by leaders and newspapers."[26] Rockefeller reconsidered the request and in February 1925 committed himself to a donation of $190,000 in memory of his mother; in May 1925, he increased the amount to $225,000.[27] With Rockefeller's commitment, the Metropolitan Board purchased the three lots adjoining the main building on its east side.[28]

The new residence, completed at a cost of $275,304.41, opened on April 7, 1926. More than three hundred people attended the opening, including white and black representatives of the National Board of the YWCA, white leaders of the New York City YWCA, and prominent black New Yorkers such as W. E. B. Du Bois and *New York Age* editor Fred R. Moore. Notably, John D. Rockefeller Jr. did not attend, as he preferred to keep his profile as philanthropist out of the public eye. The *New York Age* reported that "an interesting feature was the visit of delegations of representatives from Protestant, Catholic and Jewish boarding homes operated by the YWCA." In organizing the way in which the city's YWCA would represent itself at this significant moment in the history of its African American YWCA, the white leaders of the YWCA chose, through these delegations, to present its identity as inclusive and yet committed to racial, religious, and ethnic segregation.[29]

A revealing exchange between Cecelia Cabaniss Saunders and Rockefeller followed Rockefeller's commitment to fund the residence. Saunders and Susan P. Wortham, Emma Ransom's successor as chair of the committee of management, wrote to Rockefeller to thank him for the donation. In ways typical of this African American YWCA, Saunders and Wortham made clear their understanding of the obligation of white Christians to pay particular attention to the historical wrongs committed against African Americans; at the same time, they adopted a subservient tone, going so far as to present the end of slavery as a "gift" rather than a human right. Saunders wrote:

> Announcement was made at our Committee of Management meeting on Wednesday evening that because of your interest and generosity our dream is to be realized and we are to have a new residence building for colored women and girls . . . Naturally there was gratitude because it means that our girls are to possess the thing of which we merely dreamed, but there was also spontaneous joy because of the faith expressed in our group—such joy as only a race can feel that has not outgrown the remembrance of the transcendent gift of freedom.[30]

Saunders and Wortham then asked if he would permit them to name the new residence "Rockefeller House," both to honor his generosity and so that members could benefit from the constant reminder of the Rockefeller example in social service. In his personally written reply (an unusual case in Rockefeller's dealings with the YWCA), he wrote, somewhat condescendingly:

> As to a name for the building, while valuing highly your desire to call it Rockefeller House, both my father and I have always preferred as a rule not to have any enterprise with which we are connected named for us. Is there not some outstanding woman of the colored race after whom the house might appropriately be called, some woman the memory of whom would be an inspiration to the girls who occupy it? Some such name would please me

greatly. If, however, none comes to mind which is appropriate, I leave it with you ladies to adopt whatever name other than Rockefeller seems to you best.[31]

Saunders responded that they would in that case call the building the Emma Ransom House to honor the woman "whose spirit and life have meant so much to us."[32]

Rockefeller did not misrepresent his policy regarding use of the family name. Generally, he preferred to use such occasions to honor his mother, Laura Spelman (Rockefeller), as in the case of Laura Spelman Hall on Hudson Street, the New York City YWCA residence for white women, and Spelman College in Atlanta, a school for black women. In addition, he had already proven a commitment to the African American YWCA through his donation to the 1913 fund-raising campaign. His decision to provide funds for the residence did come, though, in response to the threat of negative publicity from black leaders and newspaper editors directed at the YWCA, one of his favored charities—a reminder of the political motivations behind some donations.

Certainly, Rockefeller's name would have lent a great deal of prestige to the African American YWCA and, in some ways, would have placed it more securely under the umbrella of the New York City YWCA, as a companion residence to the Laura Spelman Hall. At the same time, the opportunity to name after one of their own a newly constructed, state-of-the-art building that would function as the premier lodging for African American women in the mecca of Harlem provided an occasion for overflowing pride.

The Emma Ransom House quickly became a preferred temporary and long-term residence for African American women visiting the city. In its first year of operation, Cecelia Saunders reported that the facility served 8,478 transient guests, many on multiple visits to New York, and 300 permanent guests (for a term longer than one month and not exceeding three years) "from all sections of the United States, rural and urban, from South America, the West Indies, Africa, Philippines, Denmark and Canada." In 1933 the residence accommodated 2,486 different transient visitors (some of whom stayed several times during the year) and 474 permanent guests, and in 1937, 2,291 transients and 528 permanent guests. The opening of the World's Fair in New York City in 1939 brought many African American visitors to the city, resulting in tremendous strain on the facilities. The residence housed 3,484 transient guests, and the rooms registry found accommodations for the overflow. The house secretary that year reported a record number of transient guests accommodated in a single day. On August 23, 1939, the West 137th Street YWCA housed 321 guests, using the gymnasium for those who could not be given beds in the residence.[33]

In a 1936 letter to Emma Ransom, living in Wilberforce, Ohio, since her husband's election to bishop in the AME Church, Cecelia Saunders described the stress that visitors put on the branch as a whole, and on the residence in particular. Saunders wrote:

> The summer looms ahead as a very busy season for us here. The reduced railroad rates offer added inducements for travel and I sometimes think that when people start traveling sooner or later they land in New York. We have been running on an average of 40 transients a night in the residence and every room in the building is reserved during the month of July. By the time summer school people leave, the National Convention of Graduate Nurses will be meeting in New York with [the] residence for headquarters and meetings in the building and their convention is followed immediately by that of the Iota Phi Lambda Sorority, a national sorority of business women.[34]

As racism severly restricted where African Americans could find hotel accommodations, even in a city as large and cosmopolitan as New York, the Emma Ransom House's service to travelers crossed class lines. The famous and the wealthy among African American women—including Mary Church Terrell and Lugenia Burns Hope—stayed alongside working women and students—such as the young Leontyne Price and Pauli Murray—struggling to meet the cost of housing.

Residents found a great many services available. Through the Emma Ransom House and the main building, guests had access to general maid service Monday through Saturday, elevators until midnight, a message service, laundry facilities, a sewing room, a piano, a shampoo room, a beauty parlor, and shops where they could have dresses made to order, mended, pressed, or altered. Because the branch required that guests be members of the YWCA, residents also had access to all other branch services and activities.[35]

The final major project to develop the physical plant of the 137th Street YWCA during the interwar period came in 1932 with the construction of an annex to house the growing trade school. As had happened many times before, funding from John D. Rockefeller Jr. made this expansion possible. In the spring of 1930, Rockefeller informed the Metropolitan Board of the YWCA that he intended to transfer title to a lot on 138th Street, behind the African American YWCA, to the New York City YWCA. In addition, he agreed to cover expenses up to $275,000 for the construction of a new building. The building project began in April 1931 but, because of difficulties with the contractor, was not completed until February 1932. This annex provided additional rooms for Emma Ransom House guests, a four-hundred-seat auditorium, rooms for club activities, and new facilities for the trade school.[36]

Administering such a sizable physical plant that served large numbers of people from around the world proved to be increasingly expensive for the African American YWCA. The dramatic change in the budget of this branch following the move into the new building becomes clear when comparing the 1915 budget of $5,000 and the 1919 budget of $13,771 with 1922's $79,452.89. By 1936 the branch's operating budget had reached $147,000.[37] Immediately upon occupying the new building, Saunders declared her intention to make the city's African American YWCA financially independent of the Metropolitan Board. Financial independence would entail operating the Emma Ransom House at a profit and then securing the balance of the budget from among members of the community that the branch served. Saunders reported that in the first year of occupancy, the branch as a whole became 49 percent self-supporting.[38] The Emma Ransom House consistently brought in funds to help offset deficits in other areas of the branch's work, and the cafeteria also generally made a profit. However, neither the residence nor the cafeteria could provide enough money to cover the ever growing budget of the entire branch program. During the depression years, it became nearly impossible to raise large sums from residents of Harlem to support the community's YWCA. By 1935, however, Saunders reported that the branch was 87 percent self-supporting, with some funding coming from members, some from fees for services, some from donations from white and black supporters outside of New York, and a portion from the Metropolitan Board.[39]

The struggle for economic self-sufficiency sometimes engendered animosity between the white women of the Metropolitan Board and the leaders of the African American YWCA. At the end of 1920, for example, the African American YWCA found itself with a surplus of $14,037.88. The committee of management requested of the Metropolitan Board that it be allowed to use the surplus to pay the first mortgage payment on the new building. The Metropolitan Board, in light of its own financial difficulties at the time, asked the African American YWCA to return the money. In reporting this decision, the Metropolitan Board emphasized its perception of the subordinate status of the African American YWCA, arguing that "each Branch is, after all, simply a part of the whole." The minutes concluded by reminding all concerned that the funds had come from the Metropolitan Board in the first place. The committee of management returned the money and replied tersely that it would need no additional funds from the Metropolitan Board for the rest of the year.[40]

The expansion of the physical plant of the city's African American YWCA contributed to the ongoing process of broadening the mission of the organization, a process that involved reaching a growing population of African Americans and black immigrants from the Caribbean. In addition, the expense of maintaining services in the new buildings and the desire to become financially independent of the Metropolitan Board motivated Saunders and the YWCA branch to find new ways of marketing the work to an audience considerably wider than churchgoing evangelical Protestants. In reflecting on the branch's accomplishments in 1939 in particular, but in terms applicable to the organization during the interwar period in general, Saunders wrote:

> During the year 1939 the West 137th Street Branch of the YWCA has been mindful of its responsibility for getting more people to care deeply about the Association as a movement. It has sought to help people to understand that the purpose of the Association implies a belief in God; a belief in the brotherhood of man; a belief in democracy—which recognizes the worth of every person; which encourages the growth of personality; which acknowledges the right of every person to express his opinions and to share in the planning of things that concern him.[41]

In speaking of the reformulated mission of this YWCA, Saunders and the other leaders did not abandon their commitment to the organization as a religious one but, significantly, placed the belief in God—and not in Christian form in particular—in a position of only marginally greater importance than belief in brotherhood and democracy. Moreover, she defined democracy in terms familiar to evangelical Christians, that is, by emphasizing the access of each individual to participate in democracy. And while the American practice of democracy might be flawed, the African American YWCA's leaders sought to ensure that its own practice of democracy remained flawless. By making the branch building a community center and bringing in as many individuals from New York's African American communities as possible, the leaders sought to make their own democratic commitment concrete in the practice of Christian principles.

Educating for Christian Democracy

The trade school of the African American YWCA became one of the most productive means of reaching a broad population of women and men and of educating African American New Yorkers to participate in the life of the city in ways inspired by the YWCA. The educational component of the branch's program dates back to the earliest years of its work, when the training was generally geared to women entering domestic service or other service trades. The classes offered in the 63rd and 53rd Street locations included dressmaking taught by Helen Curtis, who boasted a diploma after three years' study in France. The YWCA announced the 1909 dressmaking course as "the greatest opportunity ever offered to young women of this city who want to become dressmakers" and "the only opportunity opened to our people in America to learn the French system."[42] Classes in millinery, embroidery, and basketry supplemented those in general dressmaking. For those in domestic service, or who merely wanted to improve their skills, the African American YWCA offered many courses in cooking over the years. The branch also offered courses in the general field of "business," which included skills necessary for office workers, and training in "beauty culture."[43] In addition to vocational courses, the education committee of the African American YWCA planned general development courses for its members. Over the years these included singing, English, French, Spanish, composition and letter writing, and "physical culture," or exercise.[44] As with sewing classes, this YWCA relied on the talents and training of its volunteer workers to staff the courses. As membership grew, the branch began to make use of paid workers to teach some of its courses.

In 1923 the branch reorganized its educational division, creating a trade school division with Emma Shields Penn as the full-time director. A graduate of the Virginia Normal and Industrial Institute and Fisk University and a former schoolteacher in Virginia, Penn had worked for the Woman's Bureau of the U.S. Department of Labor before moving to New York's African American YWCA.[45] Penn and Saunders grouped the courses into divisions of a business school, a beauty school, domestic arts courses, and general and cultural courses, each operating for two four-month terms annually. The business school offered core courses in stenography, typewriting, business English, filing, and bookkeeping. Beauty school courses included "hair culture," hairdressing, Marcel waving, facials, manicuring, and a special course in eyebrows and eyelashes. The domestic arts core covered sewing, dressmaking and designing, millinery, lampshades, and how to operate a power sewing machine. Tuition was low, ranging from a number of free courses in the cultural division to courses at $3, $4, and $5 per semester, and the school offered several payment options.[46]

The offerings under the general and cultural division varied depending on the instructors involved. During 1924 and 1925, for example, the division offered classes in "Correct English" and "Special English" for nonnative speakers, current literature, public speaking and parliamentary law, Bible study, and "The Charm School." That year Emma Shields Penn taught the English classes; MaBelle White Williams, the branch industrial secretary at the time, taught public speaking; and Lillian Alexander, chair of the committee of management, taught "The Charm School." Alexander, a Phi Beta Kappa graduate of the University of Minnesota, proved an appropriate choice as instructor of this course, having emerged as an important supporting figure of the Harlem Renaissance. Alexander and her husband, physician Ernest Alexander, anchored black New York society in the 1920s and 1930s, hosting exclusive parties at their New York apartment and at their country home at Greenwood Lake, New York.[47] In other years, instructors in the general and cultural division offered courses in current events, "Everyday Law for Women," "Art Appreciation," French, "Literary Appreciation Of, By, and About the Negro," "The YWCA Playhouse," and health and hygiene.[48]

The branch's cultural offerings demonstrate a complex approach to the position of African Americans vis-à-vis American national cultures and identity. At the same time that the African American YWCA participated in the Harlem Renaissance's embrace of blackness and support for cultural productions of black Americans, its leaders also promoted cultural courses aimed at "assimilating" African Americans to white American standards. Through the cultural offerings and vocational classes, the women of this YWCA conveyed to members the dual nature of their identities as African Americans, as well as the necessity of operating fluently in any American arena.

Despite the variety of general and cultural course offerings, the trade school day and evening sessions drew the largest numbers of women (and some men). From a 1927 attendance figure of 431 students in trade classes, the school grew to accommodate almost 1,500 students in 1933 and more than 3,000 in 1943.[49] In early years, the approach of this YWCA to trade education emphasized concrete training and experience in fields of employment open to African American women. Initially, the focus was on "domestic arts," sewing, and beauty care, and later, particularly as a result of labor changes during World War I, the emphasis shifted to training for clerical and factory jobs. By 1930, however, the leaders of the city's African American YWCA began to see that this approach did not fulfill its mission to advance opportunities for African American women. The brochure produced in 1931 for "The New Trade School" explained their new vision.

> The objectives of the school have grown out of an evolving experience with the educational, vocational, and employment problems of young women and their needs for adjustment in their personal and work life. The school therefore purposes: to give information concerning occupations and employment opportunities and concerning the individual's abilities and background as a basis for her vocational choices; to offer training for occupational efficiency in the major employment fields in which Negro girls are working, or in which trends indicate their possible employment, and to place and adjust trainees in their chosen vocations.[50]

The branch did not abandon its offerings to train domestics in the new version of the trade school, but did seek to systematize instruction and set standards for the women emerging from the program. The four-room "model apartment" in the annex to the main building became the venue for training domestic workers. In the training of secretaries, the new trade school expanded on its previous approach by offering courses in areas of employment from which African American women generally had been barred, in order to pose a challenge to employment discrimination in the city. Besides learning basic secretarial skills, students gained experience with office machinery. In addition, the school targeted particular professional arenas and offered courses to prepare women for civil service, to become medical and legal secretaries, and for retail sales.[51] For women preparing for the dressmaking trades, the school added training in machine pressing and dressmaking with power machines. The addition of power machines to the training of secretaries and seamstresses occasioned some controversy and conflict with the Metropolitan Board, which resisted the change because of the electrical wiring modifications necessitated by installing such machines. Anna Arnold Hedgeman, membership secretary at this YWCA from 1927 until 1933, recalled, in a letter to the editor of the *New York Post*, Saunders's considerable business acumen in making this move.

> It was this woman of insight who discovered that the garment trades would not hire Negroes because they had no experience and no union card. She also discovered that the unions would not accept them for membership because they had no experience. She bought power machines and installed them in the Harlem YWCA. Women were trained there and the vicious employer-union cycle of elimination of the Negro worker was broken.[52]

The final significant innovation in the trade school grew out of a course dealing with the care of the sick, first offered in 1935 under the household workers' division. In 1937 this became a division of nurses' aide courses, including training in home hygiene, care of the sick, and nutrition. Finally, in 1939 the trade school transformed this division into a practical nursing school through which students could receive, in local hospitals, the coursework and field training that they needed to prepare for the state Board of Regents' exam for licensed practical nurses. This division maintained the highest standard within the branch trade school in order to maintain state approval and to continue productive relationships with the hospitals that took interns; it also provided students with meals and a stipend during their six months of field work.[53] "The best thing of all," Saunders wrote to Emma Ransom in 1940, "is that when they have completed the course they are able to get work in many of the hospitals. Sea View at Staten Island will take all of the girls that we send. It is a fine work, particularly for our girls, especially since high school graduation is not a requirement for entering the course. We have been able to be very selective in the girls we have accepted because we have more applicants than we have space."[54]

Two figures of great importance in the history of African American nurses participated in the development of the practical nursing division of the trade school. Adah B. Thoms, president of the National Association of Graduate Colored Nurses from 1916 to 1923 and founder of a national registry of registered nurses, was first elected to the committee of management of the African American YWCA in 1921. Throughout her career, Thoms advocated strict standards for the nursing profession and admitted only registered nurses to her registry. Although the YWCA would deal only with the field of practical nursing, Thoms's influence in developing the program proved to be significant in designing the curriculum, setting standards, and lending the prestige of her presence to the program. Alma Vassells John, a graduate of New York University's School of Education and Harlem Hospital's School of Nursing, served as the director of the branch's practical nursing division for six years. John had also served as head nurse at Harlem Hospital, director of nursing at the hospital's school, and executive secretary of the National Association of Graduate Colored Nurses.[55] The involvement of both women made the nursing division an impressive school that was quite successful in opening the profession to African American women.

The leaders of New York's African American YWCA envisioned the trade school as a means of assisting women to live "the more abundant life" by broadening their opportunities for fulfilling employment. By offering courses and researching trends and possibilities in employment, as well as through the services of the employment bureau, the branch assisted thousands of women in finding jobs. Saunders placed a great deal of emphasis on this achievement in her annual reports. In other arenas, however, she tempered her excitement and reminded New Yorkers of the ongoing discrimination against African American women. In her testimony before Mayor Fiorello LaGuardia's Commission on Conditions in Harlem, Saunders told panel members that while her YWCA had experienced some successes, the women they worked with had faced discrimination when seeking jobs as domestics, store clerks, secretaries, and civil servants. When asked about her experiences with particular companies in the city, Saunders discussed the branch's experience with the telephone company: "We asked for employment of telephone operators at least in the Harlem area. They objected to the voices of the colored girls. We said we had someone with a lovely voice. We asked to have her tried out. The telephone company didn't agree to that. Those girls were reared in New York. No one would know whether they were colored or white."[56] One woman who worked as a member of the branch staff from 1934 until 1942 recalled that Saunders indeed had forced the telephone company to interview black women for positions.[57]

Most surprising in Saunders's testimony was her assertion that in her twenty years as executive secretary the African American YWCA had had *no* success in finding positions for African American women in businesses in Harlem. The only exceptions, she found, had come with women who were "decidedly attractive girls and very light."[58] Saunders, herself light-skinned, was clearly conflating beauty with skin color. Nevertheless, she took the opportunity on a number of occasions during her testimony to emphasize the particular difficulties that dark-skinned African American women faced in the working world. Each time she raised the issue, however, committee members failed to respond or merely changed the direction of the discussion. Saunders's testimony before the committee underscores the degree to which New York City remained a difficult environment for African American women to make advances in the area of employment.

In addition to offering vocational education through the trade school, New York City's African American YWCA embarked on a program of educating black New Yorkers, and women in particular, for responsible citizenship, a task that its leaders viewed as part of their Christian mission. The branch first began to address these issues during World War I through its monthly Woman's Forum, an "open forum for questions of vital interest."[59] As New Yorkers approached a vote on an amendment granting women suffrage within the state, the African American YWCA presented a series of forums with speakers from the

Woman's Suffrage Party. After the amendment passed, the branch invited women to a series of talks on "Preparation for Citizenship," including lectures on registering to vote and the national government. Over the next few years, the Woman's Forum would discuss candidates and political issues facing African Americans. The *New York Age* reported on a well-attended meeting just prior to the 1920 election, for example, during which the women of the branch discussed politics. "Mrs. Cecelia Cabaniss Saunders was at her best as she forcefully presented her subject, 'How I am Going to Vote and Why.' Mrs. Saunders stated that she is an enrolled Negro Republican with emphasis on 'Negro,' for she has more ties to bind her to the Negro race than to the Republican or any other party or organization."[60] Such occasions on which the leaders of the African American YWCA discussed their personal political affiliations proved to be rare, particularly when compared with the number of events that focused on the general issue of educating for responsible citizenship.

Christianizing City Politics

In addition to education as a means of broadening its base, the city's African American YWCA addressed a variety of local and national political issues. The devastating impact of economic depression during the 1930s created a crisis that strained the resources of this YWCA in a variety of ways. Unemployment among black New Yorkers reached 25 percent during the first year of the depression, homelessness increased, and jobless workers clamored for public relief.[61] Economic difficulties struck the branch as well, and Cecelia Saunders found herself forced to reduce staff and most general programs and concentrate on relief for those affected by the crisis.

This branch of the YWCA became a center through which the government administered various depression relief programs. In 1933 Saunders wrote a series of letters to the Emergency Work Bureau seeking placements for "colored 'white collar' women" in particular (to no avail). However, the Emergency Work Bureau used the 137th Street YWCA to distribute cash relief and placed unemployed people in temporary jobs at the YWCA, as did the Works Progress Administration.[62] The placement of workers seeking relief in positions at the YWCA helped the organization to remain operational under the burden of its own staff cuts in this period.[63] As a supplement to government relief, Mrs. John D. Rockefeller Jr. financed a workshop, housed at the West 137th Street YWCA, at which women did sewing work and made rag rugs out of old silk stockings, many donated by the white women of the Metropolitan Board. An average of fifty women participated in this program each week and received $4 per day plus lunch. In addition to Rockefeller's contribution of $10,000, the Woman's Bible Class of Riverside Church also dedicated funds for the workshop.[64]

New York's African American YWCA also dealt with a number of high-profile conflicts affecting black New Yorkers in the interwar period. On March 13, 1935, Harlem erupted in a night of rioting, with thousands of black residents directing violence at businesses on 125th Street. To a great degree, this riot was the culmination of the pent-up frustrations of community members who had engaged in a "Don't Buy Where You Can't Work" campaign throughout 1934. In the depth of the depression, black Harlemites demanded that the stores that they continued to support make some effort to employ African Americans. A coalition of neighborhood organizations launched picketing campaigns against stores like Blumstein's department store on 125th Street, which employed no African American women as clerks. The group won a concession from the owner that he would hire fifteen black women immediately, with more to be hired later. Other pickets did not produce successes, and in Blumstein's case, many charged that the store chose only very light-skinned African American women. By the end of 1934, the coalition that had organized the campaign had fractured over issues of method, ideology, anti-Semitism among certain groups, and corruption.[65]

On March 19, 1935, an employee at Kress's Store on 125th Street caught Lino Rivera, a sixteen-year-old boy, stealing a penknife. When in the ensuing struggle Rivera bit the employee, the store manager called the police and an ambulance for the injured man. An African American woman who had observed the incident spread the word that Rivera had been injured; this rumor, combined with the coincidental arrival of a hearse near the scene, enflamed a gathering crowd whose members thought that white police officers had killed Rivera. With some encouragement from communist organizers distributing fliers, concerned onlookers became increasingly angry. By the end of the night, fifty-seven citizens and seven police officers had been injured, seventy-five people had been arrested for participating in the riot, and a great deal of property damaged.[66]

In the aftermath of the rioting, various commentators and politicians placed the blame on communist "agitators." In response, a range of concerned African American New Yorkers called on the public to examine what they saw to be the more significant forces involved. Adam Clayton Powell Jr. and Robert W. Searle of the Greater New York Federation of Churches invited Cecelia Cabaniss Saunders and other African American leaders to meet at the YMCA to discuss the situation. Searle and Powell wrote, "The unfortunate affair in Harlem has sobered us all. Right now the focus of the City's attention is upon Harlem. It is quite apparent that in certain well known quarters there is a move to turn this attention toward a 'Red Baiting Crusade.' This would be not only a miscarriage of justice but a tragic diversion of energy."[67] Saunders wrote to Walter White, secretary of the NAACP, with a plea that the NAACP address "underlying social conditions which need to be remedied if we are not to have a recurrence."[68] According to Saunders, Harlem's large numbers of unemployed and families on relief, combined with no boys' clubs, settlement houses, recreation centers, or large playgrounds, led young people into difficulty with the law. Once in the court system, these young people had no adequate advocates. Saunders made her plea especially for young men, presenting her organization as having already undertaken to assist young female first offenders. "From time to time we have gone into the courts in the interests of certain girls whom we have known and who have been in difficulties. More of that type of thing needs to be done."[69]

As indicated in Saunders's testimony following the 1935 riot, much of the African American YWCA's involvement in New York City politics focused on conditions facing African American women attempting to make a living. The willingness, during the depression, of white women to work as domestic workers, and the ease with which they secured positions through agencies, made it increasingly difficult for African American women to maintain steady employment in this field. The scandalous "slave market" system developed out of the need of these women for some kind of work. One observer described the practice.

Every morning, rain or shine, groups of women with brown paper bags or cheap suitcases stand on corners in the Bronx and Brooklyn waiting for a chance to get some work. Sometimes there are 15, sometimes 30, some are old, many are young and most of them are Negro women waiting for employers to come to the street corner auction blocks to bargain for their labor.

If they are lucky, they get about 30 cents an hour scrubbing, cleaning, laundering, washing windows, waxing floors and wood-work all day long.

Once hired on the "slave market," the women often find after a day's backbreaking toil, that they worked longer than was ar-ranged, got less than was promised, were forced to accept clothing instead of cash and were exploited beyond human endurance.[70]

In 1938 the New York City Council held hearings to investigate the situation of these domestics. Dorothy Height, who had come from the New York City Department of Welfare in 1937 to become a case worker at the branch and then assistant director of the Emma Ransom House, testified before the council. The City Council, apparently com-pletely unaware of the situation, seemed stunned.[71] The African Ameri-can YWCA had attempted to address abuse of domestic workers as early as 1929, when it held a conference for domestic workers and em-ployers of domestics, the goal of which was "to promote a relationship of mutual regard for obligations of time, duties, privileges and wages."[72] In the aftermath of the City Council's investigation, Saunders became part of the Committee on Street Corner Markets, which sought to regulate the practice.[73]

During the 1930s, Cecelia Saunders also took on the issue of corrupt employment agencies in the South and their harsh effects on young African American migrants to New York City. In 1935, for example, she corresponded with Frances Perkins, the U.S. secretary of labor, about the practices of the People's Labor Union, Inc. in Richmond, Virginia, presenting the case of a young woman who paid a $2 fee to obtain a position as a domestic for a family of four in New York City. Saunders reported that the young woman had been promised a monthly salary of $25 but after one month of work had received only $8. The People's Labor Union had deducted $7 for bus fare and $10 for an agency fee. Saunders informed Perkins that her YWCA had dealt with many simi-lar cases and that the situation now required the attention of the federal government.[74]

Through this increasingly public role as an advocate on behalf of African American women in all aspects of their lives, the Harlem YWCA sought to extend its Christian influence into city politics. Because these issues did not stem directly from the religious lives of women, however, the focus on the political contributed to the impression that the YWCA was undergoing a process of secularization.

Girls' Work

Increasingly throughout the interwar period, New York City's African American YWCA experienced a shift in demographics, growing into an organization with a much younger membership than it had prior to World War I. In the earliest years of the branch's work, girls younger than sixteen years did not figure as a large constituency. "Young women" generally meant self-supporting women in their early twenties. In 1913, however, the branch made a special plea for girls to join the organization and instituted a "junior" membership fee of 50 cents, half the cost of adult membership. The branch also established a Camp Fire Girls club in 1912 under the direction of Helen Curtis. Like the Boy Scouts and Girl Scouts, the Camp Fire Girls used a graded honor system of achievements awarded through badges. New York's African American YWCA took advantage of the Camp Fire emphasis on outdoor activities and also used the club to teach skills such as first aid, to form a basketball team (the "Knickerbocker Five"), and to do folk dancing.[75]

In 1918 the National Board of the YWCA formed its own group for young members, the Girl Reserves, with separate programs for grade school, junior high, high school, and young employed girls.[76] The National Board chose for the emblem of the Girl Reserves a triangle with the letters "GR" in the center and bordered by the words "mind," "body," and "spirit" on each side. The YWCA sought to encourage each Girl Reserve "to build your Triangle—To find the best and grow yourself. . . but also to widen your Circle—to give the best and make better the world in which you live."[77] Girl Reserves wore a uniform consisting of a dark skirt, a white blouse, and a long, dark kerchief. Members subscribed to a code that occupied a prominent place in the guidebooks for all ages, and each agreed to try to be:

*G*racious in manner
*I*mpartial in Judgement
*R*eady for service
*L*oyal to Friends
*R*eaching toward the best
*E*arnest in purpose
*S*eeing the beautiful
*E*ager for knowledge
*R*everent to God
*V*ictorious over Self
*E*ver dependable
*S*incere at all times[78]

The code emphasized disciplining the self and turning girls' attention away from satisfying their own desires and toward working for others. In the activity book for younger girls, every action, no matter how mundane, becomes part of the overall thrust of the Girl Reserve code. Lessons in responsibility, nurturing, good housekeeping skills, and self-sacrifice are wrung out of activities presented as "adventures." Thus, a hiking trip becomes an occasion for a lesson on wearing "sensible, appropriate clothing and shoes," making "good (thin and not dry) sandwiches," and packing a lunch "carefully."[79] Many of the activities involve "finding ways to make others happier" and giving "gifts of service." Attention to health constituted a large component of the Girl Reserve's life. Older girls followed a health code, and the book for younger girls contained a health record checklist that corresponded with the items in the code. On the checklist, girls were to record bathing at least twice a week, brushing teeth, eating vegetables, washing hands, bowel movements, clean fingernails, and sleeping with windows open.[80] Girl Reserve activities also included games, songs, pageants, prayer services, and ceremonials.

In their high school years, Girl Reserves engaged in discussions of travel, music, literature, and the "world." In one section of the guidebook dedicated to "world friendship," each Girl Reserve, presumed to be white, was to examine her "attitudes toward people of other races or nations" through two exercises.[81] First, in a "public opinion test," the girls were instructed to examine a list of thirty words and cross out those words that they considered "more disagreeable than pleasing, more antagonizing than appealing" in order to begin to understand their prejudices. The list included "Prince of Wales," "Roman Catholic," "Patriotic," "Immigrant," "American Flag," "Pacifist," "Jew," "Japanese," and "Land of the Free."[82] Next, they took a test on "Americanization by Proxy vs. Proximity," in which they indicated whether they would admit certain groups of people to a variety of relationships to themselves, including citizenship, church membership, neighbors, friends, fellow workers, and kinship. The test asked the girls to rate British, Chinese, Czechs, Native Americans, Jews, Japanese, and African Americans, among other groups, according to each category.[83]

In many respects, these exercises seem constructed precisely to elicit the racist and xenophobic sentiments of white Girl Reserves. Although the "public opinion test" asked girls to designate some terms as more "disagreeable than pleasing," it seems likely that the list would prompt readers to compare the elements to one another. "American Flag," "Land of the Free," and "Patriotic" seem destined to be compared with items like "Non-English Speaking," "Immigrant," and "Bolshevik." Significantly, once the girl reader had discovered her own "likes and dislikes" through the quiz, the guidebook did not lead her beyond asking that she attempt to understand why she felt the way she did. Instead, these quizzes seem constructed to leave the reader with a sense of personal failure or sinfulness because of their "dislikes."

The guidebook for high school students contains a single image of black girls as Girl Reserves, which, rather than providing a profile of their activities, serves as an occasion for white girls to meditate on themselves. The text attached to the photograph, written by a white girl, looks forward to a banquet at which she will meet "our American sister, the colored girl. The girl who has not had the opportunities we have, who desires the same educational, economic, and religious advantages we have, who has faced snubs, jeers, and unfair criticism, but who has had so little."[84] The author continues by lauding the profound patience that "the colored girl" exhibits and ends with an affirmation in the Girl Reserves' "belief in [the colored girl's] possibilities to become a fine representative of the American Girl."[85] Just as the literature for Girl Reserves withholds full access to African American girls, the author of this caption even withholds Americanness by underscoring only the future *possibility* that black girls can be American.

Despite the invisibility of African American girls in the Girl Reserve literature, the overall flexibility of the program, as with most YWCA programs, allowed the women of New York's African American YWCA to make becoming a Girl Reserve attractive to the organization's young members. The branch encouraged young women in Harlem to join the Girl Reserves by presenting it as a fun club. A 1923 item in the *New York Age* illustrates this approach. "For girls up to eighteen years of age there is the Girl Reserve Department, with clubs for grammar school, high school and employed girls. If you really want to have a good time, girls, you should join this club. They have regular club meetings which are no end of fun, they have a glee club, too—they hike, they skate, they play basketball, they study, they have lovely parties and hilarious stunt days."[86]

The African American YWCA also included an educational component in its Girl Reserve program. The African American Girl Reserves took responsibility for educating white Girl Reserves about African American life. In 1927 this branch hosted a "Reconciliation Trip" during which white girls and boys toured Harlem and visited the YWCA. The Girl Reserves of the branch organized a program for their visitors in which they presented music and poetry by African American composers and authors and a lecture on the problems facing black youth. In addition, the group took on educational projects within the branch. In the winter of 1923, the branch's Girl Reserves produced a morality play, "The House of the Heart."[87]

The Girl Reserves did not constitute the only program for girls at the 137th Street YWCA. Indeed, by 1938 the branch's more than 1,200 junior members participated in an array of activities that kept the building brimming with young people's energy. The 1935 report of the branch's activities director paints a compelling picture.

If you have heard the laughter and tapping and splashing and irresistible jazz music issuing from the gymnasium and swimming pool on Tuesday and Thursday nights, and if you have seen the peppy young staff and volunteers who are in charge on those evenings; if you have had a glimpse of the lovely prints on the walls of the art studio, the beautifully bound books, and the exquisitely etched and hammered silver and brass work done there; if you have seen a performance by Elsie Burrows' Dancing Children, the three-year-olds up to the young sophisticates of eighteen; if you have heard the Choralites . . . , as they lift their rich voices in song; if you have seen a copy of the *Searchlight*, in which the activities for Juniors are written in charming and youthful spontaneity; . . . if you have seen the eyes of girls shining in the soft glow of candle light as they sing "Follow the Gleam" in the closing moments of a [Girl Reserve] ceremonial. . . ; if you have, then we need not write for you an annual report of the Activities Department.[88]

The branch building functioned as an afterschool center for neighborhood children, offering puppet shows, parties, craft clubs, sightseeing trips, hikes, picnics, team sports, bridge lessons, dramatics, and a game room. Discussion groups also constituted a portion of the activities for girls. There is evidence that, in addition to topics such as educational and vocational goals, current events, and the arts, the branch also conducted sex education sessions. In 1939, for example, Clara W. Alcroft, a white representative of the National Board of the YWCA, conducted six meetings for adult advisers at the branch to assist them in leading discussions on sex. She reported back to the National Board on the range of topics the group took up, some suggested by the African American women based on their experiences working with the girls: "Problems listed for discussion were petting, premarital sex relations, birth control, drinking, abnormal attitudes toward sex, homosexual relationships, attitudes about the two sexes, marriage and divorce, . . . how much do you discuss with high school girls, . . . can we do anything about the difference in training of boys and girls."[89] The list of topics covered indicates a willingness among the branch leaders to deal directly with the issues that their young constituency faced, as well as problems they feared or fantasized that young women faced.

This YWCA added a significant component to its program for young women when, during World War I, it made a summer camp available to a small number of girls. In August 1918, a group of fourteen girls, accompanied by Earle Day, the Girls' Work secretary, spent ten days at a camp on Carr's Pond in the Palisades Interstate Park. In 1920 the branch moved the camp, now called Fern Rock, to a larger site on Lake Tiorati, eight miles from Bear Mountain. The camp remained there for twenty-five years, serving hundreds of girls, ages seven to seventeen. At first summer life at Fern Rock proved rustic and challenging, with no hot water or electricity and meals delivered by a small boat from the Bear Mountain Inn. By 1927 camp attendance had reached 150, and with an adult component added in 1934, the facility became increasingly overcrowded and taxed. In 1928 the branch added enclosed cabins, an infirmary, a living room with a fireplace, and a kitchen. Finally, in 1937, the camp underwent significant renovations, emerging with a new housing unit, electricity, an enlarged main lodge, a recreation hall, and a separate kitchen and dining area for the adults. That year, 418 adults spent time at the camp, some for weeks at a time, some for only weekends, and 314 young women and girls attended. The camp's constituency originally was limited to Harlemites but, over the years, also included girls from outside New York; by 1943 campers represented fifty-four cities and nine states.[90]

Activities at Fern Rock were typical of most such camps. Jean Blackwell Hutson remembered swimming and learning to row on Lake Tiorati. Campers hiked, engaged in arts and crafts, and played a variety of sports. The camp also operated an educational program in conjunction with the American Museum of Natural History in New York City. Bernard Brown of the museum administered the program, in which the campers learned about the wildlife around them.[91]

With the increasing focus on bringing entertainment, education, new experiences, and encouragement into the lives of African American girls, the Harlem YWCA took an approach to fulfilling its mission that saw happiness—activity, joy, opportunity, fun—as central to developing spiritually committed people. In the 1935 annual report, the leaders of the branch emphasized this approach when the YWCA announced its redefined mission statement.

> For many years the YWCA defined its objective as the more abundant life for its clientele and designed its program for the physical, mental and spiritual development of young women and girls. Quite recently the organization has re-defined and re-phrased its objective and has thus stated its purpose: "To build a fellowship of women and girls devoted to the task of realizing in our common life those ideals of personal and social living to which we are committed by our faith as Christians. In this endeavor we seek to understand Jesus, to share His love for all people, and to grow in the knowledge and love of God."[92]

Leadership Training

During the interwar period, the Harlem YWCA emerged as a significant arena in which the organization's leaders—both volunteer and paid—trained, supported, and encouraged young women to engage the social, economic, and political issues that affected their lives. Cecelia Saunders proved to be a formidable and sometimes dominating force in the day-to-day operation of the branch and a profound influence on the members and staff. Dorothy Height and Anna Arnold Hedgeman, both of whom worked at the Harlem YWCA during the 1930s, recalled their sense that Saunders held an extraordinary amount of power and noted that her strength and influence drew them to the work. In 1937 Saunders invited Height to work at the branch. When Height expressed her surprise at not having to undergo interviews before members of the Metropolitan Board, Saunders replied simply, "[B]ut you see, in this branch, we look out for our own, we select our own people."[93] Hedgeman, a graduate of Hamline University in St. Paul, Minnesota, and formerly a teacher at Rust University in Holly Springs, Mississippi, had served as the executive secretary of the African American YWCAs in Springfield, Ohio, and Jersey City, New Jersey, before moving to New York. She had become increasingly frustrated by the lack of financial resources and by her constant conflicts with the white YWCA women in both cities. The subtleties of northern racism stunned her. The protection and insulation that Saunders's YWCA offered her afforded a great sense of relief. She recalled, "I would have equipment with which to work and the challenge of the largest Negro community in the nation. The wall of separation had done its work. I was completely free of and through with white people."[94] Although Hedgeman was not "through with" white people in her professional life, her six years at the African American YWCA in New York provided a respite from the kind of conflicts she had experienced previously and allowed her to leave the Harlem YWCA in a rejuvenated state.

Cecelia Saunders's strong control of the operation of the branch struck Belle Ingels, a field worker for the National Board of the YWCA, who visited the Harlem YWCA complex in 1937. She reported, "The Executive Secretary has been in her present position for twenty years. She has become the Branch to many people including the Committee of Management. Obviously she and the chairman get along fine together. Some things they decide together but many others the Executive decides alone and tells the Committee of Management about what is going on."[95] In addition, Ingels noted, Saunders served as the only connection between staff and the committee of management, and all information about the performance of staff members, or about their concerns or difficulties, reached the committee through Saunders's reports. "The staff is of high quality from the point of view of personality and training. There seems to be nothing that indicates that the staff is a group itself working in a common enterprise, though each member with whom I talked had a pride in the branch and a professional attitude toward her work. Staff members are hand picked by the Executive Secretary, which may insure their acquiescence to the status quo."[96]

Whatever its administrative difficulties, the Harlem YWCA grew to become a formidable power in the city in the interwar period and cultivated a number of impressive local and national African American female leaders. Dorothy Height, assistant director of the Emma Ransom House from 1937 until 1939, met Mary McLeod Bethune on one of her visits to the Harlem YWCA and became involved with Bethune's National Council of Negro Women. Height then went on to become director of the African American YWCA in Washington, D.C., and later a staff member at the National Board of the YWCA. Height has, since 1957, been president of the National Council of Negro Women and is one of the most influential African American women of the late twentieth century.[97]

Anna Arnold Hedgeman, membership secretary at the branch in the 1930s, also continued in YWCA work after leaving the Harlem YWCA; she served as executive secretary of the African American YWCAs in Philadelphia and Brooklyn. She later held such prestigious positions as dean of women at Howard University, member of the cabinet of Mayor Robert F. Wagner of New York City, and member of the National Advisory Council of the Department of Health, Education, and Welfare. She also served on the organizing committee of the 1963 civil rights march on Washington.[98] Georgia Myrtle Teale, director of the Emma Ransom House for a period, was later appointed dean of women at Wilberforce University, the premier educational institution of the African Methodist Episcopal Church.[99] Ruth Logan Roberts of the committee of management also served on the New York State Board of Social Welfare and as a staff member of the National Board of the YWCA.[100]

Throughout the interwar period, the Harlem YWCA served its constituency according to the community's needs and experiences. With the stress of economic difficulties, a growing and diverse population, changing national and local politics, and a shifting membership, the organization modified its approaches and transformed itself in response to its leaders' understanding of the constituency's greatest need. At times this called for attention to labor issues or politics, at others to recreation or education. Despite the varied and increasingly secular approaches that the organization felt moved to take, its leaders always underscored their sense of the Christian foundation to all the work. From their perspective, assisting young women in seeking "the more abundant life" necessarily required a recognition of the connections between spiritual, material, personal, and political well-being.

The bustling and intense atmosphere in the Harmon Foundation's film portrayal of the Harlem YWCA captured the tenor of life for the organization's members in the interwar period. African American New Yorkers, black Americans from other areas of the country, and blacks throughout the world could view the Harlem YWCA as their own community center and find staff, facilities, and programs to expand their opportunities. The most difficult challenge the organization faced came not from the economic stress of the depression nor from the approaching entrance of the United States into another war, but from ongoing interactions with white women in the New York City YWCA and in the National Board of the YWCA. This time, however, the challenge did not stem from the failure of white women to include African American women but rather from the prospect of integration coming to the New York City YWCA.

~ 7

"Against the Tide": Interracial Work and Racial Conflict

*A*T THE 1946 convention of the National Board of the YWCA, delegates adopted the "Interracial Charter," which affirmed the organization's commitment to making itself an interracial organization, rather than a biracial one with separate structures. The National Board's decision placed the YWCA among the vanguard of those organizations acting on a concern for racial justice. While African American women in the YWCA welcomed this development as beneficial, they also faced a number of potentially adverse consequences of the National Board's new policy. The loss of institutional power and authority for leaders in African American branches emerged as the most significant of these consequences. The constituents of African American YWCA branches feared most that "integration" would result in a loss of services specifically geared to the needs of their communities and would ultimately bring about the demise of their branches. Cecelia Cabaniss Saunders and the many other African American women who had devoted stunning amounts of time and energy to the YWCA had long wanted their organization to set aside its compliance with the American system of racial segregation, and African American women across the country had fought for racial equality within the YWCA for many years. For Saunders and others, however, the arrival of the long-awaited turn toward integration brought as much sadness, conflict, and difficulty as relief.

Cecelia Saunders had had many opportunities in her years at the New York City YWCA to confront racial discrimination within both the local and national associations. Two incidents illustrate the YWCA's conflicted approaches to the practice of racism. In August 1924, Walter White, then assistant secretary of the NAACP, wrote to the chair of the National Board of the YWCA concerning Lydia Gardine, a young African American woman who had applied for admission to the School of Hygiene and Physical Education at the Central (white) Branch of the New York City YWCA. Gardine, a resident of East Orange, New Jersey, had corresponded with the school, had been found eligible for admission, and had obtained an appointment for an interview. Sometime before the interview, however, Gardine received a letter from Helen McKinstry, the director of the school, saying (according to White) that "she noted on Miss Gardine's application blank that Miss Gardine is an American Negro. Miss McKinstry further stated that 'if you had only mentioned this fact on your "Eligibility Estimate" blank the matter would not have been carried this far. I am extremely sorry to be obliged to tell you that we are by terms of our arrangement with Central Branch not allowed to admit colored girls to the school.'"[1] White demanded to know the YWCA's policy concerning such situations, concluding with the request that "If such action has official sanction, that you will be good enough to advise us how the Young Women's Christian Association can label itself a Christian organization and practice such gross discrimination in direct violation of all the principles of Christianity as they are known to me."[2] Three days later, the NAACP issued a press release under the heading, "YWCA School of Hygiene Refuses Admission to Girl Because She is Colored."[3]

Mary S. Sims, head of the City Department at the National Board, replied to White with the standard National Board line about race relations within city YWCAs. Sims wrote that each local YWCA retained a great degree of autonomy and underscored that the National Board could not compel them to adhere to any set policy. Taking an approach that the NAACP would use effectively during the civil rights movement of the 1950s and 1960s regarding the relationship between state and federal laws, White argued emphatically that, as a Christian organization, the national YWCA should take a moral stand on discrimination and intervene on the local level when necessary.[4] Nevertheless, Sims told White that the National Board had turned the entire matter over to the New York City YWCA.[5]

Bertha Boody, then general secretary of the city YWCA, informed White that she was still in the process of holding meetings with the women of the "Colored Women's Branch" to reach a solution. Incredulous that the African American YWCA should be brought into the discussion at all, White responded, "To us, the issue is simply one of deciding . . . whether or not the YWCA is going to practice discrimination based not on merit or worth but on color."[6] Finally, he threatened to call a boycott of the upcoming New York City YWCA fund-raising campaign.

With White's threat, the New York City YWCA finally issued a formal statement on the exclusion of Gardine from its school. The press release described the New York City YWCA as a large organization that gathered many branches and large numbers of women from a variety of backgrounds under one umbrella. "Inter-racial contacts are receiving consideration by the civilized thinking world. They cannot be arbitrarily settled by one group. The policy of the YWCA as a whole is one of equal opportunity for all, and it is endeavoring to make its practice square with the policy."[7] And how did the YWCA seek to bring its practice into line with its policy? Through "separate but equal" accommodations. The press release described in great detail the services, facilities, and activities available to African American women at their separate West 137th Street branch. The statement concluded, "Business classes and cafeterias in other Branches are open to colored girls; and where more intimate contacts are involved, the white and colored members of the Association are working toward a better understanding and a Christian consideration which shall ensure equal opportunity for all girls without regard to race, creed or color."[8]

Lydia Gardine had applied to the YWCA's School of Hygiene and Physical Education, and yet all of the Metropolitan Board's public statements referred to it merely as the "School of Physical Education." This way of designating the school served to highlight the element of potential physical contact between black and white students. Thus, the YWCA signaled its "advanced" position on race relations by pointing to the fact that its cafeterias did not bar black women, but it also comforted whites by assuring them that there would be no black and white women sweating or exercising next to one another. For its part, the NAACP generally referred to the school as the YWCA's "School of Hygiene" in order to emphasize Gardine's desire, in pressing for admission, to further her education in the field of health and hygiene.

Neither the New York City YWCA nor the National Board took further action on Gardine's application. One can imagine the difficult situation in which African American YWCA women found themselves at this moment. At the same time that they desired to end racial discrimination, they also felt deep pride in the services that their YWCA branch offered to black New Yorkers and to other African Americans. It remained in the interest of the women of the Harlem YWCA to credit their own determination and resolve, rather than exclusion from white branches, for the high quality of their facilities and services. Such a public incident highlighting the New York City YWCA's discomfort with African American women only served to erode the reputation that Saunders, Ransom, and other leaders had worked so hard to build among black New Yorkers.

Not only did the leaders of New York's African American YWCA have to struggle to obtain equal access to YWCA programs for black members, on many occasions they found themselves embroiled in conflict over their own access to YWCA training programs. In May 1920, Cecelia Cabaniss Saunders received a form letter from Betty MacBride of the personnel division of the National Board, addressed to all branch general secretaries, inviting a representative from the branch to a summer course on physical education. The invitation also noted that those who attended would engage in a variety of recreational activities, including camping, dancing, and community singing. Saunders replied that her branch would send at least one person to the course. A few days later Saunders received a letter from MacBride withdrawing the invitation. MacBride wrote as if Saunders, and not she, had made the initial contact: "We are glad to know of your interest in the physical education course to be given this year but regret that it is impossible to have your physical director join us. It would be very profitable to her to have a course of this kind and we hope next year that the colored workers will be included in our program."[9]

Saunders did not let the matter drop. She began a correspondence with Emma Bailey Speer, then chair of the National Board, in which she asked to be informed about National Board policies concerning the exclusion of black women. "Such a courtesy," Saunders continued, "would be greatly appreciated since it will make our position with our people a little less trying; being in possession of such information we could then strive to avoid situations in which our professional etiquette and an acknowledgement of truth were the two points of our di-lemma."[10] Speer's initial reply, not preserved in the record, enraged Saunders, who fired back with a letter that described the difficulty of her position in presenting YWCA training courses as a way to "come to know the Association spirit" and then having to explain to her staff why they had been excluded. Perhaps discrimination indeed constituted the true "Association spirit," Saunders's response implied.

Speer replied that while she found Saunders's "indignation" justi-fiable, she did not feel that the situation called for action. In a stunning use of religious language as a means of evading practical responsibility, Speer counseled patience and placed her personal experience as a tour-ist on an equal footing with legal and traditional discrimination as well as systematic violence committed against African Americans. In con-cluding her letter to Saunders, she wrote:

Meanwhile let us both go forward with the infinite patience that alone can change the conditions under which such a difficulty be-comes possible. Great and painful as it is, the prejudice and misun-derstanding shown by Caucasians against the Negro race is only one of the terrible racial difficulties that face the world today. I have been where it is quite as strong against my race as against yours. I spent a winter in a country where it was dangerous for a Caucasian woman to go out alone in the street, if not impossible. I spent a summer in a country where any venture from the main highway meant foul abuse if not violence. . . . There is no way out of this darkness, in Asia or America, except the way of love. The Kingdom of God cometh not by violence, and he that believeth, neither can nor should make haste, though the temptation is heavy upon us. But though we may not make haste, neither may we rest. Day and night we must ally ourselves with those mighty processes of God that alone can make His world according to His will, filled with justice and understanding for all.[11]

African American Christians had long been accustomed to white Chris-tians' counsel of patience and faith in a divine schedule for achieving racial justice. Within the New York City YWCA, Saunders and other black women had experienced frustration with this approach, and Afri-can American women involved with the national YWCA, particularly southern women, had fought vigorously, since the end of World War I, against the attitude of passive Christian patience.

At the 1920 Sixth National Convention of the Young Women's Christian Associations, a group of southern African American women presented a petition that called for African American women to be permitted to step into leadership positions at all levels of the YWCA, national and local, and to use the authority of these positions to make policy for black women in the organization.[12] One of the petitioners, Mary Jackson McCrorey of Charlotte, North Carolina, made an impassioned plea for the women gathered at the convention to discuss seriously the issues raised in the petition.

> I don't want to touch upon anything which would offend your sensibilities, but I believe the YWCA is big enough, has enough religion of the Lord Jesus Christ in it, to face every problem which confronts the womanhood of this country and to solve it in terms of the gospel of Jesus Christ. It matters not how delicate it is, we have to face it, women, there is no question about it. The Negro women more than any other group of women are segregated, severely segregated in this country . . . Now how are the women to come into the realization of these things if this organization does not reach out its hand to bring them within its fold? Do they not deserve it? Though you may not know it, there are certain conditions which prevent you from knowing it, there is an intelligent, capable leadership among this group of women.[13]

Ironically, at the very same meeting at which the YWCA adopted the "Social Ideals of the Churches," it failed to act on the African American women's petition, continuing instead to allow the National Board's field staff for the South to set policy, a situation that the black southern women felt led to their exclusion.[14]

In the period from 1921 to 1936, as a result of their continued frustration, many African American women in the YWCA withdrew from a constant public struggle for interracial work. Some who stayed with the YWCA committed themselves more fully to the work of student YWCAs in colleges, long the more politically progressive wing of the YWCA, and others rededicated themselves to the work of city YWCAs.[15] By the late 1930s, the issue of interracial activities again became a subject of discussion, this time initiated by young women in college YWCAs. At the 1936 annual convention, students encouraged the national YWCA to take up a serious examination of the effects of segregation on the YWCA and to move toward integration. Finally, in 1940, YWCA delegates voted at the national convention to form a commission, which ultimately produced the 1944 book, *Interracial Practices in Community YWCAs*, written by Juliet Ober Bell and Helen J. Wilkins. Not surprisingly, Bell and Wilkins concluded that the YWCA indeed was segregated, and they recommended that the organization make its work fully integrated.[16]

Despite the National Board's hesitation to make a forceful statement on the question of interracial work, it nevertheless took various concrete steps to keep the issue alive. From 1932 to 1940, Frances Harriet Williams, an African American Phi Beta Kappa graduate of Mt. Holyoke College with a master's degree from the University of Chicago, served as interracial education secretary for the National Board. Williams, who had spent six years as a National Board staff member for student work during the 1920s, produced educational documents to assist young white women in the YWCA in discussing questions of race and integration in America and within the organization.[17]

"Pudge and Her Friends," a pamphlet typical of Williams's work in this capacity, begins with the fictionalized story of Patricia Platt, a young African American woman known as Pudge, at a Girl Reserve conference in the Midwest. Pudge has come from North Carolina for the conference and is one of five African American girls in attendance who find themselves bombarded with questions from the seventy-five white participants about themselves and other African Americans. "Were there other colored girls like the five there? If so, where were they? Who were these people the colored girls talked about—Walter White, . . . Booker T. Washington, . . . Frederick Douglass? What is a jim crow car like?"[18] Pudge decides to introduce all seventy-five white girls, via correspondence, to "Cousin Sue," her adult cousin and mentor. Sue provides the white girls with a nine-part study course on "The American Negro," guiding them through demographics, labor statistics, an introduction to black literature, and portraits of contemporary black leaders, among other topics. The young white women continue to correspond with Cousin Sue, one asking her advice on forming an interracial girls' club, another inquiring whether to begin calling her mother's African American seamstress Mrs. Brown rather than Mary.

In booklets like "Pudge and Her Friends," Williams focused her attention on young white women's perceptions of their African American peers. Through the lively writing and personable characters, Williams portrayed the benefits of interracial interactions for the white women in terms of broadening their perspective on the world and making them better citizens and Christians. The world of "Pudge and Her Friends" demonstrates positive developments among most of the white girls, but the struggles and complexities involved in breaking racial codes of the 1930s remain very much present. In the end, some of the white characters can move themselves only so far in terms of participating in interracial activities. Ultimately, Williams's device of using Pudge and Cousin Sue as intermediaries points to her understanding of the impediments to white women's unguided explorations of African American experiences.

While in the world of Williams's booklets the attitudes of young white women steadily changed, in the real world of the YWCA sentiment against interracial work did not shift without serious conflict. The National Board planned to take up the issue of integration as formal policy at its 1946 conference in Little Rock and circulated materials in advance of the meeting. Dorothy Height, who joined the National Board staff in 1944, embarked on a campaign to assist local YWCAs in discussions of integration. Although some white YWCA groups welcomed Height and addressed the topic, others refused to meet with her.[19]

The various protests lodged with the National Board prior to the 1946 meeting reveal the degree to which some white women in the organization saw a formal policy of integration as impossible to accept. The white women of the Birmingham, Alabama, YWCA, for example, wrote to Mary Shotwell Ingraham, president of the national YWCA, to declare themselves emphatically against integration in the YWCA. Mrs. J. H. McCary Jr., president of the Birmingham YWCA, wrote of the outrage of her membership at the YWCA's plans: "We were shocked to learn that the core purpose of the National Board is racial amalgamation . . . We have always maintained friendly relations with the negro Branch and have made every effort to further the work of the Branch among their own people. Segregation of the Branches will continue and that policy does not admit of discussion."[20]

Despite such vigorous protests, the delegates at the National Board's 1946 convention voted to adopt the "Interracial Charter," a document that recognized the potential difficulties involved in contravening the dominant modes of racial interaction, but that also pledged to do so. The charter read, in part, "As members of the Young Women's Christian Associations of the United States of America we humbly and resolutely pledge ourselves to continue to pioneer in an interracial experience that shall be increasingly democratic and Christian."[21] The convention also adopted recommendations arising from Bell and Wilkins's earlier study of interracial practices in community YWCAs. One recommendation for the National Board emphasized movement toward genuine inclusiveness and away from racial tokenism. Black women asked for full authority within the organization on an equal basis with white women. For local associations, the convention asked that programs be evaluated using the new purpose as the measure, the proposal that the Birmingham women feared most. "The implications of the Purpose [must] be recognized as involving the inclusion of Negro women and girls in the main stream of Association life."[22] Thus, staff members and volunteers would have to be educated about the purpose of the YWCA with respect to issues of race and the National Board's commitment to an inclusive membership.

With regard to changes in the parallel structure of black and white branches, the convention recommended that branches functioning specifically for African American women should, if possible, completely integrate their work into that of the white associations. The convention also recommended that where the law required segregation, efforts should be made to arrange frequent joint activities. Regardless of local laws, the YWCA asserted that African American women must always be included as full working partners in the administration of associations after any structural changes, such as combining the work of black and white branches, had been made.[23] The policies adopted at the 1946 convention constituted a significant step forward for the National Board. Significantly, the board stated openly and forcefully that African American women represented an important part of the YWCA's work and leadership.

Local YWCAs dealt with the new commitment to interracial work in a variety of ways. One common method was to declare that branches formerly designated as "colored women's" branches now become neighborhood branches serving a particular geographical area. Practically speaking, given patterns of residential segregation, such a move did not necessarily change the racial composition of these branches. White New Yorkers, few of whom lived in Harlem, did not seem likely to travel to Harlem for services that they could get in their own neighborhood YWCA. More likely, African American women who lived in Harlem or other neighborhoods would be interested in attending courses or using facilities at other YWCAs in the city. Cecelia Saunders downplayed the potentially negative effects of the new policy on the health of the branch by emphasizing that the Harlem YWCA's particular attention to African American women would keep them involved with the institution. She confessed to Reverdy Ransom, however, that she knew that it would be almost impossible to get white women to participate in Harlem branch activities.[24]

The National Board of the YWCA anticipated the difficulties that white women would face during the process of integration but did not necessarily foresee the profound conflict that it would bring for black women in the organization. In addition to the potential loss of membership in African American branches as young African American women gained access to all YWCA programs, leaders in black YWCAs faced a loss of authority over their own domain. As a result, African American women in some cases proved more resistant to integration—read as a loss of control and emphasis on African American issues—than white women. At the prospect of losing control of the African American YWCA in Oakland, California, for example, most of the African American leaders left and the members ceased participating.[25] As a post-1946 study conducted by Dorothy Sabiston and Margaret Hiller found, "Sudden changes in practice from 'segregated' to 'integrated' programs had brought the need for more interpretation in the Negro community than in the white community."[26]

In addition to the various ways that integration affected African American leaders in the YWCA, the more profound impact rested on the YWCA's girls. One leader reported to Sabiston and Hiller:

"You have no idea what you have to be continually doing to keep up the morale of Negro girls so that they can take the kinds of things they have to meet. Some of them just can't take it. It is not any fun to be in a mixed group; some girls do it because they think it is important, but it takes courage. Some of the college girls and people who have been to school together are ready for it, but the great mass of people are not, and I am interested in what happens to them."[27]

No degree of commitment to developing an integrated organization could reduce the stress that interracial activities placed on the first generation of young African American women caught in the changes.

The period during which the New York City YWCA, in accord with movement in the national YWCA, began to effect integrated work proved to be a difficult and wrenching one for African American women at the Harlem YWCA. National and local YWCAs had marshaled their resources to ease the transition for white women, who often interpreted integration as degrading their natural status and, as with the Birmingham women, necessarily leading to "racial amalgamation," or the destruction of "the white race." National and local YWCA efforts to assist white women proved largely successful, and the organization did not retreat from its commitment to the "Interracial Charter." The failure to recognize the potential psychic ruptures that integration would produce for African American women, on the other hand, left women like Saunders, who had worked productively through the Harlem YWCA for thirty-three years, with an uncertain future. In 1947 she resigned, telling Reverdy Ransom, "I believe, however, that it is not only better for me that I leave at this time, but that it is better for the work. The New York City YWCA has accepted a more advanced position in race relations; the Board of Directors will never take the same responsibility for the Harlem Branch as it takes for other branches as long as I remain with the Branch."[28]

While the implementation of the "Interracial Charter" and Saunders's subsequent resignation in 1947 brought about the end of an era for the Harlem YWCA, these two events did not directly lead to the demise of the institution as many had feared.[29] Rather, they mark the beginning of a shift in emphasis and character, a shift that required the leaders of the Harlem YWCA to balance more carefully its attention to defining and meeting the particular needs of African American New Yorkers (for following Saunders's era the branch began to include boys in its activities) and its input into the city YWCA as a whole. The issues that Saunders and other African American women in the New York City YWCA faced during the movement toward integration presaged those that confronted African Americans following the Civil

Rights Movement of the 1950s and 1960s. The ongoing struggle for activists like the women of the Harlem YWCA has been to serve their particular communities while, at the same time, pursuing an agenda of equal access and equal rights for all. As the experiences of these women during the integration process demonstrates, balancing both goals could prove arduous. The endurance of historically black institutions such as churches, fraternal organizations, sororities, and colleges, as well as of organizations struggling for a fully integrated American society, underscores the degree to which African Americans, as a group with multiple perspectives and experiences, have opted to maintain all possible avenues to "the more abundant life."

Notes

Abbreviations

CWC   Minutes of the Colored Work Committee of the National Board of
        the YWCA of the U.S.A., National Board Archives, New York;
        Record Files Collection
EC   Minutes of the Executive Committee of the 15th Street Association,
        Laura Parsons Pratt Research Center, Young Women's Christian
        Association of the City of New York
LAG   Mayor Fiorello LaGuardia Papers, Municipal Archives, Department
        of Records and Information Services, City of New York
LPPRC   Laura Parsons Pratt Research Center, Young Women's Christian
        Association of the City of New York
MB   Minutes of the Board of Directors Meetings of the YWCA of the City
        of New York, Laura Parsons Pratt Research Center, Young Women's
        Christian Association of the City of New York
NBA   YWCA of the U.S.A., National Board Archives, New York; Record
        Files Collection
RFA   Office of the Messrs. Rockefeller, Rockefeller Foundation Archives,
        Rockefeller Archive Center, Tarrytown, New York
WB   General Correspondence of the Women's Bureau, 1918–1948, Record
        Group 86, National Archives and Records Administration

Introduction

1. Throughout this work I use "black" and "African American" interchangeably. With an understanding that, throughout the period covered by the book, the women themselves would have referred to themselves as "colored" or "Negro," I prefer to use these terms only when they appear in the original sources.

2. Pauli Murray, *Song in a Weary Throat: An American Pilgrimage* (New York: Harper & Row, 1987), p. 74.

3. Ibid., p. 75.

4. Ibid., p. 60.

5. Ibid., p. 65.

6. Ibid., p. 75.

7. For more on the emergence of three generations of black professional women, see Stephanie J. Shaw, *What a Woman Ought to Be and to Do: Black Professional Women Workers During the Jim Crow Era* (Chicago: University of Chicago Press, 1996).

8. Paula Giddings, *Where and When I Enter: The Impact of Black Women on Race and Sex in America* (New York: Bantam Books, 1984); Dorothy Salem, *To Better Our World: Black Women in Organized Reform, 1890–1920* (Brooklyn, N.Y.: Carlson Publishing, 1990); Stephanie J. Shaw, "Black Club Women and the Creation of the National Association of Colored Women," *Journal of Women's History* 3, no. 2 (1991). Each of these works influences the approach of this study in their attempts to balance the national and local in discussions of organizing work among African American women.

9. See Evelyn Brooks Higginbotham, *Righteous Discontent: The Women's Movement in the Black Baptist Church, 1880–1920* (Cambridge: Harvard University Press, 1993); Anne Firor Scott, *Natural Allies: Women's Associations in American History* (Urbana: University of Illinois Press, 1991).

10. In this aspect of the project, I have been influenced by a number of works that examine middle-class African American communities as equally "authentic" black experiences as southern, rural, "folk" experiences. See Claudia Tate, *Domestic Allegories of Political Desire: The Black Heroine's Text at the Turn of the Century* (New York: Oxford University Press, 1992); Thadious M. Davis, *Nella Larsen, Novelist of the Harlem Renaissance: A Woman's Life Unveiled* (Baton Rouge: Louisiana State University Press, 1994); Willard B. Gatewood, *Aristocrats of Color: The Black Elite, 1880–1920* (Bloomington: University of Indiana Press, 1990).

1. Institutional Alliances/Institutional Appropriations

1. Elizabeth Ross received an A.B. degree from Fisk University in 1903 and an M.A. in sociology from Columbia University in 1923. Joseph J. Boris, ed., *Who's Who in Colored America: A Biographical Dictionary of Notable Living Persons of Negro Descent in America* (New York: Who's Who in Colored America Corp., 1927), p. 89. On Hunton see chapter 2.

2. Elizabeth Ross, "Report," December 3, 1908, quoted in Jane Olcott-Walters, ed., *History of Colored Work, Chronological Excerpts From Reports of Secretaries and Workers and From Minutes Showing the Development of the Work Among Colored Women, November 1907–December 1920*, p. 4, NBA.

3. Ross, "Report," March 1910, in Olcott-Walters, ed., *History of Colored Work*, p. 7, NBA; Mrs. W. A. Hunton, "Women's Clubs," *The Crisis*, July 1911; *New York Age*, August 20, 1908.

4. Ross, "Report," December 3, 1908, in Olcott-Walters, ed., *History of Colored Work*, p. 4, NBA.

5. Peter Berger, *The Sacred Canopy: Elements of a Sociological Theory of Religion* (New York: Anchor Books, 1969), pp. 35–36.

6. Mrs. Bush, "Bend the Tree While It Is Young," *Colored American Magazine* 12 (January 1907): 53.

7. Abdul R. JanMohamed, "The Economy of Manichean Allegory: The Function of Racial Difference in Colonialist Literature," in *"Race," Writing, and Difference*, ed. Henry Louis Gates Jr. (Chicago: University of Chicago Press, 1985), pp. 92–93.

8. Deborah Gray White, *Ar'n't I a Woman: Female Slaves in the Plantation South* (New York: W. W. Norton, 1981); Dorothy Sterling, *We Are Your Sisters: Black Women in the Nineteenth Century* (New York: W. W. Norton, 1984); Stephanie J. Shaw, "Black Club Women and the Creation of the National Association of Colored Women," *Journal of Women's History* 3 (fall 1991): 10–25; Gerda Lerner, "Early Community Work of Black Club Women," *Journal of Negro History* 59 (1974): 158–167.

9. Peter J. Paris's *The Social Teachings of the Black Churches* (Philadelphia: Fortress Press, 1985) provides a strong overview of this perspective.

10. I follow Evelyn Brooks Higginbotham's use of Jürgen Habermas's "public sphere" to describe the black church. Her formulation emphasizes that the exclusion of African Americans from participation in the public life of the nation moved the black church to become "an interstitial space in which to critique and contest white America's racial domination." Evelyn Brooks Higginbotham, *Righteous Discontent: The Women's Movement in the Black Baptist Church, 1880–1920* (Cambridge: Harvard University Press, 1993), p. 10.

11. See, for example, Higginbotham, *Righteous Discontent*, chapter 4; Jualynne E. Dodson, "Power and Surrogate Leadership: Black Women and Organized Religion," *Sage* 5 (fall 1988): 37–42; Sandy D. Martin, "Black Baptist Women and African Mission Work, 1870–1925," *Sage* 3 (spring 1986): 16–19.

12. See the spiritual narratives in William Andrews, ed., *Sisters of the Spirit: Three Black Women's Autobiographies of the Nineteenth Century* (Bloomington: Indiana University Press, 1986).

13. Virginia W. Broughton, *Twenty Years' Experience of a Missionary* (Chicago: The Pony Press Publishers, 1907), quoted in Higginbotham, *Righteous Discontent*, p. 70.

14. David W. Wills, "Womanhood and Domesticity in the A. M. E. Tradition: The Influence of Daniel Alexander Payne," in *Black Apostles at Home and Abroad: Afro-Americans and the Christian Mission from Revolution to Reconstruction*, ed. David W. Wills and Richard Newman (Boston: G. K. Hall, 1982).

15. Rev. Jas. H. A. Johnson, "Female Preachers," *A.M.E. Church Review* (October 1884): 103.

16. Anna Julia Cooper, *A Voice From the South* (Xenia, Ohio, 1892), p. 28.

17. Rev. James Theodore Holly, "The Divine Plan of Human Redemption in its Ethnological Development," *A.M.E. Church Review* (October 1884): 79–85.

18. Mrs. M. E. Lee, "Afmerica," *AME Church Review* (July 1885): 58.

19. Rayford Logan, *The Betrayal of the Negro* (New York: Collier Books, 1965).

20. Scholars often portray the debate over the most prudent approach to racial uplift at the end of the nineteenth century as taking place between the camps of

Booker T. Washington and W. E. B. Du Bois, with Washington advocating a retreat from politics and Du Bois, full engagement. The politics of racial uplift in the late nineteenth century encompassed a much broader spectrum of opinions, however, and both Washington and Du Bois were far more flexible in their approaches than is often conceded. Most importantly for this work, the presentation of this polarization in the literature has served to mask the contributions of women to the debate. For a discussion of the ongoing relationship between Du Bois and Washington, see David Levering Lewis, *W. E. B. Du Bois: Biography of a Race, 1868–1919* (New York: Henry Holt, 1993), and for a general discussion of the period, see August Meier, *Negro Thought in America, 1880–1915: Racial Ideologies in the Age of Booker T. Washington* (Ann Arbor: University of Michigan Press, 1963).

21. Fannie Barrier Williams, "The Awakening of Women," *A.M.E. Church Review* (April 1897): 398.

22. Evelyn Brooks Higginbotham, "African-American Women's History and the Metalanguage of Race," *Signs* (winter 1992): 251–275; Beverly Guy-Sheftall, *Daughters of Sorrow: Attitudes Towards Black Women, 1880–1920* (Brooklyn, N.Y.: Carlson Publishing, 1990).

23. "Experiences of the Race Problem. By a Southern White Woman," *Independent* 56 (March 17, 1904), quoted in Guy-Sheftall, *Daughters of Sorrow*, p. 46.

24. Mrs. Bush, "Bend the Tree While it is Young," *Colored American Magazine* 12 (January 1907): 54.

25. See Higginbotham, *Righteous Discontent*, chapter 7.

26. Indianapolis *Freeman*, July 28, 1906, quoted in Willard B. Gatewood, *Aristocrats of Color: The Black Elite, 1880–1920* (Bloomington: University of Indiana Press, 1990), p. 142.

27. See Dorothy Salem, *To Better Our World: Black Women in Organized Reform, 1880–1920* (Brooklyn, N.Y.: Carlson Publishing, 1990), pp. 34–35; Gatewood, *Aristocrats of Color*, p. 142.

28. Ida B. Wells, *Crusade for Justice: The Autobiography of Ida B. Wells*, ed. Alfreda Duster (Chicago: University of Illinois Press, 1970), p. 18–20. On the Rev. Love incident, see, for example, *Washington Bee*, September 21, 1889.

29. Topeka *Plaindealer*, February 7, 1902, in Gatewood, *Aristocrats of Color*, pp. 245–246.

30. Higginbotham, *Righteous Discontent*, chapter 4.

31. Fannie Barrier Williams, "Club Movement Among Negro Women," in *Progress of a Race*, ed. J. W. Gibson and W. H. Crogman (Atlanta: J. L. Nichols, 1903), pp. 220–226.

32. Higginbotham, *Righteous Discontent*, chapter 4.

33. Elizabeth Wilson, *Fifty Years of Association Work Among Young Women, 1866–1916: A History of Young Women's Christian Associations in the United States of America* (New York: National Board of the YWCAs of the U.S.A., 1916; reprint, New York: Garland Publishing, 1987), pp. 13–18; Richard Carwardine, *Transatlantic Revivalism: Popular Evangelicalism in Britain and America, 1790–1865* (Westport, Conn.: Greenwood Press, 1978), pp. 15, 162. Although the New York group was the first in the United States to organize itself under the principles generally accepted to be the trademarks of the YWCA, the group founded in Boston in 1866 was the first to use the name Young Women's Christian Association. The New York Young Ladies' Christian Association changed its name to the Young Women's

Christian Association in 1876. Mary S. Sims, *The Natural History of a Social Insti-tution—The Young Women's Christian Association* (New York: The Woman's Press, 1936), pp. 5–6; Elizabeth Wilson, *Fifty Years*, p. 55.

34. Early on the YWCA based its understanding of "evangelical" on the YMCA definition: "And we hold those churches to be evangelical which, maintain-ing the Holy Scriptures to be the only infallible rule of faith and practice, do believe in the Lord Jesus Christ (the only begotten of the Father, King of kings, Lord of lords, in whom dwelleth the fullness of the God-head bodily, and who was made sin for us though knowing no sin, bearing our sins in his own body on the tree) as the only name under heaven given among men whereby we must be saved from ever-lasting punishment, and unto life eternal." Resolution—1879 Portland Convention of the Young Men's Christian Association, in Elizabeth Wilson, *Fifty Years*, p. 257.

35. *Tenth Annual Report of the Officers of the Young Women's Christian Association of the City of New York* (New York, 1881), p. 9.

36. *Fifth Annual Report of the Young Women's Christian Association of New York* (New York, 1878), p. 9.

37. "Methods of Christian Work," 1893, quoted in Elizabeth Russell Hendee, *The Growth and Development of the Young Women's Christian Association: An Interpre-tation* (New York: The Woman's Press, 1930), p. 28; Harriet Taylor, "City Depart-ment," *Evangel* (June 1898): 5–7, quoted in Sims, *Natural History*, pp. 45–46.

38. "Social Entertainments," *Faith and Works* 4 (August 1879): 185, quoted in Sims, *Natural History*, p. 12.

39. *Ninth Annual Report of the Officers of the Young Women's Christian Association of the City of New York* (New York, 1880), p. 7.

40. *Second Annual Report of the Officers of the Young Ladies' Christian Union* (New York, 1873), p. 6.

41. David I. Macleod, *Building Character in the American Boy: The Boy Scouts, YMCA, and Their Forerunners, 1870–1920* (Madison: University of Wisconsin Press, 1983), pp. xvi, 3, 27.

42. G. Stanley Hall, *Adolescence: Its Psychology and Its Relations to Physiology, An-thropology, Sociology, Sex, Crime, Religion and Education* (New York: Appleton, 1905); Macleod, *Building Character*, p. 27.

43. Hall, *Adolescence*, pp. 632–642.

44. Ibid., p. 649.

45. Macleod, *Building Character*, pp. 47–49, 128–129; Mary Ross Hall and Helen Firman Sweet, *Women in the Y.M.C.A. Record* (New York: Association Press, 1947), pp. 10–14; Helen Bittar, "The YWCA of the City of New York: 1870–1920" (Ph.D. diss., New York University, 1979), p. 34.

46. Janet Forsythe Fishburn, *The Fatherhood of God and the Victorian Family* (Philadelphia: Fortress Press, 1981), pp. 15, 139–144, 149; Robert T. Handy, *The Social Gospel in America, 1870–1920: Gladden, Ely, Rauschenbusch* (New York: Oxford University Press, 1966).

47. Sims, *Natural History*, p. 47; Grace Wilson, *The Religious and Educational Philosophy of the Young Women's Christian Association* (New York: Teachers College Bureau of Publications, 1933), pp. 14–16.

48. Salem, *To Better Our World*, p. 47.

49. Monroe N. Work, *Negro Year Book and Annual Encyclopedia of the Negro* (Tuskegee, Ala., 1912), p. 95.

50. Gatewood, *Aristocrats of Color*, p. 241; interview with Dorothy I. Height in *The Black Woman Oral History Project*, vol. 5, ed. Ruth Edmonds Hill and Patricia Miller King (Westport, Conn.: Meckler Publishing, 1991), p. 77.

51. Salem, *To Better Our World*, pp. 47–48.

52. Olcott-Walters, *History of Colored Work*, p. 7; Salem, *To Better Our World*, p. 49.

53. Hunton, *Beginnings Among Colored Women* (New York: YWCA, circa 1914), p. 6.

2. African American Women in Networks

1. In 1905 the YWCA at 7 East 15th Street, founded in 1871, served as the central branch of a group of YWCAs that included the Margaret Louisa Home and Restaurant, the Westside Settlement at 460 West 44th Street, and the Seaside Home in Asbury Park, New Jersey. In addition, a separate YWCA founded in 1891 and located in Harlem served Dutch Christian women of that neighborhood. *YWCA of the City of New York Record of the Year 1902*; MB, March 13, 1911, LPPRC.

2. EC, January 19, 1905, LPPRC.

3. EC, February 2, 1905, LPPRC.

4. W. E. B. Du Bois, "The Black North: A Social Study—New York City," *New York Times*, November 24, 1901.

5. Ibid.

6. *The New York Freeman*, April 17, 1886.

7. Mary White Ovington, *Half a Man: The Status of the Negro in New York City* (1911; reprint, New York: Negro Universities Press, 1969), p. 122.

8. Walker credited this group of women with raising $3,000 to benefit the YMCA that Walker helped to found at Mt. Olivet in 1899. On African American men in the YMCA in New York, see Nina Mjagkij, *Light in the Darkness: African-Americans and the YMCA, 1852–1946* (Lexington: University of Kentucky Press, 1994).

9. Silas Xavier Floyd, *Life of Charles T. Walker, D.D.* (Nashville: National Baptist Publishing Board, 1902), pp. 108, 112; Gilbert Osofsky, *Harlem: The Making of a Ghetto, Negro New York, 1890–1930* (New York: Harper & Row, 1963), p. 15.

10. L. A. Scruggs, *Women of Distinction: Remarkable in Works and Invincible in Character* (Raleigh, N.C.: L. A. Scruggs, 1893), pp. 30–32; I. Garland Penn, *The Afro-American Press, Its Editors* (Springfield, Mass.: Willey, 1891), pp. 375–376; Henry Davenport Northrop, Joseph R. Gay, and I. Garland Penn, *The College of Life, or Practical Self-Educator: A Manual of Self-Improvement for the Colored Race* (n.p.: Horace C. Fry, 1900), p. 102; Frances R. Keyser, "Victoria Earle Matthews," in *Homespun Heroines and Other Women of Distinction*, by Hallie Q. Brown (Xenia, Ohio, 1926), pp. 208–216. For more on Matthews as a literary figure, see Hazel V. Carby, *Reconstructing Womanhood: The Emergence of the Afro-American Woman Novelist* (New York: Oxford University Press, 1987).

11. Brooklyn existed as a municipality separate from New York until 1898.

12. *The Woman's Era* 1, no. 1 (March 24, 1894).

13. *The Woman's Era* 1, no. 4 (July 1894).

14. *The Woman's Era* 1, no. 8 (November 1894); 1, no. 9 (December 1894).

15. *The Woman's Era* 2, no. 5 (August 1895); 2, no. 12 (May 1896).

16. *The Woman's Era* 2, no. 5 (August 1895).

17. *The Woman's Era* 2, no. 9 (January 1896).

18. *Annual Report*, White Rose Industrial Association, 1912.

19. Keyser, "Victoria Earle Matthews," in *Homespun Heroines*, by Brown, p. 214.

20. Floris Barnett Cash, "Radicals or Realists: African-American Women and the Settlement House Spirit in New York City," *Afro-Americans in New York Life and History* 15 (January 1991): 10.

21. *Annual Report*, White Rose Industrial Association, 1912.

22. Keyser, "Victoria Earle Matthews," in *Homespun Heroines*, by Brown, p. 212.

23. *Annual Report*, White Rose Industrial Association, 1911.

24. New York *Evening Post*, reprinted in *New York Age*, July 6, 1905.

25. Florence Spearing Randolph, a native of Charleston, South Carolina, became a licensed AMEZ preacher in 1897 and was ordained deacon by Bishop Alexander Walters in 1901 and elder in 1903. Joseph J. Boris, ed., *Who's Who in Colored America* (New York: Who's Who in Colored America Corp., 1927), p. 248. Also see Bettye Collier-Thomas, "Minister and Feminist Reformer: The Life of Florence Spearing Randolph," in *This Far by Faith: Readings in African-American Women's Religious Biography*, ed. Judith Weisenfeld and Richard Newman (New York: Routledge, 1996).

26. *Annual Report*, White Rose Industrial Association, 1911, 1912.

27. *Fifth Annual Report of the Free Kindergarten Association for Colored Children*, November 1, 1900, New York City, New York, in *Black Heritage in Social Welfare*, ed. Edyth L. Ross (Metuchen, N.J.: Scarecrow Press, 1978), p. 234.

28. Dorothy Salem, *To Better Our World: Black Women in Organized Reform, 1880–1920* (Brooklyn, N.Y.: Carlson Publishing, 1990), pp. 68, 70, 82.

29. *New York Age*, June 23, 1888.

30. See Elisabeth Lasch-Quinn, *Black Neighbors: Race and the Limits of Reform in the American Settlement House Movement, 1890–1945* (Chapel Hill: University of North Carolina Press, 1993).

31. A variety of difficulties hamper attempts to recover biographical information for all committee members, particularly those in the early years. Records at the YWCA of the City of New York archives do not contain such information, and the fact that more than half of the committee's members between 1905 and 1910 were unmarried when they were active at the YWCA presents additional difficulties in locating information on those who married and changed their names.

32. *Twenty-Two Years' Work of the Hampton Normal and Agricultural Institute at Hampton, Virginia* (Hampton: Normal School Press, 1893), p. 83. Lucy Robinson also appears in the 1906–1907 *Trow General Directory of the Boroughs of Manhattan and Bronx, City of New York* as widowed and residing at 15 East 22nd Street.

33. *New York Age*, June 4, 1908.

34. Richard R. Wright Jr., *Centennial Encylopaedia of the African Methodist Episcopal Church* (Philadelphia: Book Concern of the A.M.E. Church, 1916), p. 237; Richard R. Wright Jr., *Encyclopaedia of the African Methodist Episcopal Church* (Philadelphia: Book Concern of the A.M.E. Church, 1947), p. 285.

35. *New York Age*, March 13, 1913.

36. EC, February 9, 1905, LPPRC.

37. *Thirty-Fifth Annual Report of the YWCA of the City of New York* (1906), p. 10; John W. Leonard, ed., *Who's Who in New York City and State* (New York: L. R. Hammersly, 1907); *Social Register* (New York, 1904, 1905, 1907).

38. *Seventy-Eighth Annual Report of the Woman's Branch of the New York City Mission and Tract Society* (February 1911), p. 3.

39. EC, November 2, 1905, LPPRC.

40. See, for example, EC, March 23, 1905, November 14, 1907, LPPRC; *Thirty-Fifth Annual Report of the YWCA of the City of New York* (1906), p. 27.

41. See, for example, *Thirty-Fifth Annual Report of the YWCA of the City of New York* (1906), p. 10.

42. EC, March 23, 1905, LPPRC.

43. Rayford W. Logan and Michael R. Winston, eds., *Dictionary of American Negro Biography* (New York: W. W. Norton, 1982), p. 54; *New York Age*, June 19, 1928, March 7, 1907.

44. EC, December 19, 1907, LPPRC.

45. EC, January 9, 1908; April 30, 1908, LPPRC. Bowles left this YWCA to teach in the public school system in Cincinnati and then took a position as a caseworker for Associated Charities in Columbus before returning to the YWCA's National Board. Logan and Winston, eds., *Dictionary of American Negro Biography*, p. 54; Joseph J. Boris, ed., *Who's Who in Colored America* (New York: Who's Who in Colored America Corp., 1929), p. 43.

46. EC, April 30, 1908; May 7, 1908; May 14, 1908, LPPRC.

47. Gretchen Maclachlan, "Addie Waites Hunton," in *Black Women in America: An Historical Encyclopedia*, ed. Darlene Clark Hine (Brooklyn, N.Y.: Carlson Publishing, 1993).

48. Addie W. Hunton, *William Alphaeus Hunton: A Pioneer Prophet of Young Men* (New York: Association Press, 1938), p. 17; Nina Mjagkij, "History of the Black YMCA in America, 1853–1946" (Ph.D. diss., University of Cincinnati, 1990), pp. 73–74, 80.

49. *New York Age*, June 18, 1908; July 9, 1908; August 20, 1908.

50. EC, October 1, 1908; October 8, 1908, LPPRC.

51. *New York Age*, September 2, 1909.

52. *New York Age*, September 9, 1909.

53. EC, January 7, 1909; February 4, 1909; February 11, 1909, LPPRC.

54. *The Woman's Era* 2, no. 4 (July 1895).

55. In 1896 the National Federation of Afro-American Women merged with the National League of Colored Women to become the National Association of Colored Women.

56. *New York Age*, February 14, 1908. Jones, a graduate of the Women's Medical College of Pennsylvania, went on to help found the Lincoln Settlement House in Brooklyn in 1908 and to work for the Committee for Improving the Conditions of Negroes in New York, one of the organizations that later became the National Urban League. Florence Barnett Cash, "Radicals or Realists: African American Women and the Settlement House Spirit in New York City," *Afro-Americans in New York Life and History* 15 (January 1991): 12.

57. *New York Age*, June 4, 1908.

58. *New York Age*, November 26, 1908; February 18, 1909.

59. *New York Age*, August 5, 1909; EC, May 3, 1909, LPPRC.

60. EC, April 14, 1910; May 5, 1910, LPPRC.

61. EC, November 3, 1910, LPPRC.

62. EC, March 23, 1911, LPPRC.

63. MB, May 8, 1911, LPPRC; *Seventy-Eighth Annual Report of the Woman's Branch of the New York City Mission and Tract Society* (February 1901), p. 43.

64. MB, October 9, 1911, LPPRC.

65. The merger brought together the YWCA at 7 East 15th Street, the Harlem YWCA at 72 West 124th Street, the West Side Branch at 501 West 50th Street, the Bronx YWCA at 329 East 176th Street, the French Branch at 124 West 16th Street, the Studio Club at 35 East 62nd Street, the International Institute at 108 East 30th Street, the Central Club for Nurses at 132 East 45th Street, and the African American YWCA. See Helen Bittar, "The YWCA of the City of New York: 1870–1920" (Ph.D. diss., New York University, 1979) for more on the history of the merger and the New York City YMCA's role in encouraging consolidation of YWCA work.

66. MB, May 8, 1911, LPPRC.

67. MB, December 11, 1911, LPPRC. Other Metropolitan Board budget items for that year included: board of directors, $3,767; International Institute, $7,500; West Side Branch, $3,500; Harlem Branch, $1,000; Nurses' Club, $1,000.

68. *New York Age,* January 11, 1912.

69. EC, February 2, 1905, LPPRC; *New York Age,* April 26, 1906; April 25, 1907; October 3, 1907; October 10, 1907; December 22, 1910; June 1, 1911; June 15, 1911; June 22, 1911.

70. Leonard left New York again in 1916 when she married the Rev. Albert H. Scott, pastor of the Fourth Methodist Episcopal Church in Boston. *New York Age,* October 5, 1911; December 17, 1914; April 27, 1916.

71. *Colored American Magazine* 10 (February 1906): 117; *New York Age,* January 6, 1910; March 17, 1910; January 12, 1911; June 15, 1911; August 18, 1912; April 10, 1913; May 22, 1915.

72. James Walker Hood, *One Hundred Years of the African Methodist Episcopal Zion Church; or The Centennial of African Methodism* (New York: A.M.E. Zion Book Concern, 1895), p. 537; *New York Age,* November 26, 1908; August 3, 1911.

73. Joseph J. Boris, ed., *Who's Who in Colored America* (New York: Who's Who in Colored America Corp., 1929), p. 94; *New York Age,* April 1, 1909; January 12, 1911; January 11, 1912; August 1, 1912; November 7, 1912. James L. Curtis's family belonged to the Washington, D.C., black elite. His brother, Austin Maurice Curtis, was a prominent physician from Raleigh, North Carolina, who became the director of the Freedman's Hospital. Austin's son, A. M. Curtis Jr., a graduate of Howard Medical School, became the house physician at Tuskegee in 1913. Willard Gatewood, *Aristocrats of Color: The Black Elite, 1880–1920* (Bloomington: Indiana University Press, 1990), p. 49; Thadious M. Davis, *Nella Larsen, Novelist of the Harlem Renaissance: A Woman's Life Unveiled* (Baton Rouge: Louisiana State University Press, 1994), p. 92.

74. Bittar, "YWCA of the City of New York," p. 47.

75. EC, March 23, 1911, LPPRC.

76. *New York Age,* July 6, 1911; September 14, 1911; October 5, 1911.

77. MB, October 9, 1911, LPPRC.

78. *New York Age,* January 27, 1910.

3. Constructing a Mobile Private Space

1. *The New York Freeman*, March 21, 1885; Richard T. W. Smith, "Militant Negro Churchmen: Fighters in the World's Battle for the Triumph of God's Kingdom on Earth," *Colored American Magazine* 1 (March 1907).

2. Roi Ottley and William J. Weatherby, eds., *The Negro in New York: An Informal Social History* (New York: New York Public Library and Oceana Publications, 1967), p. 135.

3. *The New York Freeman*, November 13, 1886; April 5, 1890, in *Aristocrats of Color: The Black Elite, 1880–1920*, by Williard Gatewood (Bloomington: Indiana University Press, 1990), p. 222.

4. James Weldon Johnson, *Along This Way* (New York: Penguin Books, 1990), pp. 170–177; Timothy J. Gilfoyle, *City of Eros: New York City, Prostitution, and the Commercialization of Sex, 1790–1920* (New York: W. W. Norton, 1992), p. 210.

5. *New York Age*, June 13, 1907; June 20, 1907.

6. EC, December 13, 1906; December 20, 1906; January 10, 1907; January 14, 1907; March 14, 1907; April 4, 1907, LPPRC.

7. Mary P. Ryan, *Women in Public: Between Banners and Ballots, 1825–1880* (Baltimore: Johns Hopkins University Press, 1990), p. 176.

8. These riots supposedly gave rise to the neighborhood's name, offering a comparison with battles of the Spanish-American War. See Gilbert Osofsky, *Harlem: The Making of a Ghetto, Negro New York, 1890–1930* (New York: Harper & Row, 1963), p. 13; Mary White Ovington, *Half a Man: The Status of the Negro in New York City* (1911; reprint, New York: Negro Universities Press, 1969), p. 39.

9. *New York Age*, July 11, 1907.

10. *New York Age*, February 14, 1907.

11. Ryan, *Women in Public*, p. 149. According to Adrian Cook's figures, 241 of the rioters identified were male and nineteen were female. More than half were between the ages of twenty-one and forty; most were factory workers or unskilled laborers, while some were skilled tradesmen. The vast majority of those identified as rioters were Irish, most of these born in Ireland. Adrian Cook, *The Armies of the Streets: The New York City Draft Riots of 1863* (Lexington: University Press of Kentucky, 1974), pp. 195–198.

12. See James M. McPherson, *Ordeal by Fire: The Civil War and Reconstruction* (New York: Knopf, 1982), p. 360; Ottley and Weatherby, eds., *Negro in New York*, pp. 116–118.

13. James Weldon Johnson, *Black Manhattan* (1930; reprint, New York: Da Capo Press, 1991), p. 52; Ryan, *Women in Public*, p. 151; Cook, *Armies of the Streets*, pp. 77–78.

14. Cook, *Armies of the Streets*, pp. 199–200, 312, n. 24.

15. Ibid., pp. 132, 134–135, 203.

16. Ibid., pp. 79–80, 312 n. 30.

17. Some of the press reports refer to her as May Eno. I have used Enoch throughout.

18. *The People vs. Arthur J. Harris*, October 29, 1900, in Osofsky, *Harlem*, p. 47.

19. *The Sun*, August 16, 1900; *New York Herald*, August 16, 1900.

20. See Gilfoyle, *City of Eros*, p. 208, for a map of houses of prostitution in the area.

21. *New York Herald*, August 16, 1900; August 17, 1900.

22. *The Sun*, August 18, 1900.

23. *The Sun*, August 20, 1900.

24. *The Sun*, August 22, 1900; August 24, 1900; *New York Herald*, August 25, 1900.

25. The committee's membership included Bishop Walters of the African Methodist Episcopal Zion Church and Bishop Derrick of the African Methodist Episcopal Church. *New York Herald*, August 19, 1900.

26. [Frank Moss], *Story of the Riot: Persecution of Negroes by Roughs and Policemen, in the City of New York, August, 1900* (New York, 1900).

27. *New York Herald*, August 18, 1900; Herman W. Knox, ed., *Who's Who in New York: A Biographical Dictionary of Prominent Citizens of New York City and State* (New York: Who's Who Publications, 1918), p. 782.

28. *The Sun*, August 18, 1900.

29. *Story of the Riot*, back cover.

30. See, for example, *Story of the Riot; New York Tribune*, August 17, 1900; *The Sun*, August 16, 1900.

31. *Story of the Riot*, pp. 1, 5.

32. John Gilmer Speed, *Harper's Weekly*, December 22, 1900.

33. Herbert G. Gutman, *The Black Family in Slavery and Freedom, 1750–1925* (New York: Vintage Books, 1976), p. 506.

34. Ibid., p. 450; Ovington, *Half a Man*, p. 35.

35. Gutman, *Black Family*, p. 522.

36. Ibid., p. 508.

37. Ibid., p. 451.

38. *Harper's Weekly*, December 22, 1900.

39. See Hazel V. Carby, "Policing the Black Woman's Body in an Urban Context," *Critical Inquiry* 18 (summer 1992): 738–755, for a discussion of Kellor's contribution to fostering a sense of "moral panic" concerning black women in cities.

40. Frances A. Kellor, "Assisted Emigration from the South," *Charities* 15 (October 7, 1905): 13.

41. Kellor, "Assisted Emigration," p. 13.

42. Ovington, *Half a Man*, p. 148.

43. *Story of the Riot*, pp. 60–61.

44. EC, November 3, 1910, LPPRC.

45. Nannie Helen Burroughs, "The Colored Woman and Her Relation to the Domestic Problem," in *The United Negro: His Problems and His Progress, Containing the Addresses and Proceedings of the Negro Young People's Christian and Educational Congress, Held August 6–11, 1902*, ed. I. Garland Penn and J. W. E. Bowen (1902; reprint, New York: Negro Universities Press, 1969), p. 328.

46. Claudia Tate, "Allegories of Black Female Desire; or, Rereading Nineteenth-Century Sentimental Narratives of Black Female Authority," in *Changing Our Own Words: Essays on Criticism, Theory, and Writing by Black Women*, ed. Cheryl A. Wall (New Brunswick, N.J.: Rutgers University Press, 1989), p. 99.

47. Penn and Bowen, eds., *The United Negro*, pp. 433–434.

48. Ibid., p. 434.

49. Addie W. Hunton, "A Deeper Reverence for Home Ties," *The Colored American Magazine* 12 (January 1907): 59.

50. Emma S. Ransom, "The Home-Made Girl" (n.p., 1905), p. 1.

51. Ibid., p. 4.

52. Ibid., p. 3.

53. Ibid., p. 5.

54. Ibid., p. 6.

55. *YWCA of the City of New York, Thirty-Fifth Annual Report* (New York, 1906), p. 43; EC, December 3, 1906, April 4, 1907, LPPRC; MB, May 12, 1913, LPPRC.

56. The branch needed $25 a month to supplement the $60 appropriation from 15th Street in order to meet the rent. EC, September 4, 1905, LPPRC; *New York Age*, December 14, 1905.

57. *New York Age*, February 10, 1910.

58. *New York Age*, December 14, 1905.

59. *YWCA of the City of New York, Thirty-Ninth Annual Report* (New York, 1910), p. 23; *New York Age*, November 26, 1908.

60. *New York Age*, December 6, 1906; March 10, 1910; June 1, 1911.

61. *New York Age*, March 18, 1909.

62. *New York Age*, July 27, 1911.

63. *New York Age*, April 26, 1906; September 20, 1906; May 7, 1908; May 6, 1909; November 25, 1909; May 1, 1911; January 18, 1912. For additional information on Grace Campbell, see *New York Age*, January 18, 1912; March 28, 1912; January 30, 1913; May 15, 1913; July 24, 1913; December 21, 1918; Mark Naison, *Communists in Harlem During the Depression* (New York: Grove Press, 1983), pp. 5–7, 20–22. On DeLaney, see Sandy D. Martin, "Spelman's Emma B. DeLaney and the African Mission," in *This Far by Faith: Readings in African-American Women's Religious Biography*, ed. Judith Weisenfeld and Richard Newman (New York: Routledge, 1995), pp. 220–235.

64. It is difficult to determine with certainty at all times the boundary between the writers in the *Age* and the leadership of this branch of the YWCA. Because T. Thomas Fortune and Fred R. Moore, the editors and publishers of the paper, sometimes attended meetings and (based on a reading of various editorials and feature articles on the branch) greatly valued and supported the work of the African American women in this YWCA, it is not unlikely that a reporter sometimes also attended Sunday meetings and other events. It is just as likely, however, that the weekly accounts of YWCA activities in this paper were placed by a "correspondent" who, as with correspondents from local churches and other groups, was also a member of the organization.

65. *New York Age*, February 6, 1908; February 14, 1908; July 18, 1907; April 28, 1910; June 8, 1911; September 21, 1911.

66. *New York Age*, October 3, 1907; December 5, 1907; May 4, 1911; January 1, 1907; August 10, 1911.

67. Osofsky, *Harlem*, pp. 63–64; Philip Foner and Ronald L. Lewis, eds., *The Black Worker, vol. V, 1900–1919* (Philadelphia: Temple University Press, 1980), pp. 34–39; *New York Age*, June 21, 1906.

68. *New York Age*, May 17, 1906; August 23, 1908; May 12, 1910; June 15, 1911.

69. *New York Age*, June 27, 1907; July 2, 1908; April 14, 1910; June 1, 1911.

70. *New York Age*, June 27, 1907; April 15, 1909; April 14, 1910; June 1, 1911.

71. Carby, "Policing," p. 741.

4. Building on the Urban Frontier

1. On Battles, see *New York Age*, March 25, 1915; Richard R. Wright, *Centennial Encyclopedia of the AME Church* (Philadelphia: Book Concern of the A.M.E. Church, 1916), p. 331. Incorporated into New York City in 1873, Harlem's boundaries have never been firmly defined. Gilbert Osofsky places the nineteenth-century boundaries at 110th Street to 155th Street between the East River and Morningside and St. Nicholas Avenues. Gilbert Osofsky, *Harlem: The Making of a Ghetto* (New York: Harper, 1971) pp. 75, 235.

2. *New York Age*, May 29, 1913.

3. James Weldon Johnson, *Black Manhattan* (1930; reprint, New York: Da Capo Press, 1991), pp. 3–4.

4. Leonard Thompson and Howard Lamar, "Comparative Frontier History," in *The Frontier in History: North America and Southern Africa Compared*, ed. Howard Lamar and Leonard Thompson (New Haven: Yale University Press, 1981), p. 7.

5. Ibid., p. 10.

6. *Harlem Rides the Range* is the title of a 1939 "all-colored cast" cowboy film.

7. *New York Herald*, December 24, 1905.

8. "Heart of Harlem Now Invaded by Negroes," *Harlem Home News*, July 28, 1911, quoted in Osofsky, *Harlem*, p. 107. See Osofsky, *Harlem*, p. 105, for more on war as a metaphor in this particular contest.

9. Osofsky, *Harlem*, p. 106.

10. T. Dunbar Moodie's study, *The Rise of Afrikanerdom: Power, Apartheid and the Afrikaner Civil Religion* (Berkeley: University of California Press, 1980), demonstrates connections between aspects of Dutch Reformed theology and the development of a racialized, nationalist theology among Afrikaners in South Africa in the eighteenth and nineteenth centuries. An unexplored question, beyond the scope of this study, concerns the potential relationship between Dutch Reformed theology among white Harlemites and their response to the "invasion" of Harlem by African Americans.

11. *The Crisis*, March 1914, July 1914.

12. *Harlem Home News*, April 7, 1911.

13. Ibid.

14. *New York Age*, January 29, 1914.

15. *New York Age*, May 26, 1910; January 19, 1911; June 8, 1911; August 18, 1912; January 16, 1913; January 30, 1913; March 6, 1913; January 8, 1914; February 12, 1914; May 21, 1914; July 30, 1914; September 17, 1914.

16. *The Crisis*, March 1914.

17. Osofsky, *Harlem*, p. 94.

18. Ibid., pp. 88–89, 117.

19. Ibid., pp. 110–112.

20. *New York Age*, April 24, 1913.

21. *New York Age*, May 18, 1911.

22. MB, May 12, 1913.

23. *New York Age*, January 11, 1912; December 31, 1914; *The Crisis*, December 1915, June 1917; *Colored American Magazine* 10 (February 1906): 117.

24. *New York Age*, May 22, 1913.

25. *New York Age*, July 17, 1913.

26. MB, February 9, 1914; October 5, 1914; *New York Age*, July 17, 1913.

27. Helen Bittar "The YWCA of the City of New York, 1870–1920" (Ph.D. diss., New York University, 1979), p. 50; *Financial Report of the Joint Campaign Committee of the Young Women's and Young Men's Christian Associations on the Results of the $4,000,000 Campaign Fund*, January 22, 1917.

28. Reverdy C. Ransom, *The Pilgrimage of Harriet Ransom's Son* (Nashville: AME Sunday School Union, n.d.), p. 203.

29. Ibid., pp. 203–204.

30. In addition to these projects, the money was also used for the Central Club for Nurses at 132 East 45th Street; a boarding home; and property improvements on the West Side Branch at 50th Street and Tenth Avenue. *Financial Report of the Joint Campaign Committee of the Young Women's and Young Men's Christian Associations on the Results of the $4,000,000 Campaign Fund*, January 22, 1917, pp. 7–10.

31. *New York Age*, October 30, 1913; November 13, 1913.

32. *New York Age*, October 30, 1913.

33. Ibid.

34. Jane Olcott-Walters, *History of Colored Work, Chronological Excerpts From Reports of Secretaries and Workers and From Minutes Showing the Development of the Work Among Colored Women, November 1907–December 1920*, p. 24, NBA; Monroe N. Work, *Negro Year Book and Annual Encyclopedia of the Negro* (Tuskegee, Ala., 1915), p. 191.

35. "Women Pass Men in Y.M.C.A. Campaign," unidentified clipping, November 1913, Mary Gould Papers, NBA.

36. *New York Age*, November 13, 1913; "Women Pass Men in Y.M.C.A. Campaign."

37. *New York Age*, October 30, 1913; November 6, 1913; November 13, 1913. On Lafayette Hall, see Osofsky, *Harlem*, pp. 108–109.

38. *New York Age*, November 6, 1913; November 13, 1913; November 20, 1913.

39. *New York Age*, November 20, 1913.

40. *New York Times*, November 14, 1913; *New York Age*, November 20, 1913.

41. *New York Age*, November 13, 1913; *The Crisis*, January 1914; *New York Times*, November 11, 1913.

42. *New York Times*, November 11, 1913; November 26, 1913; "Women Pass Men in Y.M.C.A. Campaign."

43. "Women Pass Men in Y.M.C.A. Campaign."

44. *Financial Report of the Joint Campaign Committee*, January 22, 1917, p. 3.

45. *New York Times*, November 26, 1913; *Financial Report of the Joint Campaign Committee*, January 22, 1917, p. 3.

46. *New York Age*, November 27, 1913.

47. *New York Times*, November 8, 1913.

48. *The Crisis*, January 1914.

49. *The Crisis*, December 1914.

50. *New York Age*, April 8, 1915.

51. *New York Age*, May 7, 1914.

52. *New York Times*, November 26, 1913; *Financial Report of the Joint Campaign Committee*, January 22, 1917, p. 3.

53. BD, April, 12, 1915.

54. Starr J. Murphy to George W. Perkins, July 3, 1912, folder 463, box 41, Welfare Interests—Youth Files—YWCA—New York City—Contributions, 1912–1917, Record Group 2, RFA.

55. MB, November 8, 1915.

56. MB, December 13, 1915.

57. Ibid.

58. MB, March 13, 1916; December 11, 1916.

59. See G. W. Bromley, *Atlas of the City of New York—Borough of Manhattan* (Philadelphia: G. W. Bromley, 1914).

60. Williard B. Gatewood, *Aristocrats of Color: the Black Elite, 1880–1920* (Bloomington: University of Indiana Press, 1990), p. 14; Robert C. Morris, *Reading, 'Riting and Reconstruction: The Education of Freedmen in the South, 1861–1870* (Chicago: University of Chicago Press, 1981), pp. 103, 271–272.

61. *Fisk News* 32 (March 1959): 4; Dorothy Salem, *To Better Our World: Black Women in Organized Reform, 1880–1920* (Brooklyn, N.Y.: Carlson Publishing, 1990), pp. 130–131.

62. *New York Age*, August 18, 1912; May 8, 1913.

63. Olcott-Walters, *History of Colored Work*, p. 19; *New York Age*, February 13, 1913; October 31, 1912.

64. *New York Age*, January 1, 1914; March 26, 1914.

65. Beresford Sylvester Briggs Trottman, *Who's Who in Harlem: The 1949–1950 Biographical Register of a Group of Distinguished Persons of New York's Harlem* (New York: Magazine & Periodical Printing & Publishing, 1950), p. 39.

66. *New York Age*, July 16, 1914.

67. *New York Age*, July 23, 1914.

68. *Journal of the Eighth Annual Assembly of the Woman's Convention Held in the First Baptist Church of Lexington, Kentucky, September 16–21, 1908* (Nashville: National Baptist Publishing Board, 1909), p. 243, quoted in Evelyn Brooks Higginbotham, *Righteous Discontent: The Women's Movement in the Black Baptist Church* (Cambridge: Harvard University Press, 1993), p. 208.

5. Wars at Home and Abroad

1. AME Bishops' Memorial to Congress (1919), quoted in Daniel Alexander Payne, *History of the African Methodist Episcopal Church*, ed. Charles Spencer Smith (Nashville: Publishing House of the AME Sunday School Union, 1922), p. 395.

2. *The Christian Index*, September 11, 1919, quoted in Robert T. Kerlin, ed., *The Voice of the Negro* (New York, 1920; reprint, New York: Arno Press, 1968), p. 180.

3. James Weldon Johnson, *Black Manhattan* (1930; reprint, New York: Da Capo Press, 1991), p. 152; Carole Marks, *Farewell—We're Good and Gone: The Great Black Migration* (Bloomington: Indiana University Press, 1989), p. 122.

4. *War Work Bulletin*, June 13, 1919.

5. United War Work Campaign posters.

6. *War Work Bulletin*, November 8, 1918.

7. "The Colored Girl a National Asset," National Board of the Young Women's Christian Association, January 1919.

8. *New York Age*, March 29, 1917.

9. *The Crisis*, May 1917, p. 111.

10. Quoted in Arthur E. Barbeau and Florette Henri, *The Unknown Soldiers: Black American Troops in World War I* (Philadelphia: Temple University Press, 1974), p. 12; *The Messenger*, January 1918, in *A Documentary History of the Negro People in the United States*, vol. 3, by Herbert Aptheker (New York: Citadel Press, 1973), p. 195.

11. Johnson, *Black Manhattan*, p. 233.

12. *Nineteenth Annual Session of the Woman's Convention* (1918), quoted in Evelyn Brooks Higginbotham, *Righteous Discontent: The Women's Movement in the Black Baptist Church* (Cambridge: Harvard University Press, 1993), p. 225.

13. Higginbotham, *Righteous Discontent*, pp. 225–226.

14. Barbeau and Henri, *Unknown Soldiers*, p. 17.

15. U.S. Army, War College, *Colored Soldiers in the U.S. Army* (Washington, D.C.: Government Printing Office, 1942), p. 4, in *Unknown Soldiers*, by Barbeau and Henri, p. 31.

16. Elliott Rudwick, *Race Riot at East St. Louis* (Cleveland: Meridian Press, 1966); David Levering Lewis, *W. E. B. Du Bois, Biography of a Race, 1868–1919* (New York: Henry Holt, 1993), pp. 536–537; Barbeau and Henri, *Unknown Soldiers*, pp. 23–26.

17. *New York Age*, August 2, 1917; Nell Irvin Painter, *Standing at Armageddon* (New York: W. W. Norton, 1987), pp. 337–338; Johnson, *Black Manhattan*, pp. 236–237.

18. Johnson, *Black Manhattan*, p. 237.

19. Barbeau and Henri, *Unknown Soldiers*, p. 27.

20. Ibid., p. 44.

21. Ibid., pp. 71–72.

22. Quoted in Barbeau and Henri, *Unknown Soldiers*, pp. 72–73.

23. Ibid., pp. 73, 111.

24. Ibid., p. 116; W. Allison Sweeny, *History of the American Negro in the Great World War* (n.p., 1919), pp. 146–149.

25. Johnson, *Black Manhattan*, p. 245.

26. Stephen Vaughn, *Holding Fast the Inner Lines: Democracy, Nationalism, and the Committee on Public Information* (Chapel Hill: University of North Carolina Press, 1980), p. 207.

27. Quoted in Vaughn, *Holding Fast*, p. 124.

28. *Year Book of the Young Women's Christian Associations of the U.S.A.* (New York, 1917), p. 93. In 1916–1917 the YWCA recognized the Baltimore, Brooklyn, Denver, Indianapolis, Kalamazoo, Montclair, New York City, Philadelphia, Richmond, Rochester, St. Louis, Washington, and Yonkers African American associations.

29. Jane Olcott, *The Work of Colored Women* (New York: Colored Work Committee—War Work Council of the National Board YWCA, n.d.), p. 133.

30. *Report of the Commission on Social Morality from the Christian Standpoint, Made to the Fourth Biennial Convention of the YWCAs of the U.S., Richmond, Virginia, April 9–13, 1913*, in *The Christian Approach to Social Morality* (New York: National Board of the YWCA, 1913), p. 88.

31. William J. Robinson, M.D., *Sex Knowledge for Women and Girls* (New York: The Critic & Guide Company, 1917), p. 9.

32. Ibid., p. 11.

33. Ibid., p. 12.

34. "The Consecration of the Affections," Lecture II, in *The Christian Approach to Social Morality*, p. 46.

35. *Report of the Commission on Social Morality from the Christian Standpoint.*

36. *War Work Bulletin*, August 21, 1917.

37. "The Girl You Leave Behind" (New York: YWCA National Board, n.d.).

38. Addie Hunton and Kathryn Johnson, *Two Colored Women with the American Expeditionary Forces* (New York: Brooklyn Eagle Press, n.d.).

39. Will Irwin, "Conquering an Old Enemy" (New York: American Social Hygiene Association, 1920), p. 2.

40. James H. Jones, *Bad Blood: The Tuskegee Syphilis Experiment* (New York: The Free Press, 1993), p. 24.

41. Daniel David Quillian, "Racial Peculiarities as a Cause of the Prevalence of Syphilis in Negroes," *Medical Era* 20 (1911): 417, and James M. McIntosh, "The Future of the Negro Race," *Transactions of the South Carolina Medical Association* 41 (1891): 186, quoted in *Bad Blood*, by Jones, p. 25.

42. The Tuskegee experiment represents the most egregious form of this inattention. In this experiment, the U.S. Public Health Service observed 399 African American men who were infected with syphilis over a period of forty years and, as part of the study, withheld information and proper treatment from them. See Jones, *Bad Blood*, for a full-length treatment of the study.

43. Dr. Max J. Exner to Charles O. Heydt, April 5, 1917, folder 426, box 39, Welfare Interests—Youth Files—YWCA—National Board—Sex Lectures—1913–1918, Record Group 2, RFA.

44. CWC, January 12, 1918, NBA; *War Work Bulletin*, August 30, 1918; *New York Age*, September 28, 1918; *The Crisis*, October 1918.

45. *Report of the Social Morality Committee, War Work Council, National Board, Young Women's Christian Associations, July 1917, to July 1919.* Whipper, one of four female graduates of Howard University Medical School's class of 1903, had worked as a physician at Collegiate Institute in West Virginia and at Tuskegee Institute, and therefore was familiar with health issues at colleges. In the 1920s, she served as an assistant medical officer for the Children's Bureau of the Department of Labor and traveled in the South instructing midwives. She later founded the Ionia Rollin Whipper Home for Unwed Mothers in Washington, D.C. Brown received a B.S. degree from Cornell University and graduated from Howard University Medical School in 1904. Sara W. Brown, M.D., "Fundamentals of Race Progress," *Southern Workman* (December 1921): 538; Sara W. Brown, M.D., "Colored Women Physicians," *Southern Workman* (December 1923): 580–593; Carole Ione, *Pride of Family: Four Generations of American Women of Color* (New York: Summit Books, 1991), pp. 24–25.

46. *Budget of the War Work Council, National Board of the YWCA, Estimates to Cover Necessary Expenditures, June 1917–June 1918*, box 39, folder 432, War Work Campaign—1917–1920, Record Group 2, RFA.

47. For more on Hope, see Jacqueline A. Rouse, *Lugenia Burns Hope: Black Southern Reformer* (Athens: University of Georgia Press, 1989).

48. Jane Olcott, *The Work of Colored Women* (New York: Colored Work Committee War Work Council, National Board, n.d.), p. 135.

49. Olcott, *The Work of Colored Women*, pp. 17–18.

50. CWC, January 25, 1918, NBA.

51. Ibid.

52. *War Work Bulletin*, August 30, 1918.

53. *War Work Bulletin*, July 11, 1919.

54. *New York Age*, May 4, 1918.

55. *New York Age*, June 15, 1918.

56. *New York Age*, May 24, 1917; June 14, 1917; September 27, 1917.

57. *New York Age*, February 9, 1918; April 6, 1918; July 29, 1918; Alice Dunbar Nelson, "Negro Women in War Work," in *The American Negro in the World War*, by Emmett J. Scott (n.p., 1919), reprinted in *Black Heritage in Social Welfare*, ed. Edyth L. Ross (Metuchen, N.J.: Scarecrow Press, 1978), p. 395.

58. *Journal of the National Medical Association* 10 (January–March 1918): 52–53.

59. *New York Age*, January 26, 1918.

60. *New York Age*, December 8, 1917.

61. *New York Age*, June 28, 1917; January 19, 1918; February 2, 1918; April 20, 1918; May 14, 1918.

62. *War Work Bulletin*, September 28, 1917.

63. *New York Age*, October 25, 1917; November 22, 1917.

64. Olcott, *The Work of Colored Women*, p. 79; CWC, February 23, 1918, NBA.

65. MB, March 11, 1918; *New York Age*, June 29, 1918; June 14, 1919; July 5, 1919; August 30, 1919; Olcott, *The Work of Colored Women*, pp. 79–80. On Fisher, see Debra Newman Ham, "Ruth Anna Fisher," in *Black Women in America: An Historical Encyclopedia*, ed. Darlene Clark Hine (Brooklyn, N.Y.: Carlson Publishing, 1993).

66. *New York Age*, February 1, 1917.

67. *New York Age*, August 23, 1917.

68. *New York Age*, September 20, 1917.

69. *New York Age*, January 26, 1918; March 30, 1918; May 11, 1918; December 21, 1918; Cecelia Cabaniss Saunders, "A Half-Century of the Harlem Branch of the Young Women's Christian Association," rough draft typescript, 1955, p. 6, LPPRC.

70. *New York Age*, March 23, 1918; February 1, 1919; April 5, 1919; May 17, 1919.

71. Saunders, "Half-Century," p. 5.

72. *War Work Bulletin*, December 6, 1918.

73. On McDougald, who eventually became the first black female school principal in New York and chaired the African American YWCA's employment and industries committee, see Beresford Sylvester Briggs Trottman, *Who's Who in Harlem: The 1949–1950 Biographical Register of a Group of Distinguished Persons of New York's Harlem* (New York: Magazine & Periodical Printing & Publishing, 1950), p. 21, and Olivia Pearl Stokes in *The Black Women Oral History Project*, vol. 9, ed. Ruth Edmonds Hill and Patricia Miller King (Westport, Conn.: Meckler Publishing, 1991), p. 135.

74. Olcott, *The Work of Colored Women*, p. 81.

75. *New York Age*, March 22, 1919.

76. *War Work Bulletin*, May 3, 1918.

77. See David R. Roediger, *The Wages of Whiteness: Race and the Making of the American Working Class* (London: Verso Press, 1992).

78. CWC, January 25, 1919, NBA.

79. *New York Age*, December 7, 1918; March 5, 1919; CWC, February 7, 1919, NBA.

80. James Weldon Johnson, "The Making of Harlem," *Survey Graphic* VI, no. 6 (March 1925): 637; M. A. Harris, *A Negro History Tour of Manhattan* (New York: Greenwood Publishing, 1968), pp. 98–99.

81. Saunders, "Half Century," p. 6; MB, October 14, 1919, p. 2; *New York Age*, November 22, 1919. The YWCA adapted the Blue Triangle symbol from the YMCA's Red Triangle. "The base is Spirit, and the two sides are Knowledge and Health. This means that the Blue Triangle girl is physically fit, is mentally and morally trained and filled with an understanding spirit." *The Girl Reserves, A Manual for Leaders* (1918), p. 45, in *The Girl Reserve Movement of the Young Women's Christian Association: An Analysis of the Educational Principles and Procedures Used Throughout Its History*, by Catherine S. Vance (New York: Bureau of Publications, Teacher's College, 1937), pp. 43–44.

82. *Blue Triangle News*, January 16, 1920.

83. Minnie M. Newman, *Handbook of Racial and Nationality Backgrounds* (New York: National Board of the YWCA, 1922).

84. Olcott, *The Work of Colored Women*, p. 122.

85. *New York Age*, October 25, 1919.

86. MB, January 13, 1919; February 10, 1919; December 8, 1919.

6. Black America's Community Center

1. *Y.W.C.A., Harlem, New York* (Harmon Foundation, 1940), HF247, National Archives and Records Administration.

2. Janet Forsythe Fishburn, *The Fatherhood of God and the Victorian Family* (Philadelphia: Fortress Press, 1981), p. 15.

3. *Proceedings of the National Convention of the Y.W.C.A.* (1920), quoted in Grace H. Wilson, *The Religious and Educational Philosophy of the Young Women's Christian Association* (New York: Teacher's College, 1933), pp. 84–85.

4. Wilson, *Religious and Educational Philosophy*, p. 85.

5. Alain Locke, "Enter the New Negro," *Survey Graphic* VI, no. 6 (March 1925): 630.

6. Jervis Anderson, *This Was Harlem: A Cultural Portrait, 1900–1950* (New York: Farrar, Straus, Giroux, 1981), p. 186.

7. James Weldon Johnson, *Black Manhattan* (1930; reprint, New York: Da Capo Press, 1991), p. 163.

8. See, for example, Arthur Huff Fauset, *Black Gods of the Metropolis* (Philadelphia: University of Pennsylvania Press, 1944); Howard Brotz, *The Black Jews of Harlem: Negro Nationalism and the Dilemma of Negro Leadership* (New York: Schocken Books, 1970); Jill Watt, *God, Harlem, USA* (Berkeley, 1992); Robert Weisbrot, *Father Divine and the Struggle for Racial Equality* (Urbana: University of Illinois Press, 1983); Hans A. Baer and Merrill Singer, *African-American Religion in the Twentieth Century: Varieties of Protest and Accommodation* (Knoxville: University of Tennessee Press, 1992).

9. Cecelia Cabaniss Saunders, "A Half-Century of the Harlem Branch of the Young Women's Christian Association," rough draft typescript, 1955, p. 71, LPPRC.

10. Interview with Olivia Pearl Stokes in *The Black Women Oral History Project*, vol. 9, ed. Ruth Edmonds Hill and Patricia Miller King (Westport, Conn.: Meckler Publishing, 1991), p. 138.

11. MB, January 19, 1920; April 12, 1920; May 18, 1921.

12. *New York Age*, February 14, 1920.

13. Interview with Olivia Pearl Stokes in *Black Women Oral History*, vol. 9, ed. Hill and King, pp. 142–143.

14. Interview with the author, July 29, 1992.

15. Saunders, "Half-Century," p. 9.

16. Adah B. Thoms, *Pathfinders: A History of the Progress of Colored Graduate Nurses* (New York: Kay Printing House, 1929), pp. 214, 217.

17. Saunders, "Half-Century," p. 41.

18. Ibid., p. 69.

19. Ibid., pp. 6, 80, 96, 107, 133; New York City YWCA brochure, folder 459, box 41, Welfare Interests—Youth Files—YWCA—New York City—Pledge, 1927–1928, Record Group 2, RFA.

20. Anna Arnold Hedgeman, *The Trumpet Sounds: A Memoir of Negro Leadership* (New York: Holt, Rinehart & Winston, 1946), p. 45.

21. Anna Arnold Hedgeman to the editor, *New York Post*, March 10, 1958; interview with Dorothy I. Height in *Black Women Oral History*, vol. 5, ed. Hill and King, p. 66.

22. Telephone interview with Florence Ellis Dickerson, July 19, 1995.

23. James Weldon Johnson, "The Making of Harlem," *Survey Graphic* VI, no. 6 (March 1925), p. 637; *New York Times*, December 28, 1923.

24. Mrs. William Rossiter to Raymond Fosdick, folder 484, box 43, Welfare Interests—Youth Files—YWCA—New York City—Harlem, 1925, Record Group 2, RFA.

25. W. S. Richardson to Mrs. William Rossiter, May 13, 1924, folder 484, box 43, Welfare Interests—Youth Files—YWCA—New York City—Harlem, 1925, Record Group 2, RFA.

26. W. S. Richardson to John D. Rockefeller Jr., December 15, 1924, folder 484, box 43, Welfare Interests—Youth Files—YWCA—New York City—Harlem, 1925, Record Group 2, RFA.

27. W. S. Richardson to Mrs. Edward Perry Townsend, January 3, 1924; W. S. Richardson to Mrs. Edward Perry Townsend, February 7, 1925; W. S. Richardson to Mrs. Edward Perry Townsend, May 11, 1925, folder 484, box 43, Welfare Interests—Youth Files—YWCA—New York City—Harlem, 1925, Record Group 2, RFA.

28. Saunders, "Half-Century," p. 11.

29. Mrs. Edward Perry Townsend to John D. Rockefeller Jr., December 27, 1926, folder 484, box 43, Welfare Interests—Youth Files—YWCA—New York City—Harlem, 1925, Record Group 2, RFA; *New York Age*, April 17, 1926.

30. Cecelia Saunders and Susan P. Wortham to John D. Rockefeller Jr., May 12, 1925, folder 484, box 43, Welfare Interests—Youth Files—YWCA—New York City—Harlem, 1925, Record Group 2, RFA.

31. John D. Rockefeller Jr. to Cecelia Saunders and Susan P. Wortham, May 25, 1925, folder 484, box 43, Welfare Interests—Youth Files—YWCA—New York City—Harlem, 1925, Record Group 2, RFA.

32. Cecelia Saunders to John D. Rockefeller Jr., June 20, 1925, folder 484, box 43, Welfare Interests—Youth Files—YWCA—New York City—Harlem, 1925, Record Group 2, RFA.

33. Saunders, "Half-Century," pp. 14, 48, 66, 87.

34. Cecelia Cabaniss Saunders to Emma Ransom, June 27, 1936, LPPRC.

35. "Information Booklet for Our Guests," 1937–1938, LPPRC.

36. MB, October 20, 1930; April 20, 1931; December 21, 1931; February 15, 1931; press release, April 5, 1930, LPPRC.

37. Vera Scott Cushman to John D. Rockefeller Jr., December 6, 1915, folder 463, box 41, Welfare Interests—Youth Files—YWCA—New York City—Contributions, 1912–1917, Record Group 2, RFA; MB, January 13, 1919, LPPRC; Saunders, "Half-Century," pp. 10, 55.

38. Saunders, "Half-Century," p. 7.

39. Ibid., p. 55.

40. MB, February 21, 1921; March 21, 1921.

41. Saunders, "Half-Century," p. 91.

42. *New York Age*, April 1, 1909.

43. *New York Age*, February 14, 1907; May 4, 1908; September 11, 1913; November 1, 1919; September 25, 1920.

44. *New York Age*, November 5, 1908; May 20, 1909; September 22, 1910; February 16, 1911; July 17, 1913; October 19, 1916; January 11, 1917; September 25, 1920.

45. *Fisk News* 32 (March 1959): 4; Saunders, "Half-Century," p. 11; Jackson Davis to John D. Rockefeller Jr., October 11, 1929, folder 487, box 43, Welfare Interests—Youth Files—YWCA—New York City—Harlem, Additional Land and Building, 1930–1934, Record Group 2, RFA; Gerda Lerner, ed., *Black Women in White America: A Documentary History* (New York: Vintage Books, 1992), p. 252.

46. "Business School," 1923–1924; "Educational Classes," 1924–1925, West 137th Street YWCA, LPPRC.

47. Thadious M. Davis, *Nella Larsen, Novelist of the Harlem Renaissance: A Woman's Life Unveiled* (Baton Rouge: Louisiana State University Press, 1994), pp. 227, 291.

48. "Educational Classes," 1925–1926, 1927–1928, 1932–1933, West 137th Street YWCA, LPPRC.

49. Saunders, "Half-Century," pp. 14, 32, 118.

50. "The New Trade School," 1931–1932, West 137th Street YWCA, LPPRC.

51. "The New Trade School," 1931–1932; "The Trade School," 1932–1933, 1935–1936, West 137th Street YWCA, LPPRC.

52. Anna Arnold Hedgeman to the editor, *New York Post*, March 10, 1958.

53. "The Trade School," 1935–1936, 1937–1938, 1939–1940, West 137th Street YWCA, LPPRC.

54. Cecelia Cabaniss Saunders to Emma Ransom, June 24, 1940, LPPRC.

55. Beresford Sylvester Briggs Trottman, *Who's Who in Harlem* (New York: Magazine & Periodical Printing & Publishing, 1950), p. 28.

56. Cecelia Cabaniss Saunders, testimony before Mayor's Commission on Conditions in Harlem, Hearing on Racial Discrimination in Employment, April 13, 1935, box 3770, LAG.

57. Telephone interview with Florence Ellis Dickerson, July 19, 1995.

58. Cecelia Cabaniss Saunders, testimony before Mayor's Commission on Conditions in Harlem, April 13, 1935, box 3770, LAG.

59. *New York Age*, September 13, 1917.

60. *New York Age*, November 6, 1920.

61. Cheryl Lynn Greenberg, *"Or Does It Explode?" Black Harlem in the Great Depression* (New York: Oxford University Press, 1991), p. 42.

62. Saunders, "Half-Century," pp. 30, 90.

63. Telephone interview with Florence Ellis Dickerson, July 19, 1995.

64. MB, December 15, 1930; January 19, 1931; April 20, 1931; Saunders, "Half-Century," pp. 22–23.

65. Greenberg, *Or Does It Explode*, pp. 114–131.

66. Ibid., pp. 3–4.

67. Robert W. Searle and A. Clayton Powell Jr. to Cecelia Cabaniss Saunders, March 22, 1935, LPPRC.

68. Cecelia Cabaniss Saunders to Walter White, March 28, 1935, LPPRC.

69. Ibid.

70. Louise Mitchell, "Slave Markets Typify Exploitation of Domestics," *The Daily Worker*, May 5, 1940, in *Black Women in White America*, ed. Lerner, p. 230. The average weekly wage for a full-time domestic worker in New York City in 1934 was $12.25, thus making it far cheaper for white women to engage day labor at these markets, since many paid as little as 15 cents an hour. See Alice Kessler-Harris, *Out to Work* (New York: Oxford University Press, 1982), pp. 270–271; Greenberg, *Or Does It Explode*, p. 79.

71. *New York Times*, May 19, 1938; interview with Dorothy I. Height in *Black Women Oral History*, vol. 5, ed. Hill and King, pp. 60–63.

72. *New York Age*, March 9, 1929.

73. Saunders, "Half-Century," p. 84.

74. Cecelia Cabaniss Saunders to Frances Perkins, March 29, 1935, box no. 85, New York State file, WB.

75. *New York Age*, November 7, 1912; May 22, 1913; September 11, 1913.

76. Catherine Stuart Vance, *The Girl Reserve Movement of the Young Women's Christian Association: An Analysis of the Educational Principles and Procedures Used Throughout Its History* (New York: Bureau of Publications, Teachers College, Columbia University, 1937).

77. *An Adventure Book for Younger Girls: Girl Reserve Grade and Junior High School Series* (New York: The Woman's Press, 1927), p. 6.

78. Ibid., p. 35.

79. Ibid., pp. 16, 13, 14, 20.

80. Ibid., pp. 36–37; *Guide Book for Senior High School Girl Reserves* (New York: The Woman's Press, 1928), p. 63.

81. *Guide Book*, p. 90.

82. Ibid., p. 94.

83. Ibid., p. 95.

84. Ibid., p. 125.

85. Ibid., p. 125.

86. *New York Age*, February 17, 1923.

87. Saunders, "Half-Century," p. 15; *New York Amsterdam News*, February 21, 1923.

88. Saunders, "Half-Century," p. 49.

89. Clara W. Alcroft, Report on Course on Sex Education, March–May 1939, New York City—Harlem, NBA.

90. *New York Age*, August 18, 1918; *New York Amsterdam News*, June 20, 1923; MB, October 15, 1928; Saunders, "Half-Century," pp. 15, 40, 64, 78, 121, 159.

91. *New York Amsterdam News*, April 18, 1923; interview with Jean Blackwell Hutson, July 29, 1992.

92. Saunders, "Half-Century," p. 46.

93. Interview with Dorothy I. Height in *Black Women Oral History*, vol. 5, ed. Hill and King, p. 52.

94. Anna Arnold Hedgeman, *The Trumpet Sounds: A Memoir of Negro Leadership* (New York: Holt, Rinehart & Winston, 1946), p. 41.

95. Belle Ingels, field worker, Laboratory Division, "1937 Summary Sheets for the West 137th Street Branch," p. 4, New York City—Harlem, NBA.

96. Ibid., p. 20.

97. Interview with Dorothy I. Height in *Black Women Oral History*, vol. 5, ed. Hill and King; Eleanor Hinton Hoytt, "Dorothy I. Height," in *Black Women in America: An Historical Encyclopedia*, by Darlene Clark Hine (Brooklyn, N.Y.: Carlson Publishing, 1993), pp. 552–554.

98. Paula F. Pfeffer, "Anna Arnold Hedgeman," in *Black Women in America*, by Hine, pp. 549–552.

99. Bishop Richard R. Wright Jr., *The Bishops of the AME Church* (Nashville: AME Sunday School Union, 1963), pp. 291–292.

100. Adele Logan Alexander, "Ruth Logan Roberts," in *Black Women in America*, by Hine, p. 986.

7. Interracial Work and Racial Conflict

1. Walter White to the chairman of the National Board of the YWCA, August 26, 1924, New York City—Harlem, NBA.

2. Ibid.

3. NAACP press release, August 29, 1924, New York City—Harlem, NBA.

4. Walter White to Mary S. Sims, September 3, 1924, New York City—Harlem, NBA.

5. Mary Sims to Mabel Cratty, September 22, 1924; Eva D. Bowles to Walter White, September 23, 1924; Mary Sims to Walter White, September 24, 1924, New York City—Harlem, NBA.

6. Walter White to Bertha M. Boody, November 6, 1924, New York City—Harlem, NBA.

7. Press release, YWCA of the City of New York, November 17, 1924, LPPRC.

8. Ibid.

9. Betty MacBride to general secretaries, May 14, 1920; Cecelia Cabaniss Saunders to Betty MacBride, May 17, 1920; Betty MacBride to Cecelia Cabaniss Saunders, May 20, 1920, New York City—Harlem, NBA.

10. Cecelia Cabaniss Saunders to Mrs. Robert Bailey Speer, May 25, 1920, New York City—Harlem, NBA.

11. Emma Bailey Speer to Cecelia Cabaniss Saunders, May 30, 1920, New York City—Harlem, NBA.

12. "What the Colored Women Are Asking of the YWCA," in *Black Women in White America: A Documentary History*, ed. Gerda Lerner (New York: Vintage Books, 1992), pp. 480–484.

13. *Report of the Proceedings. Sixth National Convention of the Young Women's Christian Associations of the United States of America*, Cleveland (New York: National Board of the YWCA, 1920), pp. 121–122.

14. See Jacqueline Dowd Hall, *Revolt Against Chivalry: Jessie Daniel Ames and the Women's Campaign Against Lynching* (New York: Columbia University Press, 1993), pp. 83–86, and Dorothy Salem, *To Better Our World: Black Women in Organized Reform, 1880–1920* (Brooklyn, N.Y.: Carlson Publishing, 1990), pp. 243–246, for more on this conference and various follow-up meetings.

15. Frances Sanders Taylor, "'On the Edge of Tomorrow': Southern Women, the Student YWCA, and Race, 1920–1940" (Ph.D. diss., Stanford University, 1984), p. 29.

16. Juliet O. Bell and Helen J. Wilkins, *Interracial Practices in Community YWCAs: A Study Under the Auspices of the Commission to Gather Interracial Experience as Requested by the 16th National Convention of the YWCAs of the USA* (New York: National Board of the YWCA, 1944).

17. Interview with Frances Harriet Williams in *The Black Women Oral History Project*, vol. 10, ed. Ruth Edmonds Hill and Patricia Miller King (Westport, Conn.: Meckler Publishing, 1991), pp. 276–292; "Biography of Frances Harriet Williams," October 2, 1945, National Council of Negro Women file, box 5, OPA.

18. Frances Harriet Williams, *Pudge and Her Friends* (New York: The Woman's Press, 1938), p. 1.

19. Susan Lynn, *Progressive Women in Conservative Times: Racial Justice, Peace, and Feminism, 1945 to the 1960s* (New Brunswick, N.J.: Rutgers University Press, 1992), pp. 47–48.

20. Mrs. J. H. McCary Jr. to Mrs. Henry Ingraham, March 29, 1944, Young Women's Christian Association file, OPA.

21. "Interracial Charter," in Dorothy Sabiston and Margaret Hiller, *Toward Better Race Relations* (New York: The Woman's Press, 1949) p. 180.

22. Ibid., p. 182.

23. Ibid., pp. 182–183, 185–186.

24. Cecelia Cabaniss Saunders, "A Half-Century of the Harlem Branch of the Young Women's Christian Association," rough draft typescript, 1955, p. 162, LPPRC; Cecelia Cabaniss Saunders to Reverdy Ransom, July 16, 1947, LPPRC.

25. Lynn, *Progressive Women*, p. 54.

26. Sabiston and Hiller, *Better Race Relations*, p. 62.

27. Ibid., pp. 21–22.

28. Cecelia Cabaniss Saunders to Reverdy Ransom, March 12, 1947, LPPRC.

29. The New York City YWCA closed the Emma Ransom House in 1960 and sold the African American YWCA's property to the Abyssinian Baptist Church in 1961. These closings took place in the context of large-scale budget cuts. From that point on, the New York City YWCA has operated various activities centers in Harlem on a much smaller scale than the West 137th Street branch.

Index